DOING SOCIAL PSYCHOLOGY

DOING SOCIAL PSYCHOLOGY

EDITED BY DOROTHY MIELL AND
MARGARET WETHERELL

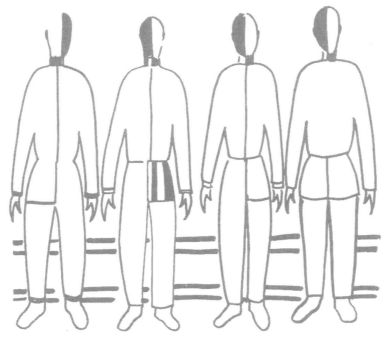

SAGE Publications
London • Thousand Oaks • New Delhi
In association with

The Open
University

Cover illustration: Kasimir Malevich, *Sportsmen*, *c.*1928–32, oil on canvas, 142 × 164cm., State Russian Museum, St Petersburg.

The Open University, Walton Hall, Milton Keynes, MK7 6AA.
First published 1998.

SAGE Publications Ltd
6 Bonhill Street,
London, EC2A 4PU

SAGE Publications Inc.
2455 Teller Road,
Thousand Oaks,
California 91320

SAGE Publications India Pvt Ltd
32, M Block Market, Greater Kailish – 1
New Delhi 110 048

British Library Cataloguing in Publication Data
A catalogue record for this book is available from the British Library.
ISBN 0 7619 6049 X
ISBN 0 7619 6050 3 (pbk)

Library of Congress catalog record available

Edited, designed and typeset by the Open University.
Printed and bound in the United Kingdom by The Cromwell Press, Trowbridge, Wiltshire.
This text is based on materials which form part of an Open University course *D317 Social Psychology: Personal Lives, Social Worlds*. Details of this and other Open University courses can be obtained from the Course Reservations Centre, PO Box 724, The Open University, Milton Keynes MK7 6ZS. For availability of this or other course components, contact Open University Worldwide Ltd, The Berrill Building, Walton Hall, Milton Keynes MK7 6AA.

1.1
B/d317copubi1.1

Contents

INTRODUCTION

by Margaret Wetherell and Dorothy Miell

Doing Social Psychology is intended as a practical manual for social psychology and other psychology students. It gathers together eight worked research examples. These examples are designed for use in practical classes and also should prove invaluable models for any student attempting to construct their own research project perhaps for their third year dissertation. Each chapter takes a particular methodology, such as experimental investigation, content analysis, depth interviewing, survey and questionnaire research, and shows the student how to use this approach to investigate a topic such as person perception, media representations or group interaction. Each step in the research process is carefully described, including the analysis of results and the process of writing up a report. Students are encouraged, however, to be creative in the choice of topic, samples and analysis, and other research examples are referenced for more background on a method, research issue or area of investigation.

The book is fuelled by our belief that social psychology is a practical activity. As teachers of social psychology we believe that our task is to encourage students to *do* social psychology as well as read it, think it, write it and pass exams in it. Doing, of course, has a number of resonances. In a sense we do social psychology whenever we notice something about people's activities in social life, view these through the lens of theory, and wonder about the origins and implications of such phenomena, suspending or critically examining our normal taken-for-granted frames of reference. But doing social psychology also involves learning specific sets of methodological conventions or practices and acquiring investigative tools. It is about knowing how to tailor a method to a social psychological problem, understanding the epistemological fit between theory and method, knowing how to operationalize, how to use the tried and tested procedures, how to act in line with ethical principles, and then how to communicate the findings, convincing others of the logic and benefits of the research which has been conducted.

Teachers of psychology know from experience that the best way of communicating these skills is through a process of active and hands-on learning. Students need many opportunities to practice. Yet the process of designing adequate practical classes is an onerous one, as is the business of supervising the projects and dissertations of individual students at undergraduate and postgraduate levels. Good practicals which 'work' are jealously guarded, carried by lecturers from institution to institution, their origins often lost in the mists of time. Typically, 'good' practicals are those which have been worked over and revised, customized and re-customized, on numerous occasions.

One of our main aims in producing this book was to add to the communal stock of good practicals and projects. The exercises in this book have been thoroughly tested on several, and in some cases very many, generations of Open University students (literally thousands of students). They are written by experienced teachers and researchers acting as consultants for the Open University. The authors draw on their own research expertise and the process of teaching research methods in their own universities. Each chapter is written from the student's point of view and addresses the student directly using the accessible learning style characteristic of Open University course materials.

These practicals are used in the Open University with students doing a third level course who have been asked to design and conduct their own piece of research. However, our student group includes a number who have no previous experience of psychology, or no second level experience, and perhaps few previous educational qualifications. We suggest that these projects are most appropriate as practical classes for second and third year students, but could also be modified for first year general psychology classes and for A-level students, and could also prove a useful stimulus for a graduate class or for acquainting a PhD student with an unfamiliar methodology.

Classes based on these practicals could be taught in a number of ways. Students could work in groups independently following the instructions in a chapter at their own pace, but coming together with the rest of the class for comparison of results and discussion of the theoretical background and methodological issues raised. Alternatively, a tutor or lecturer could take a class through each stage and then ask the students to read the book as a resource to remind them of the procedures they have used, the theoretical rationale, and to give them guidance on completing an assignment. The book could also be used in advance of practical classes to prepare students and familiarize them with bodies of theory, methodological approaches and the practical requirements of different methods. Although students are given guidance about which simple statistical tests to use, these tests are not explained in detail as we assume that standard statistical handbooks already in use with courses will be available.

Most of the practicals will require several class sessions with a period of active data gathering in between as students, for instance, administer questionnaires to their sample, conduct their interviews, or conduct a content analysis of magazines. Methods can also be used flexibly, applied to a different topic from those suggested here, or in combination as part of a larger individual or group project which might include both qualitative and quantitative dimensions (such as media analysis combined with a survey, or diary methodology and depth interviewing, or experimental research and structured observation of group processes). At the end of this introduction, there is a summary of each practical providing a quick guide to the methods employed, and the aims and requirements. Note that each chapter contains ethical advice but it is the responsibility of each student and their supervisor to ensure compliance to ethical principles such as the guidelines issued by the British Psychological Society.

The book is designed to stand alone, but it may also be read with profit with other textbooks of social psychology. It is a companion volume to the four other published books which make up the Sage/Open University series in social psychology: *Understanding the Self* (edited by Richard Stevens), *Social Interaction and Personal Relationships* (edited by Dorothy Miell and Rudi Dallos), *Identities, Groups and Social Issues* (edited by Margaret Wetherell) and *Theory and Social Psychology* (edited by Roger Sapsford *et al.*). Where readers of this book need information about substantive issues in social psychology, the authors have often suggested one or more of these four books as a good source, because they were all put together at much the same time and inspired by the same general 'vision' of what the discipline of social psychology is and could be.

As part of that 'vision' we have included a range of methods in social psychology in this book, with more emphasis than perhaps is usual on qualitative methods such as structured observation (Chapter 3), repertory grids (Chapter 6), content and thematic analysis (Chapter 7), depth interviewing (Chapter 8) and discourse analysis (Chapter 2), as well as experimental research (Chapters 1 and 5), questionnaire and survey research (Chapter 4), quantitative content analysis (Chapter 7), quantitative diary research (Chapter 2) and the use of descriptive statistics in observation (Chapter 3). A number of experimental and correlational designs used in social psychology have been omitted in favour of a more representative spread. Our definition of social psychology has thus been inclusive rather than exclusive and we have included methods that are also relevant to clinical psychologists, humanistic psychologists and sociologists.

If nothing else, we hope this collection will persuade the reader of the variety, interest and potential of social psychological investigations, and we hope these practicals will help new generations of students attain their educational objectives.

Chapter by chapter summaries

Chapter 1: An experimental investigation of primacy and perseverance effects in person perception

Students are taken through the conduct of an experiment stage by stage, replicating and extending Asch's original study on person perception. A detailed discussion of the concepts of primacy and perseverance is provided. The experiment compares the responses of four groups of participants given different sequences of purported reference letters to rate. It sets up a between-subjects design and uses simple statistics (Mann-Whitney test or independent samples t-test). All the materials required to run the practical are provided in an appendix.

Requirements

The experiment requires around 40 subjects (10 per group) but could be demonstrated with as few as 16. The stimulus materials and response sheets will need to be photocopied.

Options

This practical could be run in one class session as a demonstration using the students as the subjects. Alternatively, the students could act as the experimenters and collect their own data which could be pooled and analysed in a subsequent class session. A further possibility is to first generate the data by running the experiment with other groups and then base the practical session around the students analysing the data provided for them. If more data were collected, then more complex forms of statistical analysis could also be demonstrated.

Chapter 2: Relationships, social networks and social interaction: an exploration in diary methodologies

This practical demonstrates a variety of ways of analysing people's accounts of their relational lives collected using diaries of daily interactions. Students can either use themselves as the subject (collecting records of their interactions for 28 days) or involve one other person. The diaries can be organized for quantitative analysis (correlational investigations using rating scales of topics such as social networks and significant social interactions) or for qualitative analysis (discourse analysis of open-ended accounts investigating personal constructions of relationships and intersubjectivity). The practical teaches the students how to formulate relevant research questions, provides a step-by-step guide to discourse analysis and, for the quantitative option, discusses the appropriate statistics. Diary sheets to complete are also provided.

Requirements

This practical involves a relatively long-term commitment to data collection on the part of the student and their collaborator (if one of the dyadic options is selected). If a dyadic option is chosen, special attention needs to be paid to ethical issues. The appropriate number of diary sheets will need to be photocopied.

Options

This practical could be adapted as a class demonstration run over two sessions by collecting data for a shorter period and trying out the analytic techniques suggested. The discourse analysis could be used as a self-contained exercise and applied to literary accounts of relationships, for instance, or other textual material.

Chapter 3: Structured observation and the investigation of group interaction

This practical involves the structured observation of two group interactions. Students are asked to observe established groups interacting in their natural settings such as family, friendship or work groups and to collect independent accounts from two participants. They are given background on a range of topics they could investigate, such as verbal and non-verbal variables and the relationship with gender and status, interactive sequences and intra-group processes such as forming coalitions, sub-groups and scapegoating. Insider and outsider perspectives are compared and the process of reflexively checking out analytic inferences about group process is described. Students are introduced to Bales's analysis and to sociograms. They are shown how to record non-verbal behaviour frequencies, and are advised on how to present their results using descriptive statistics.

Requirements

Students need access to groups willing to be observed. Use of an audio recorder and/or a video camera is optional.

Options

This practical could be run over two sessions with an intervening period of independent data collection. It could also be adapted to run in one session in a classroom using small groups convened among the students, perhaps discussing some controversial issue or making a complex decision where other students act as the observers, and perhaps then swapping roles. Alternatively, it could be used with prepared or available video material of group interactions for students to analyse in the classroom.

Chapter 4: Designing a survey and constructing a questionnaire

This practical provides a complete guide to survey research noting the topics it is appropriate to investigate using this method. Some research questions are outlined and students are encouraged to formulate their own question and hypothesis. The process of designing a questionnaire is described including the advantages and disadvantages of different types of layouts and question formats. Students are instructed in how to code the data, construct summary tables and perform appropriate statistical tests to test hypotheses.

Requirements

If the students are to collect data for questionnaires they have designed themselves, then they will need access to appropriate samples and will need to photocopy questionnaires.

Options

This practical could be used in parts. Thus, one session could be based around the process of defining a research question and then designing a survey and questionnaire where students are assessed on the questionnaire they produce. If it is impractical for students to collect their own data, another session could be based on prepared or fabricated data which they learn to code, organize and present using the chapter as a guide.

Chapter 5: An experimental investigation of framing effects and decision making

This practical sets up an experiment on the ways in which the framing of dilemmas affects subsequent decision making. The original studies of Tversky and Kahneman on the psychology of choice are presented as background. Students are given two options. They can prepare their own dilemmas (they are instructed in how to do this) and develop some hypotheses to test using the chi-square statistic, or examine in detail the verbal protocols subjects generate as they work on the dilemmas. Background on protocol analysis is included.

Requirements

Access to between 4 to 40 subjects depending on the option chosen. Photocopies of instruction sheets.

Options

This practical has multiple uses. It could be used as a demonstration of framing effects or to teach students how to do protocol analysis. Equally, students could be set the task of designing their own dilemmas and collecting and analysing their own data over two practical sessions.

Chapter 6: Glances into personal worlds: the construction and analysis of repertory grids

This practical introduces students to Kelly's idiographic approach to the study of subjective experience. Students can choose to use themselves as the subject, interrogating their own constructs, or compare constructs with one other person. The procedures for generating, administering and analysing a repertory grid are described in detail as well as extensions of the research through laddering or conversational elaboration.

Requirements

If a second person is involved, conformity to ethical principles needs to be monitored. An audio recorder is desirable but not necessary to extend the research.

Options

This practical could be run over two class sessions with the students doing some independent work on their grids before the second session. Alternatively, if each student acts as their own subject, it could be run as one session in class demonstrating the repertory grid.

Chapter 7: Social representations of gender in the media: quantitative and qualitative content analysis

This practical shows the student how to apply the theory of social representations to conduct an analysis of magazines and the meanings associated with femininity and masculinity. Students are instructed in the theory and method of quantitative and qualitative content analysis including a guide to sampling textual material and the process of narrowing down research questions. The project includes detailed background material on social representations research and develops its own worked examples. Suggestions are included about applying the approach to other topics such as health and illness.

Requirements

Students need to collect or have access to a pool of women's and men's magazines.

Options

This practical could be run over two class sessions with students conducting the analysis in between. Alternatively, if the magazine material were provided in advance, the practical could be adapted so that the students were taken through the analysis stage by stage as a demonstration, perhaps combined with a lecture on social representations theory and/or preliminary reading of the chapter.

Chapter 8: Discovering subjective meanings: depth interviewing

This practical demonstrates how to conduct a depth interview of some aspect of one other individual's experience. It focuses on the procedures involved in the selection of an informant and the process of preparing an interview guide and conducting the interview as well as the principles of interpretative analysis. This method is located for the student within the perspectives and aims of experiential psychology. Students are given a number of options for further research, for triangulation and to validate their findings, such as conducting a second interview, comparing initial findings with other autobiographical material produced by the participant, negotiating a joint account with the participant or enlisting another researcher to interview the same person.

Requirements

The student must have access to a person willing to give up several hours for the research. An audio recorder is highly desirable but suggestions are also given for how to base the analysis on note-taking. Ethical issues are crucial in all practicals but particularly so for this one and teachers and supervisors will need to vet students' choice of topics, clarify the distinctions between interviewing and counselling and to ensure anonymity and informed consent.

Options

This practical will need to be run over two or more class sessions with the first session devoted to formulating the research aims, preparing the guide and planning the validation procedure and the second session occurring after the data collection.

CHAPTER 1

AN EXPERIMENTAL INVESTIGATION OF PRIMACY AND PERSEVERANCE EFFECTS IN PERSON PERCEPTION

by Patrick McGhee

Contents

PART A: INTRODUCTION

1 You never get a second chance to make a first impression: the psychology of primacy and perseverance

1.1 Objectives of the person perception project

'You never get a second chance to make a first impression' or so the saying goes. This experimental project will test that contention in relation to applying for psychology courses.

Our first impression of someone is very powerful and often quite unaffected by any later information we may gain about that person. This is referred to as the 'primacy' effect in social psychology. Even when the information we have based our first impression on turns out to be completely false, we still find it difficult if not impossible to discount that information completely. We call this the 'perseverance' effect. This experimentally-based project will help you explore empirically some of the key issues related to these two phenomena as they apply to person perception. You will also be invited to consider and discuss some of the *implications* of such 'primacy' and 'perseverance' effects as they affect our everyday lives, and what if anything the study of these phenomena can tell us about the *role of experiments* in social psychology generally.

By the end of the project you should have achieved the following objectives:

1   Acquired a thorough grasp of the concepts of primacy and perseverance as they relate to person perception.

2   Carried out an experimental investigation of the phenomena and offered a critical discussion of the relevant theories.

3   Achieved the ability to assess critically the distinctive contribution of experiments in the area of person perception including the methodological limitations of the technique.

1.2 Primacy

We have probably all found ourselves at one time or another heavily influenced by the very first piece of information we have 'picked up' about another person. For example, at a party you overhear someone called Fred being described as 'intelligent' and this triggers a mental set for you about Fred (that he says clever things, wears glasses and is quiet and unassuming, perhaps – or whatever your image is of an 'intelligent person'). Then a few minutes later you overhear that Fred is an 'envious' person. The chances are (if you behave in the way that psychologists argue most people do – and it is quite possible of course that you do not) that you will weight the first piece of information you heard about this mysterious Fred person (that he is intelligent) more than the second piece (that he is envious) and finish up with an overall impression of Fred that is largely positive (reflecting your information that he is intelligent).

Non-psychologists might ask: Is this phenomenon of any importance for our everyday lives? Does it matter? The answer to this must surely be 'yes'. While it might be the case that casual impressions of other partygoers and their friends are hardly the most important concerns in anyone's life, the same psychological processes are at work in court-rooms, party political broadcasts, in classrooms and medical consultations and so are of immense consequence to all our lives. And remember, every single person you have ever met, telephoned or written to or who has ever seen you *in your entire life* has had a first impression of you.

We will return to Fred and the party later, but let us consider first some of the research and theory which relates to the area of the psychology of primacy effects.

A number of psychological researchers have shown through question-naires and real-life studies that our first observations of other people (be they face-to-face or in writing) are not only given undue weight when we come to make global judgements about those people, but also that these impressions are long-lasting. In one classic study, Asch (1946) listed the traits of a target person (list A) and presented it to one group of par-ticipants and then gave another group of participants the same list of traits but in a different order (list B).

List A: intelligent – industrious – critical – stubborn – envious

List B: envious – stubborn – critical – industrious – intelligent

The result was that when the participants given list A were asked to ex-pand upon these brief sketches they constructed a much more positive image of the target person (that is, the person to whom the adjectives supposedly referred) than the participants who had been presented with list B.

The primacy effect can be defined as follows:

> The process whereby our first impression of another person causes us to interpret his or her subsequent behaviour in a manner consistent with the first impression.
>
> (Aronson et al., 1994, p.128)

Of course in real life we do not usually get to know someone through a list of trait adjectives conveniently drawn up for us. In order to look more directly at real life a study by Bernadette Park (1986) involved asking seven participants to meet weekly in a small group over a period of seven weeks. At the end of each session participants wrote down their impressions of each of the others. After the seventh session, each participant was asked to rate the others again, but this time for general personality characteristics. It was found that the best predictor of these final overall impressions was the set of ratings made by the participants after the *first* meeting. Indeed, Park found that week-by-week judgements of others were heavily influenced by impressions formed at the first meeting (even though these were obviously based on fairly limited information at the time).

As well as having strong influences on our immediate impressions of a participant, our first impressions, Park's study suggests, are difficult to change and this has indeed been shown in many other studies. In experiments of perceptions of *ability* (as distinct from personality), judges tend to give higher ratings to targets who perform well on early tasks but poorly on later ones, than to targets who perform poorly on early tasks but better on later ones (for example, Jones *et al.*, 1968). It would seem that once we have formed our initial impression about others, information which is inconsistent with that initial impression is ignored or reinterpreted to fit with what we have already decided. Aronson (1995) suggests that there are two mechanisms which lead to primacy effect phenomena: *attention decrement* and *interpretative set*. The attention decrement explanation involves the idea that judges simply get tired, careless or distracted as they receive more information about the same target. The interpretative set explanation argues that early pieces of information directly influence the *meanings* of later ones. For example, if we have been told that Fred is 'extroverted', how can we make sense of being told later that he is also 'cautious'. A schema or prototype (see Lalljee, 1996) is being triggered by the concept of 'extrovert' into which the idea of Fred being 'cautious' just does not fit. Similarly, any later trait term which is in any way ambiguous (for example 'ambitious') will be construed in a manner consistent with the initial impression.

Bernstein *et al.* (1994) suggest four reasons why our first impression of a target is so resistant to change, even when later information contradicts it.

BOX I   Reasons for the resilience of first impressions

1   People tend to be overconfident in their initial judgements and do not feel the need to revise them in the light of later information.

2   People construe subsequent information in ways which are consistent with the immediate impression formed after the first exposure to new information; for example, the new employee who makes a good impression at her first team meeting is likely to have her subsequent periods of silence at later meetings interpreted as 'intelligent listening', rather than as 'shyness'.

---

3   People remember general impressions better than specific contradicting events that happen subsequently.

4   In face-to-face interactions people tend to act in ways which elicit from the other person behaviour which helps confirm the original impression given off.

Source: Adapted from Bernstein *et al.* (1994), pp.611–12

Of course we can consider each of these explanations and raise questions about *why* humans are like this, *why* people 'tend to be overconfident in their initial judgements and do not feel the need to revise them in the light of later information' (Bernstein *et al.*, 1994)? It should be said first of all that to relate the phenomena of person perception to underlying cognitive and social dynamics *does* constitute a form of explanation, even if there are still more 'why' questions to be raised. (Compare, for example, the situation where a mechanic might be asked why a car keeps making 'that dreadful grinding noise when slowing down'. The mechanic might say 'because the brake pads are worn'. This is still a helpful explanation of sorts – even if you want to go on to ask 'yes, but *why* are the brake pads worn?').

First impressions and their resilience are probably side-effects of the way in which human cognitive systems have evolved to deal with the short-term survival problems presented by an environment where fast identification of familiar objects is essential. However, the social structures that host our institutional and cultural systems have evolved much more rapidly than the brain structures that host our cognitive systems. Our cognitive systems evolved to deal with the perception of a limited range of simple objects where first impressions – even if they were not always accurate – were at least accurate sufficiently often for practical survival purposes (for example, the speed of our prey and the presence of other predators meant there was not much time for anything more than a first impression). In contrast, the complex judgements of other people that we are expected to make as mature, responsible, accountable and literate adults in socially complex settings in the twenty-first century are a minefield for our cognitive systems which originally evolved to deal with practical hunting-and-gathering tasks and for survival (though, of course, our nervous systems have immense flexibility and capacity to learn).

Interestingly, some workers in the area of animal research have recently suggested that some animals, including pigeons and monkeys, demonstrate primacy effects in memory experiments similar to those demonstrated by humans in studies of recall of visual stimuli such as abstract snowflake-like designs (Wright, 1994) and rats in terms of spatial location (Kesner *et al.*, 1994). Nevertheless, other researchers argue that these primacy effects are artefacts (that is, irrelevant artificialities) caused by the way animals are tested and the statistical analyses used (for example, Gaffan, 1994). On balance, however, the evidence would seem to support the view that some animals at least demonstrate what we can validly call a 'primacy effect' in memory. It would be interesting therefore to explore whether first impressions between two monkeys have the same kind of disproportionate influence on subsequent social interactions as first impressions do between two humans.

In contrast to this point of view, some social constructionist social psychologists might argue that primacy effects (such as they are in the real world) are part of the rituals of social interaction whereby we learn to expect others to be consistent in the identity they present of themselves in social episodes with us. In other words, it is perfectly reasonable to assume that someone who behaves in a friendly manner at the beginning of a conversation is not then going to switch to an aggressive style later, because there are unwritten social rules about 'face' and 'self-presentation' that say one has to present a consistent and coherent image when interacting with others (Goffman, 1959). As for the experimental results which are not directly predictable from this point of view (suggesting there might be more going on here than mere social etiquette), social constructionists would argue that the strange tasks participants are asked to complete in pencil-and-paper tests are meaningful only in the artificially complex settings of laboratories with elaborate experimental designs.

Whatever the cause of primacy effects there is little doubt that they exist and no doubt of their importance. Although folk psychology tells us about the importance of first impressions, it remains an intriguing and robust phenomenon which seems to relate to something very fundamental in our psychological make-up and something which still exercises the imagination of a range of social psychologists.

And yet the psychology of person perception still has another fascinating phenomenon to describe which shows us that first impressions seem not only to be 'influential' but in a sense virtually indestructible.

1.3 Perseverance

So far we have seen that once we have formed an initial impression of someone, subsequent information is unlikely to have much impact on our final or overall judgements of that individual. In these cases participants are trying to give weight to evidence that points one way initially and then the other way subsequently. Overall, information that is consistent with the initial impression is given more weight than information that is inconsistent with the initial impression. In other words, we seem to take heed only of early information in forming impressions of people even if that information is only 'half the story'.

But what if the initial information given is not even 'half the story' but *completely false*? Let us return to the scenario of the party gossip mentioned earlier. If you remember, you overheard originally that Fred is 'intelligent', and then heard subsequently that he is 'envious' (and you constructed an image of Fred that reflects intelligence more than enviousness – that is, an image influenced more by the first impression).

What if you *then* overheard another conversation at the party where someone said 'Yes, I agree with what you said earlier, I think Ted *is* intelligent'. You suddenly realize that *no-one* had said that *Fred* was intelligent at all – you had misheard – they had been talking about Ted at that point and then only subsequently moved on to talk about Fred (and his enviousness). Assuming you still have some interest in Fred's personality at this point – what would your overall final impression of him be? A straightforward image of an envious person (whatever that might mean for you)? In fact, social psychological research in this area has clearly shown that the original impression of Fred as intelligent will still have a subtle influence on your overall impression of Fred now *even though that information has been shown to be completely erroneous.*

In the present context, the idea for the experiment to be carried out here is to test the hypothesis that an invalid piece of information about a subject will still influence the judgement of a group of people even after the information has been shown to be totally untrue and the group believe they have completely expunged it from their minds.

A common example of perseverance, which we have all seen on television, is when in a courtroom scene a witness exclaims that the defendant is guilty because she knows that he has been tried and found guilty of many similar offences over several years. Since evidence about previous convictions is (normally) inadmissible in court, the presiding judge at this point is compelled to direct the jury to 'disregard the witness's last statement'! Clearly, no matter how hard members of the jury might try to disregard the information, few psychologists would suggest that jurors are likely to be unaffected by what they have heard – even if the jurors believe that they really have disregarded the witness's exclamation (see, for example, Thompson *et al.*, 1981). In a study carried out by Elizabeth Loftus in 1974, it was found that 68 per cent of mock jurors were still prepared to return guilty verdicts against a defendant even when the only witness against him was revealed to the jury to be legally blind after giving evidence of what she had seen. (In comparison, only 18 per cent of jurors returned guilty verdicts when the witness was not used at all.)

The same phenomenon is also dramatically shown in a classic study by Ross and his colleagues (Ross *et al.*, 1975). In this study, judges observed a fellow-student attempting to solve 25 puzzles. Half the judges were told that the target had correctly solved 24 out of the 25 puzzles, but the other half were told that the target had correctly solved only 10 of the 25. Later, the same participants were told that in fact the information on the target's success rate had been completely false and that the information on the target's performance had been provided on an entirely random basis. Ross now asked the participants to predict how many puzzles of a similar nature the target would get correct in a future similar test. Even although the initial information had been declared to be bogus (and participants indicated that they fully accepted this), participants who had been told originally that the target had got 24 out of the 25 correct now predicted on average that the target would get 19 correct next time, whereas those participants who had originally been told that the participant had only got 10 correct now predicted on average that the target would only get around 14 correct next time!

In the same series of studies, Ross and his colleagues carried out the experiment again but this time, rather than ask participants to make predictions regarding future performance about others, they got participants to make predictions about *themselves*. It was found that participants who were given initial positive feedback on their performance on a task predicted better future performance on similar tasks for themselves compared with participants who had been given initial negative feedback *even though in both cases participants were told that this initial feedback was completely bogus, entirely determined on a random basis and entirely unconnected to their real performance on the task.*

Apart from anything else, the Ross *et al.* experiments should make us think very carefully about carrying out an experiment or simulation where participants are led to believe negative things about themselves, since post-experimental debriefing ('do not worry, you are not really unattractive/unintelligent/weak at problem solving, we just told you that for the sake of the experiment') may still leave a substantial degree of residual low self-esteem amongst participants.

Why does this perseverance effect occur so powerfully? One explanation is that while participants who are told to disregard information they were presented with earlier may 'delete' this from their representation of the target, they do not delete inferences they drew on the basis of that original information. The main reason why the original information can be disregarded while the inferences drawn from it are not is simply because some inferences are not always very accessible to the cognitive system. For example, suppose I told you on Monday that I watched Susan training at the weekend and believe she is likely to win the county swimming championships. On Monday evening you might, consciously or subconsciously, draw out various inferences from this 'fact'. You might, in particular, infer that Mary, Susan's trainer, is very skilled. But suppose that when I see you on Tuesday I say I did not mean Susan at all I meant Sarah, I had seen Sarah training *not* Susan. You would immediately consciously disregard the idea that Susan is likely to win the championship. However, the inference that Mary is a good trainer remains in your cognitive belief system even though the original grounds for drawing the inference have now been discarded. If asked about Susan's chances of winning you would not rate them particularly highly, but if asked about Mary's skills as a trainer you would rate her quite highly (but possibly be a bit unsure as to why!).

In such situations something curious can happen – your assessment of Susan's chances might eventually become quite positive. Why? Because you start to draw inferences from your (still enduring) belief that Mary is a good trainer (and presumably will help Susan's technique etc.). And we say to the person who tells us that the original information was false that despite what they say we actually believe it to be true anyway. Of course, if you have *acted* on what now turns out to be bogus information you might want to justify your action in order not to appear foolish and to save face (see Johnson and Seifert, 1994, for a critical discussion of the idea that perseverance effects are caused by undiscarded inferences).

Interestingly, there would appear to be clear individual differences in the extent to which people are prone to these kinds of perseverance effects. Davies (1993) has found that belief perseverance was greater for participants who scored higher on a separate measure of dogmatism (a tendency towards inflexibility and certainty in attitudes and beliefs). It would appear that dogmatic individuals are less able (or less willing) to think of reasons why unexpected outcomes might occur.

1.4 The experimental approach to person perception

The area of person perception is one which is typically studied from an *experimental* perspective and this project is designed to help you explore some of the above ideas using this approach.

It is generally quite straightforward to get participants to give ratings of other participants or of hypothetical persons ('targets') along various dimensions, and social psychologists have been attracted by the idea of simple procedures that can be applied to a range of settings and theoretical problems. The experimental approach in person perception, of course, typically involves constructing two or more versions of the same description of an individual (usually but not always hypothetical) which constitute the experimental manipulation. Participants are then allocated *randomly* to these two or more conditions in order to make sure that any differences in perceptions of the two versions cannot be attributed to differences between the individual characteristics of the perceivers (it would be absurd, for example, if Asch had given list A above to participants who were generally very pleasant, polite and generous, and list B to participants who were cynical, critical and rude – since then he would not have known whether any differences in ratings of the two lists were caused by aspects of the lists, or aspects of the raters. Of course, Asch made certain that he randomly allocated the participants to the two lists so that different ratings could only have been caused by the lists, not by subject differences).

PART B: DATA COLLECTION

2 The project

The project you are going to carry out involves replicating and extending Asch's (1946) experiment in a more externally valid context (that is, in a context which has more relevance to the real world). Instead of showing participants a bare list of words, this study will involve a series of reference letters for a student applying for a Masters course in Psychology (the results might be particularly interesting to if you are thinking of applying for Masters courses yourself).

You will be allocating participants randomly to one of four groups (two experimental and two control groups). You will be presenting two experimental groups of participants with the same set of references and each group will be asked to give their opinion on the suitability of the applicant. However, one experimental group of participants will be presented with the letters such that the first is positive and the last negative, and the other experimental group with the first letter negative and the last letter positive.

Participants in all four groups will be asked to write down their judgements after they have seen all the letters. The primacy effect hypothesis is that the positive-negative sequence will lead to more positive judgements than the negative-positive sequence.

In order to assess the perseverance hypothesis, a final letter will be presented to both sets of participants (i.e. all four groups) explaining that, due to an administrative error, the first letter refers to a different candidate and should be set aside. The perseverance effect will be tested by comparing the results in the experimental groups with those in two control groups that see a neutral letter first. You will be able to test whether the perseverance effect works for both positive and negative information.

2.1 Hypotheses

In this study you will be testing the following hypotheses:

1   Positive information followed by negative information for a target will lead to more positive judgements than negative information followed by positive information (primacy hypothesis).

2   Participants will make more positive judgements of targets when initial positive information is presented first but discredited, than of targets where neutral information is presented first but discredited (positive perseverance hypothesis).

3 Participants will make more negative judgements of targets when initial negative information is presented first but discredited, than of targets where neutral information is presented first but discredited (negative perseverence hypothesis).

2.2 Design

There will be four groups of participants as indicated in Table 2 below, each of which will be exposed to a different sequence of letters. There are four reference letters (1–4), two instruction letters (R and D) and one control letter (C).

For clarity the seven letters are described in Tables 1 and 2.

Table 1 The seven letters

Letter code	Content	Function
Letter R	Letter requesting judgement	Tells participants what they are about to read.
Letter 1	Very positive	These letters give participants information about the applicant. The *sequence* of presentation will constitute the primacy manipulation.
Letter 2	Positive	
Letter 3	Negative	
Letter 4	Very negative	
Letter D	Letter telling participants to discount first letter (either 1 or 4)	The perseverance hypothesis predicts that participants will still be influenced by what they discount after reading this letter
Letter C	Control letter	This letter is the first letter to be presented to participants in the control groups. If the experimental groups really are discounting the information contained in their original letters, their ratings should be similar to those obtained when this control letter is discounted.

Table 2   Design of experiment and sequence of letters

	Order of presentation	
	Positive – Negative	**Negative – Positive**
Experimental	Group A: R, 1, 2, 3, 4, D	Group B: R, 4, 3, 2, 1, D
Control	Group C: R, C, 2, 3, 4, D	Group D: R, C, 3, 2, 1, D

Note that Groups A and B differ only in terms of the *sequence* of letters 1–4, that Groups A and C, and B and D differ from each other only in terms of the *first letter* in their sequence. It is essential in experimental research to make the conditions being compared identical to each other in every way apart from the dimension that constitutes the experimental comparison itself.

Constructing the comparisons

In order to test the primacy and perseverance hypotheses as efficiently as possible, it is necessary to take *two* sets ratings from all groups. The *first* set will be the ratings given after reading their fourth letter (whether that is letter 1 or letter 4). This will provide the data for testing the primacy hypothesis. The *second* set of ratings are taken after Letter D has been read – this provides the data for the perseverance hypotheses (one on positive and one on negative perseverance).

In order to test Hypothesis 1 (the primacy hypothesis), Group A ratings before discounting will be compared with Group B ratings before discounting. The prediction is that the Group A ratings will be more positive (because of the primacy of positive information in Group A).

In order to test Hypothesis 2 (positive perseverance hypothesis), Group A ratings after discounting will be compared with Group C ratings after discounting. The prediction is that the Group A ratings will be more positive (because, despite the instruction to Group A to discount the early positive information, the positive effects of that information will persevere).

In order to test Hypothesis 3 (negative perseverance hypothesis), Group B ratings after discounting will be compared with Group D ratings after discounting. The prediction is that the Group D ratings will be more positive (because, despite the instruction to Group B to discount the early negative information, the negative effects of that information will persevere).

(Note that all groups contribute two sets of ratings – once before discounting and once after discounting. These two sets of ratings are not directly compared so there are no statistical problems in running the experiment like this.)

The function of Groups C and D

Groups C and D are *control groups*. They are necessary to use as a standard against which we can compare the 'discounted' ratings of A and B respectively. Note that it would not be enough just to give participants in group C and D only the last four letters. We need to give them a control letter which we ask them to discount otherwise we would not be comparing like with like.

2.3 Running the experiment

Booklets

You will need approximately 40 participants for this experiment (approximately 10 per condition) but any number can be tested simultaneously without too much difficulty so this number of participants should not take too long to test.

The simplest way to run the experiment is to use a set of questionnaire-type booklets. You will need to construct four booklets (one for each group) which will consist of different combinations of the letters presented in the Appendix. Note that each letter is labelled 'Letter R', 'Letter 1' and so on. You should make sure these labels *do not appear* on the copies you use in your booklets. Each booklet will also require the same briefing sheet (also supplied in the Appendix) at the front, and two response sheets.

You should construct your booklets as per Table 2 above, adding briefing sheets at the front, and the response sheets. The two response sheets should be inserted, one just after the fourth letter (for the testing of the primacy hypothesis), and one just after the discounting letter (to test the perseverance hypothesis). Your dependent variable will be ratings of the target's (i.e. the applicant's) suitability for the MSc course. (Although a response sheet is prepared for you in the Appendix, you may want to alter this for added realism, or because you want to test the effect of primacy and perseverance on more than one dependent variable.)

Procedure

The most straightforward arrangement is to access a class of 40 or so students who are asked to complete the booklets one page at a time, turning over each *page when directed by the experimenter to do so.*

Alternatively, you can issue the response sheets only and project the letters on to an overhead projector, but this is rather less satisfactory.

Bear in mind ethical considerations regarding informed consent and freedom to withdraw. There is, however, little or no prospect of harming any of your participants in this study (though their faith in admissions systems may emerge somewhat diminished).

Be careful to ensure that booklets are distributed randomly to participants and avoid contamination between conditions by keeping your participants as far apart from each other as possible – and prohibited from speaking to each other, of course.

2.4 Analysing the results

Completing the data matrix grids

All your comparisons are between-participants so you should use either a *Mann-Whitney* test *or* an *independent samples* t-test.

Testing the hypotheses

For each of the three hypotheses you should have a significant or non-significant result.

The comparisons that you will be making are directly linked to each hypothesis and are worth repeating:

In order to test Hypothesis 1 (the primacy hypothesis), Group A ratings before discounting will be compared with Group B ratings before discounting. The prediction is that the Group A ratings will be more positive (because of the primacy of positive information in Group A).

In order to test Hypothesis 2 (positive perseverance hypothesis), Group A ratings after discounting will be compared with Group C ratings after discounting. The prediction is that the Group A ratings will be more positive (because, despite the instruction to Group A to discount the early positive information, the positive effects of that information will persevere).

In order to test Hypothesis 3 (negative perseverance hypothesis), Group B ratings after discounting will be compared with Group D ratings after discounting. The prediction is that the Group D ratings will be more positive (because, despite the instruction to Group B to discount the early negative information, the negative effects of that information will persevere).

Rejecting or not rejecting the experimental hypotheses

If your statistical test is significant at the 5 per cent one-tailed level for any given hypothesis, then you do not reject that experimental hypothesis (note that you never actually 'accept' an experimental hypothesis. This is because in statistics we can never really prove a hypothesis is 'true', we can only reject those that clearly are not true. A good hypothesis is one which consistently fails to be rejected).

If you find that Hypothesis 1 is supported (i.e. Group A had higher ratings than Group B before discounting), this suggests that Asch's primacy effect is *robust,* in the sense that it holds good beyond simple lists of trait terms.

If you found support for Hypothesis 2 (i.e. Group A after discounting was still higher than Group C after discounting), this would suggest that participants *were* influenced by the positive first letter they saw (even if only slightly) despite trying to discount it.

If you found support for Hypothesis 3 (i.e. Group B after discounting was still lower than Group D after discounting), this would suggest that participants *were* influenced by the negative first letter they saw (even if only slightly) despite trying to discount it.

If you found support for *both* hypotheses 2 and 3, this would suggest that perseverance works for both positive and negative material. However, if you found that only one of these hypotheses was supported, then you should try to think through why that might be the case. Whatever your results you will find some pointers in the references and further reading at the end of this chapter which will help you interpret your results.

2.5 Writing the report

You will find detailed advice on writing research reports in Chapter 10 of Banister *et al.* (1994).

You will need to begin with a title and an abstract. The *abstract* is meant to be a self-contained summary of the entire experiment, indicating the general area of the work, the method used and including a brief statement of whether or not the hypothesis being tested was supported. The *introduction* is where you provide the general rationale for the study and some of the background. You will want to briefly review the work of Asch (primacy) and Ross (perseverance) and some of the general issues around the notion of 'person perception'. You should discuss the rationale for the hypotheses you tested. In the *method* section you need to give clear details of your participants, materials and procedure in such a way that someone reading the report will know exactly what you did and could repeat it.

Present the summary of your statistical analyses clearly in the *results* section, with degrees of freedom and probablility values of your tests. Actual computations should be in a separate appendix (where you should also attach copies of your stimulus materials). The *discussion* section is where you interpret your results in the light of relevant theories. You should also be critical of the approach you used – how internally and externally valid do you feel it was? Could you have improved the study in any way – if so, how? What aspects of person perception have and have not been illuminated by the study? You should also discuss the underlying assumptions of the experimental approach to studying social psychological phenomena such as person perception. Finally, don't forget to list all the *references* you have referred to at the end of your project report.

References

Aronson, E., Wilson, T.D. and Akert, R.M. (1994) *Social Psychology: The Heart of the Mind*, New York, Harper Collins.

Asch, S.E. (1946) 'Forming impressions of personality', *Journal of Abnormal and Social Psychology*, vol.41, pp.258–90.

Banister, P., Burman, E., Parker, I., Taylor, M. and Tindall, C. (1994) *Qualitative Methods in Psychology: A Research Guide*, Buckingham, Open University Press.

Bernstein, D.A., Clarke-Stewart, A., Roy, E.J., Srull, T.K. and Wickens, C.D. (1994) *Psychology*, (3rd edn), Boston, MA, Houghton-Mifflin.

Davies, M.F. (1993) 'Dogmatism and the persistence of discredited beliefs', *Personality and Social Psychology Bulletin*, vol.19, pp.692–9.

Gaffan, E.A. (1994) 'Primacy in animal working memory – artefacts', *Animal Learning and Behaviour*, vol.22, pp.231–2.

Goffman, E. (1959) *Presentation of Self in Everyday Life*, Garden City, NY, Doubleday Anchor.

Johnson, H.M. and Seifert, C.M. (1994) 'Sources of the continued influence effect: when misinformation in memory affects later inferences', *Journal of Experimental Psychology: Learning, Memory and Cognition*, vol.20, pp.1420–36.

Jones, E.E., Rock, L., Shaver, K.G., Goethals, G.R. and Ward, L.M. (1968) 'Pattern of performance and ability attribution. An unexpected primacy effect', *Journal of Personality and Social Psychology*, vol.10, pp.317–40.

Kessner, R.P., Chiba, A.A., Jacksonsmith, P. (1994) 'Rats do show primacy and recency effects in memory for lists of spatial locations: a reply to Gaffan', *Animal Learning and Behaviour*, vol.22, pp. 214–18.

Lalljee, M. (1996) 'The interpreting self: an experimentalist perspective', in Stevens, R. (ed.) *Understanding the Self*, London, Sage/The Open University.

Loftus, E.F. (1974) 'The incredible eyewitness', *Psychology Today*, vol.8, no.7, pp.116–19.

Park, B. (1986) 'A method for studying the development of impressions in real people', *Journal of Personality and Social Psychology*, vol.51, pp.907–17.

Ross, L., Lepper, M. and Hubbard, M. (1975) 'Perseverance in self-perception and social perception: biased attributional processes in the debriefing paradigm', *Journal of Personality and Social Psychology*, vol.30, pp.880–92.

Thompson, W.C., Fong, G.T. and Rosehan, D.L. (1981) 'Inadmissable evidence and jury verdicts', *Journal of Personality and Social Psychology*, vol.5, pp.117–33.

Wright, A.A. (1994) 'Primacy effects in animal memory and human nonverbal memory', *Animal Learning and Behaviour*, vol.22, pp.219–23.

Further reading

These readings provide background information and more detail on primacy and perseverance effects.

Betz, A.L., Gannon, K.M. and Skowronski, J.J. (1992) 'The moment of tenure and the moment of truth: when it pays to be aware of recency effects in social judgments', *Social Cognition*, vol.10, pp.397–413.

Klein J.G. (1991) 'Negativity effects in impression formation: a test in the political arena', *Personality and Social Psychology Bulletin*, vol.17, pp.412–18.

Martijn, C., Spears, R., Van der Pligt, J., Jakobs, E. (1992) 'Negativity and positivity effects in person perception and inference: ability versus morality', Special Issue: Positive-negative asymmetry in affect and evaluations: Part I, *European Journal of Social Psychology*, vol.22, pp.453–63.

Mumma, G.H., and Wilson, S.B. (1995) 'Procedural debiasing of primacy/anchoring effects in clinical-like judgments', *Journal of Clinical Psychology*, vol.51, pp.841–53.

Singh, R., Onglatco, M.L.U., Sriram, N. and Tay, A.B.G. (1997) 'The warm-cold variable in impression formation: evidence for the positive-negative asymmetry', *British Journal of Social Psychology*, vol.37, pp.457–77.

Yzerbyt, V.Y. and Leyens, J.P. (1991) 'Requesting information to form an impression: the influence of valence and confirmatory status', *Journal of Experimental Social Psychology*, vol.27, pp.337–56.

Acknowledgements

I would like to thank Dorothy Miell, Christopher Wooldridge and the Open University D317 course team for their helpful advice on earlier drafts of this project and June Asprey, Karen Hough, Barry Eyre and Linda Thompson for their helpful suggestions for clarifying these notes.

Appendix: Stimulus materials and response sheets

Stimulus materials and response sheets are to be found on the following pages.

Briefing Sheet

PLEASE DO NOT TURN OVER ANY PAGES UNTIL ASKED TO DO SO

For the purposes of this study you are asked to put yourself in the role of the admissions tutor for an MSc in Applied Psychology.

You are considering the application of a Mr Smith who is currently an undergraduate at Daubhill University.

You are having difficulty making up your mind on the applicant because his application form has good and bad points.

You have therefore written to the Psychology course leader at Daubhill University asking for a reference for Mr Smith for the three main final year modules that he is doing.

The letters in this booklet are the references you receive. You should only turn over the pages when told to do so. Under no circumstances should you turn the pages back to read previous information once you have been asked to move on.

After some of the letters you are asked to give your judgement on the academic suitability of the applicant.

Please do not speak to anyone during the course of the experiment.

PLEASE DO NOT TURN OVER ANY PAGES UNTIL ASKED TO DO SO

Letter R

Department of Experimental Psychology
Daubhill University
Westshire
United Kingdom

Tel: 01266 987654

Fax: 01266 980000
Email: *enquiries@daub.ac.uk*

Doctor B. Hill
Admissions Tutor
MSc Applied Psychology
Southchester University
Southchester
Markshire
United Kingdom

6 May 1998

Dear Dr Hill,

MSc Applied Psychology

Thank you for your request for a reference for Mr Smith regarding his application for the above course. I have asked his final year tutors to write to you individually with their references. You should be receiving these over the next few days.

Please let me know if you require any further information.

Yours sincerely,

M. Jones

Dr M. Jones
Course Leader, BSc Psychology

Letter 1

Department of Experimental Psychology
Daubhill University
Westshire
United Kingdom

Tel: 01266 987654
Fax: 01266 980000
Email: *enquiries@daub.ac.uk*

Doctor B. Hill
Admissions Tutor
MSc Applied Psychology
Southchester University
Southchester
Markshire
United Kingdom

8 May 1998

Dear Dr Hill,

<u>MSc Applied Psychology</u>

Thank you for your request for a reference for Mr Smith regarding his application for the above course.

Mr Smith has been extremely committed to his studies in Module 319. His attendance has been excellent and his contributions to the class have been outstanding. His seminar papers have been strikingly original and they are always very well prepared. Although he is not quite our very best student, he picks up complex ideas straight away. He has a superb grasp of the key concepts and ideas in the area and should do extremely well in this part of his final exams. I confidently expect him to achieve a first class mark in this module. I would strongly recommend his application to your course without any reservations at all.

Please let me know if you require any further information.

Yours sincerely,

P. Green

Dr P. Green
Module Tutor, Module 319

Letter 2

Department of Experimental Psychology
Daubhill University
Westshire
United Kingdom

Tel: 01266 987654
Fax: 01266 980000
Email: *enquiries@daub.ac.uk*

Doctor B. Hill
Admissions Tutor
MSc Applied Psychology
Southchester University
Southchester
Markshire
United Kingdom

8 May 1998

Dear Dr Hill,

<u>MSc Applied Psychology</u>

Thank you for your request for a reference for Mr Smith regarding his application for the above course.

Mr Smith has been conscientious in his studies in Module 365. His attendance has been very good and his contributions in seminars have been generally good. Mr Smith has a sound understanding of the key ideas in this area and will ask questions where he is unsure. If he puts in the effort over the next few weeks I anticipate that he will get a good Upper Second class mark for this module.

Please let me know if you require any further information.

Yours sincerely,

R. White

Dr R. White
Module Tutor, Module 365

Letter 3

Department of Experimental Psychology
Daubhill University
Westshire
United Kingdom

Tel: 01266 987654
Fax: 01266 980000
Email: *enquiries@daub.ac.uk*

Doctor B. Hill
Admissions Tutor
MSc Applied Psychology
Southchester University
Southchester
Markshire
United Kingdom

8 May 1998

Dear Dr Hill,

MSc Applied Psychology

Thank you for your request for a reference for Mr Smith regarding his application for the above course.

Mr Smith has found Module 342 rather challenging though he has applied himself as required. When he has attended seminars he has listened to others rather than offer ideas himself. He has found some of the more advanced ideas just a little over his head, to be fair, but he is absorbing enough to get through. I am sure Mr Smith would be the happy to achieve a mark around the Lower Second division in his final exams and I think he is probably just about capable of it, though I worry about the clarity of his written English under examination conditions.

Please let me know if you require any further information.

Yours sincerely,

Dr S. Gold
Module Tutor, Module 342

Letter 4

Department of Experimental Psychology
Daubhill University
Westshire
United Kingdom

Tel: 01266 987654
Fax: 01266 980000
Email: *enquiries@daub.ac.uk*

Doctor B. Hill
Admissions Tutor
MSc Applied Psychology
Southchester University
Southchester
Markshire
United Kingdom

8 May 1998

Dear Dr Hill,

<u>MSc Applied Psychology</u>

Thank you for your request for a reference for Mr Smith regarding his application for the above course.

Mr Smith has unfortunately found Module 355 very difficult. His attendance has been rather sporadic and he has never explained this satisfactorily, as far as I am concerned. His seminar papers have been dreadfully rushed and he makes little or no attempt to listen to, let alone act on, feedback. Although not the weakest student in the class, he has found advanced concepts very difficult to grasp, largely because he appears to lack some of the basics which he should really have picked up earlier in the degree. Although Mr Smith is a pleasant enough student, I really do find it difficult to support his application without some reservations.

Please let me know if you require any further information.

Yours sincerely,

Dr T. Brown
Module Tutor, Module 355

Letter D

Department of Experimental Psychology
Daubhill University
Westshire
United Kingdom

Tel: 01266 987654
Fax: 01266 980000
Email: *enquiries@daub.ac.uk*

Doctor B. Hill
Admissions Tutor
MSc Applied Psychology
Southchester University
Southchester
Markshire
United Kingdom

10 May 1998

Dear Dr Hill,

MSc Applied Psychology

It has been brought to my attention that an error has been made in the recent correspondence to you regarding Mr J.F. Smith. It would appear that the very first letter you received was in fact referring to Mr J.S. Smith who is also doing our BSc Psychology degree. You should of course disregard the information contained in that letter, as it has no bearing on Mr J.F. Smith's application.

I do apologise for this embarrassing error and hope you will accept our apologies.

Please let me know if you require any further information about Mr J.F. Smith.

Yours sincerely,

M. Jones

Dr M. Jones
Course Leader, BSc Psychology

Response sheet

Please indicate your judgement of the academic suitability of this applicant for the course given all the information you have been given about him so far. Please circle a number rather than any words.

Very
unsuitable   1   2   3   4   5   6   7   Very
suitable

Letter C

Department of Experimental Psychology
Daubhill University
Westshire
United Kingdom

Tel: 01266 987654
Fax: 01266 980000
Email: *enquiries@daub.ac.uk*

Doctor B. Hill
Admissions Tutor
MSc Applied Psychology
Southchester University
Southchester
Markshire
United Kingdom

8 May 1998

Dear Dr Hill,

<u>MSc Applied Psychology</u>

Thank you for your request for a reference for Mr Smith regarding his application for the above course.

Mr Smith has found Module 339 fine overall and has performed fairly similarly to other students. There are no problems with his attendance and his contributions are sensible enough. Like most students he enjoys some parts of the module more than others. He will get a pretty average mark in the module overall, possibly a good Lower Second or possibly a low Upper Second.

Please let me know if you require any further information.

Yours sincerely,

W. Gray

Dr W. Gray
Module Tutor, Module 339

Response sheet

Please indicate your judgement of the academic suitability of this applicant for the course given all the information you have been given about him so far. Please circle a number rather than any words.

Very
unsuitable   1   2   3   4   5   6   7   Very
suitable

CHAPTER 2

RELATIONSHIPS, SOCIAL NETWORKS AND SOCIAL INTERACTION: AN EXPLORATION IN DIARY METHODOLOGIES

by Patrick McGhee with Dorothy Miell

Contents

1 Introduction

1.1 The project

This project deals with the psychological interpretation of accounts given by people of their everyday experiences in relationships. The project is based around data collected by you (and, if you wish, by a partner, friend or colleague also) using a 'diary' format.

This project should contribute directly to your substantive understanding of the social psychology of personal relationships. As Miell and Dallos (1996) note, the recent rapid increase in social psychological research in personal relationships has drawn on traditional research methodologies and assumptions and has been criticized on the grounds that it has not adequately addressed certain key features of all relationships such as (i) joint construction of relationships, (ii) time and relationship development, and (iii) the diversity of relationship functions. This project attempts to address each of these issues directly or indirectly.

The project is in four phases.

Phase 1: Introduction

During this phase you should read sections 1 and 2 of this guide which contain information on the aims of the project and a critical introduction to the methodology you will use. During this phase you will begin to develop your hypotheses and the research questions which you will seek to address from the data collected.

Phase 2: Data collection

In this phase you (and possibly another person) fill in a simple diary sheet once a day for 28 days. Master copies of these sheets are provided for you (see Appendix). These sheets take about 10 minutes to complete and are kept on one side by you until the end of the 28-day period when you will analyse the responses according to specific social psychological research principles. The process of data collection is fully described in section 3 of this guide.

Phase 3: Analysis of data

Section 4 of this guide describes phase 3, analysis of the data, and for the quantitative options (i.e. options 3 and 4) should not be read until you have fully completed the data collection phase.

Phase 4: Writing the report

Section 5 describes how to write up the report both in terms of presenting your findings according to standard conventions for scholarly reports and in terms of what to emphasize and what you can safely leave out. In particular, this section contains instructions and suggestions for writing up your project in an appropriate format for submission as a formal report.

1.2 Aims and objectives of the project

The goal of this project is to help you develop your understanding of some of the key themes of the social psychology of relationships including social networks, relationship functions, communication in relationships and intersubjectivity. The project will also help you consider the advantages and disadvantages of the diary technique as a research methodology and the differing approaches of qualitative and quantitative analyses of individuals' experiences in relationships.

In practical terms the project involves you (and, optionally, a partner, colleague or friend) keeping a special type of structured 'diary' over 28 days and then at the end of that period interpreting the significance of the data recorded therein. In particular, this project will be exploring the ways in which we *construct* our conceptions of self and relationships over time, and how those conceptions emerge and are negotiated in our everyday social and practical activities.

You will also have the opportunity, if you wish, to analyse the ways in which two individuals can offer *differing*, even contradictory, accounts of the same relationship.

A further aim of this project is to give you the opportunity to collect and interpret empirical data of your own in a systematic and focused manner so that you can come to informed conclusions about the applicability of key theories in social psychology to *your* life situation.

Since this project can be done with a quantitative/nomothetic dimension, or as an exclusively qualitative/social constructionist (hence hermeneutic) activity, you will find yourself able to think through the practical and methodological consequences of adopting one or other perspective. This should consolidate your understanding of the differences between these two approaches (see Stevens, 1998, where he discusses the differences between nomothetic and hermeneutic epistemologies).

Finally, and very importantly, this project will give you the chance to use a specific and increasingly common technique in social psychology, the diary method, in order that you can critically evaluate the usefulness of the approach.

1.3 Diary technique: the basics

The diary technique, for present purposes, involves a participant either filling in a brief questionnaire at the end of their day, completing simple rating scales measuring various aspects of the important interactions that have taken place during that day, or writing a longer and more open-ended description. Typically, the participant also records data on the relationship, on how long the interaction lasted, where it took place, and so on. This 'daily log' of social interactions enables the researchers to collect data day-by-day rather than having to rely upon questions such as, 'What kind of important social interactions have you experienced in the past month?'

1.4 Theory and method in studying personal relationships

We will now consider the way in which the diary technique might be able to address some of the issues raised by the researchers who take a critical view of how best to study the *meaningful* processes and structures of personal relationships rather than the objective publically observable behaviours only (see Miell and Dallos, 1996; Duck 1994; Burnett *et al.*, 1987). There are several possibilities and you must reflect carefully on which one(s) you are going to focus on, and just as importantly which ones you are going to ignore.

Practical project tip

The diary technique lends itself to many empirical questions. You must be careful to resist the temptation to analyse all of the questions or issues that it can address. Within the context of this project you are recommended to focus on only two or three key questions. In this kind of project you will be demonstrating a greater degree of competence by addressing a small number of questions in depth rather than a large number superficially. A wide range of possibilities are discussed in these briefing notes, but you should treat them as a menu of suggestions and not as a checklist of questions you must gather data on and analyse. Your primary task in the early stages of the diary project is to narrow down the issues you want to analyse. Your tutor will be able to advise you on whether the analyses you anticipate doing are too ambitious, too modest or appropriate in terms of the project as a piece of work within the course or module you are taking.

The link between social interactions and relationships in general is discussed by Alan Radley (1996). Radley considers different ways in which we can interpret social interaction through knowledge of context. In particular, he emphasizes how context itself can be altered through crucial 'moves' in the social exchanges between two people. In relation to this project you might want to consider whether or not a diary approach can help us identify these context changes. You might also want to consider Radley's discussion of 'social episodes as ceremonial occasions' (*ibid.*, section 6.4). If there is a ceremonial or formal event scheduled for you within the 28-day period the diary project will cover, then it might be interesting to explore some of the ideas that Radley raises in his discussions through a diary approach.

Dallos (1996a) reviews a number of theoretical ideas which may lend themselves to analysis with a diary methodology, such as the attributions people make over time within relationships and the processes of interaction amongst triads. The diary project would allow you to do this through one of the options where both you and a partner keep a diary. If both of you share an acquaintance or relation then, in principle, you could examine how interactions between the three of you develop over the 28-day period.

Health warning!

You should strongly resist adopting a pseudo-therapeutic role when discussing the diary contents with your partner or friend. You should make it clear to them that that is not what the project is about. Even if *you* are very clear about this in your own mind, you need to be aware that *others* might see you as being in a position to adopt such a therapeutic role. You need to be alert to this and avoid assuming a role which is being projected on to you. There are also a range of ethical issues that need to be addressed in this area, and these are discussed more fully below.

Dallos (1996b) discusses the idea of *change* in relationships, covering theories and empirical studies in the areas of friendship, leaving home and the family life cycle generally. A study using a day-by-day diary technique might be well suited to the idea of relationship change. Even if friendship choice and leaving home are not issues which you anticipate will be central to your life over the 28-day recording period, the *idea* of transformation as presented by Dallos could offer some powerful concepts with which to analyse your diary account.

Miell and Croghan (1996) present a wide range of material which is especially useful for this project and which raises a number of issues which you may wish to explore empirically through the diary method. For example, the idea of social networks (their diversity and function) can be investigated through recording in the diaries the range of individuals with whom you come into contact and the kinds of interaction you have with them. You might be surprised by the relative frequency and importance of the interactions you have within your personal ('significant others'), exchange, interactive and global networks (see Miell and Croghan, 1996, section 2.1). Miell and Croghan also provide many interesting ideas related to forms of exchange in relationships, and a diary study monitoring 'give-and-take' across a period of time might help develop your understanding of equity, interdependence and communality in real everyday relationships. Issues of power and ambiguity are also addressed by Miell and Croghan, and you may want to consider analysing the ways in which relationships (through social interactions) address the ambiguities, contradictions and boundaries of power.

1.5 Conceptual background to diary studies

Research into personal relationships has been criticized for running before it can walk. Specifically, elaborate and complex models have been put forward to *explain* behaviour in relationships when the behaviour to be explained is not itself adequately *described* (an example of this might be the more mathematically involved versions of equity and exchange theory discussed by Miell and Croghan, 1996, and by Argyle, 1996). Diary methods were developed in the late 1970s and early 1980s partly as a means of addressing this problem. In other words, the diary technique was seen initially as a way of describing how relationships are actually conducted outside of the laboratory (and outside of the limitations of restrictive standard questionnaires).

Much research on personal relationships is based on relationship questionnaires, yet it has been known for some time that even participants who are attempting to present the truth, as they see it, are likely to present their relationship development as being more smooth and more positive in retrospect than they described it at the time *as* it developed (Miell, 1987). It was widely believed amongst psychologists that diaries directly addressed some of the main problems of questionnaires. For example, questionnaires which asked questions such as 'To what extent would you describe your conversations with your partner as generally rewarding?' were seen as being highly problematic for a number of reasons. How could participants remember their interactions? How could they give a single tick on a scale to describe what 'generally' happened? Were the questions relevant to the features of the participants' relationships? Such questionnaire studies, by asking for a general summary statement about the relationship at this moment in time, inevitably emphasized the *states* of relationships rather than the important *processes* of relationships (Duck and Sants, 1983). Diary studies were seen as a way of 'getting up close' to relationships. In this context, diary studies were seen as a necessary adjunct to studies like those of Byrne (1971), which looked at the relationship between perceived similarity and liking in artificial laboratory settings, and which were high on internal validity but low on external validity.

> **Internal and external validity in personal relationship research**
>
> *Internal validity* is the extent to which an instrument (e.g. a rating scale of relationship satisfaction) actually does measure what it claims to measure (i.e. relationship satisfaction in actual relationships). If the instrument does accurately measure what it claims to, then it is said to be *high* in internal validity and research carried out using that measure is considered correspondingly more useful.
>
> *External validity* is the extent to which the results of a study can in principle be applied to 'real life', *external* to the conditions under which the original study was performed. Typically, research carried out in a laboratory (the majority of social psychology experiments and questionnaire studies) is seen as being low in external validity, and therefore problematic in terms of its application to the outside world.

In personal relationship research, studies based on diaries are seen as possessing fairly high external validity (inasmuch as they attempt to be records of relationships as they happen over a period of time). However, as with other areas of social psychology there is generally a trade off: as external validity is improved, internal validity is compromised (because experimenter control is reduced) and vice versa.

Many diary studies in this tradition contributed significantly to achieving the aims of improving the external validity of personal relationship research and generally providing adequate accounts of what people did in their everyday relationships. Most noteworthy was the early work of the Rochester Group in the USA which found interesting results from diary studies, such as the fact that general life satisfaction was best predicted (for both male and female participants) by the number of *female* acquaintances the participant reported interacting with over the period of the study (Wheeler and Nezleck, 1977). Similarly, UK research, for example, by Duck and Miell (1982) studying friendships, found that satisfaction ratings were the best predictors of estimated future duration of the relationship, and (somewhat counter-intuitively) that ratings by males of intimacy in interactions were greater than those made by females.

More recently, however, diaries have become less an instrument designed to accurately monitor relationships 'up close' and more an opportunity for helping individuals articulate their *interpretations* of their immediate experiences in and of relationships. It is now recognized that diary sheets filled in each evening reporting on the interactions and relationship experiences of that day cannot and should not be used as unproblematic records of what 'actually' happened, but rather should be treated as just another form of account, constructed by a individual in a particular context, and involving a search for significance and a construction of meaning (e.g. Wetherell and Maybin, 1996; and Potter, 1996).

An interesting early example of this interpretative or more social constructionist approach to the diary methodology can be found in the work of Sue Wilkinson (1987). She arranged for pairs of participants who had never met before to meet over a 4 to 6-week period and to record their impressions of each other, and of the impression-formation process itself, in an open-ended way. Participants were encouraged to reflect upon their views of the other's views of them. Amongst a number of intriguing findings, Wilkinson found that monitoring of the other remained extensive over most of the 4 to 6 weeks, until the couples hit a 'transition point' where either: (i) the relationship became 'stuck', at which point the monitoring of impressions being formed hit a plateau and then tailed off, the couples apparently no longer motivated to monitor impressions; or (ii) the relationship 'took off', when it appeared to have developed a momentum of its own, and perceptions of each other seemed less conspicuous.

A common characteristic of the accounts gathered by Wilkinson in her research is the very different perspectives offered by participants on the same relationship. For example, one woman 'F' states to the researcher after a couple of meetings with 'C':

> I sense there is a barrier of some sort between C and myself but can't quite place it. Although we superficially talk as equals there is something extra on her side – is it she treats me or I feel she treats me as one would a child? – listening, nodding, and feeding back some points. I can't quite fix it.
>
> *(ibid., p.53)*

However, 'C' has quite a different view:

> My first impression that I could make a friend of F has not changed ... My basic requirements for friendship are sense of humour, integrity/dependability, interesting ... I judge that F meets these requirements. (We are) two people with mutual interests who like to talk.
>
> *(ibid., p.53)*

As Wilkinson notes, 'Not surprisingly, this relationship never really "takes off" ' (*ibid.*, p.53).

Diary methodology is *not* a single technique but one common characteristic is that the participant completes some kind of written statement about what they have experienced in their social interactions and/or personal relationships on a day-by-day basis. The statement might be tightly structured by the researcher in the form of a mini questionnaire – for example, a series of rating scales which the participant ticks off as appropriate (this was the basic approach of Wheeler's Rochester team). Alternatively, at the other end of the spectrum is the entirely open-ended approach such as that used by Wilkinson. Here, participants are only given some general guidance at the outset about what types of issue to cover and are largely left to construct their statements as they wish. These relationship accounts can be seen as types of personal 'texts'

(Potter, 1996; Sapsford, 1998) which lend themselves to analysis from a discourse analytic perspective.

As you might anticipate, the 'mini questionnaire' approach is usually pursued by researchers who subscribe to an experimentalist scientific model of social psychology and who seek to pursue quantitative analyses of data (Lalljee, 1996; Argyle, 1996). By contrast, researchers who employ open-ended diary methods tend to subscribe to more social constructionist-orientated perspectives (see Wetherell and Maybin, 1996). Thus, the decision to include (and analyse) a mini questionnaire is more than just a 'technical' methodological decision on the part of researchers; it is also a commitment to a particular philosophy and set of assumptions regarding the interpretation of relationships.

2 The fieldwork

2.1 The project options

There are four options in this project.

Option 1	*Theme:*	Personal constructions of relationships
	Methods:	Qualitative
	Participants:	Just you
Option 2	*Theme:*	Intersubjectivity
	Methods:	Qualitative
	Participants:	You and a partner, colleague or friend
Option 3	*Theme:*	Social networks
	Method:	Quantitative
	Participants:	Just you
Option 4	*Theme:*	Significant social interactions
	Method:	Quantitative
	Participants:	You and a partner, colleague or friend

Over a period of four weeks you will complete a 'diary'. On each day of this period you will collect data. This will be either (i) an open-ended response section only (qualitative), or (ii) a structured response sheet (quantitative). You will collect this data either (i) on your own ('individual') or (ii) with a friend, colleague or partner ('dyad' – NB *the term 'dyad' or 'dyadic' means two people*). Thus your project will fall into one of four categories. Each option has an associated 'theme'. For the qualitative/individual option (option 1) the theme is *personal constructions of relationships*. For the qualitative/dyadic (option 2) the theme is *intersubjectivity*.

For the quantitative/individual option (option 3) the theme is *social networks*. For option 4 (the quantitative/dyadic option) the theme is *significant social interactions*. Whichever option you adopt you will be expected to focus on the relevant theme in terms of the research questions you adopt and in terms of your write-up.

2.2 Choosing an option

It should be noted that none of these options is any more difficult than any other. They each have their own specific challenges in terms of question formulation, data collection, data analysis, data interpretation and links to theory. As is very often the case in research methodology, each option with which you are faced entails different advantages and disadvantages, and it is important that you consider these costs and benefits before committing yourself to one path or another. Further, when it comes to interpreting and assessing your results, you should be aware of the implications of having used one method rather than another. We can consider now the choices you are faced with one by one.

Individual vs. dyadic?

Are you going to collect data on your own, or are you going to invite someone else to complete a diary too, the data from which you will then analyse? This decision involves practical, analytic, ethical and personal considerations.

In *practical* terms, if there is not a specific other person with whom you have an ongoing relationship (personal, social or occupational), then you simply chose option 1 or 3 by default. Note that if you choose options 1 or 3 you will still need to be in a position where you have some interactions with other people (even if only by telephone). On the other hand, you might have such a relationship but it may be impractical for the other person to complete 28 sheets on 28 consecutive days.

In *analytic* terms, you may prefer to focus primarily on issues to do with self and look in detail at how one person (you) experiences relationships, social interaction and social networks, rather than focusing on any one relationship and its joint construction. You should note however that, whether you select an individual option (1 or 3) or a dyadic option (2 or 4), you will be able (and expected) to address *some* issues relating to both self and relationships. The option you choose implies a difference in approach and in the type of data you will be collecting, but the general issues remain broadly the same.

If you choose one of the individual options, then your analytic approach will be, at least in part, particularly concerned with developments over *time*. Although the data-collection period is only 28 days, you may well still find a number of clear developments, troughs and peaks of perceptions and experiences coming through. Additionally, you might find that certain days of the week or times of the day have characteristic regularities for you as an individual.

If you choose one of the dyadic options, you will not only have twice as much data, but you will have twice as many alternatives in terms of the questions you can address. In the qualitative dyadic option (option 2) the focus is first and foremost on how you and your partner see the relationship between the two of you. This means that the accounts given in the diaries should reflect interactions that occur between you more than anything else. In this option you will have a collection of 56 daily qualitative accounts (28 from 2 persons). The theme of this option is *intersubjectivity*. In this option you will be exploring the ways in which the diary accounts differ from each other and yet are also similar to each other (there are other aspects which will be explained to you more fully later in this guide). In general terms, you will need to look for aspects of personal accounts of relationships, as given by your partner and yourself, and explore the subtleties of meaning in each account. The ways in which the accounts develop over time is also likely to be an aspect of your analysis.

However you conduct your research, it is crucial that *ethical* considerations are paramount. Quite apart from the general moral consideration that we should be sensitive to the consequences of our actions for others, as psychologists it is important that we develop our appreciation of ethical considerations in conducting research.

Finally, in *personal* terms you need to think very carefully about what it means to select one option over another in terms of individual vs. dyadic. Every set of personal circumstances will be different, and there is certainly no reason to expect that this project will cause any particular personal difficulties for you, but there are a number of personal issues you might well want to reflect on before finally selecting either an individual option or a dyadic option.

If you do choose a dyad option, you should not feel that it is necessary or even preferable to use a partner with whom you are in an ongoing emotional or 'romantic' relationship. The project can work just as well with a friend, a work colleague or even a relative. Indeed, although you might find the idea of doing a diary project with your 'romantic' partner very intriguing, there are very good grounds for aiming to do this project with someone who is *not* in such a relationship with you. (The wording of the rest of this guide will often refer to 'partner' and draw upon some examples from romantic relationships, but you should not see this as conveying any kind of expectation or encouragement to focus on that kind of relationship.)

If you choose one of the dyadic options, then obviously at the end of the data-collection period you as the researcher will need to analyse the diary sheets from the other person. You will no doubt be very interested in how your partner, friend, work colleague or relative saw various events and episodes over the 28-day period (notwithstanding the fact that you may have jointly discussed some of these issues as part of normal everyday conversations). It is also important that you are sensitive to the differences in perspective that will inevitably arise when you review the accounts that have been generated. There is no single 'correct' account of an event or process – the dyadic options revolve around exploring the ways in which such accounts frame and express experience in different ways, not which is 'right' and which is 'wrong'.

Think carefully about how you might react to such differences. Would you be surprised? uneasy? intrigued? If you believe you might feel uncomfortable in any way, you might want to chose an alternative option.

Qualitative vs. quantitative data collection

Here you need to think about whether you are going to adopt an essentially social constructionist or more quantitative/experimentalist approach to data collection.

In the qualitative options, you (and, for the dyadic option, the other participant) will be required to write an open-ended account of the subjective experience of social interactions with significant others, and the relevant relationships. If you attempt option 1 you will be focusing on the way in which you construct your relationships as an individual. One possible way of making sense of the range of different relationships you are involved in, and come into contact with, is suggested by Weiss (1974). He discusses a range of *functions* that different relationships serve. You might want to focus on how you make sense of what you 'get out of' relationships. It is not compulsory for you to focus on the notion of relationship functions in option 1, but you may find such a focus useful. The defining theme of option 1 is the idea of the *personal construction of relationships and relationship experience*. Your own personal constructions could take many forms but you will be invited to review the metaphors, narratives, categories, and interpretative repertoires generally with which you construct your own account of your lived experiences. One of the issues you might wish to explore within this option, for example, is the ways in which your personal accounts are reflections of public accounts evident in the wider cultures and subcultures in which you live or have lived.

If you *do* decide to emphasize the role of relationship *functions* in your analyses in option 1 of this project, you will need to focus not so much on what the functions of your relationships *really* are, but more on how you *construct* the meaning of those relationships and their function.

By contrast, in option 3 (the quantitative individual option) you will be correlating two variables, such as the correlation between perceived 'satisfaction' in episodes of social interaction and perceived 'empathy' in the same episodes (you will be doing this with several pairs of variables). The information from the correlations will help you test hypotheses regarding the key features of relationships and the interactions which take place within them. For example, you might want to test hypotheses relating to the different aspects of interaction (e.g. between interaction satisfaction and interaction disclosure), between different aspects of relationships (relationship duration and relationship commitment), or between aspects of relationships and aspects of interactions (relationship duration and interaction disclosure).

The focus of option 3 is on social networks. (See Miell and Croghan, 1996, pp.268–77 for general background information on this topic.)

In the quantitative dyadic option (option 4) you will be correlating your ratings of, say, communication clarity in interactions with the ratings given by your partner, friend, work colleague or relative *for those same interactions*.

For all four options you will be given further guidance on how to analyse your data in section 4. For the quantitative options you will need to consult a statistical textbook to show you precisely how to carry out the statistical tests. For the qualitative options you are given a series of suggestions on how to interpret the accounts given by yourself (and by your participant partner for option 2) applying a discourse analysis to the diary entries.

Getting the feel of discourse analysis

At this point you should have a reasonable overview of what the different options in this project involve. However, for the qualitative options you may not have had time to think through exactly what discourse analysis actually involves or the kind of approach it takes to social psychological issues. We strongly recommend that you spend some time considering this before proceeding. The simplest way to get a feel for discourse analysis of the kind relevant to this project is to look at section 4.1 of this guide and you will be able to decide whether or not you are intrigued enough to attempt option 1 or 2 and attempt to analyse *your* everyday writing about relationships. If you feel that the analysis of discourse is *not* what you want to do then you are advised to tackle either option 3 or option 4.

In all of the options the standard procedure would be to instruct participants (including yourself) to set aside the diary sheets day by day, and not consult them retrospectively. This is the way all previous studies have operated, and for the sake of simplicity you are probably wise in this instance to do the same. However, just because it is the common practice does not mean it is necessarily correct. In particular, if you are considering a qualitative option you might want to pause and think about this issue just a little bit more deeply ...

To set aside, or not to set aside:

Please answer the following question before reading on.

Why do you think researchers normally insist that their participants set aside their diary sheets (usually in an envelope) immediately after completion?

If your answer to the above was along the lines of, 'To avoid later diary sheet completion being "contaminated" by earlier ones', then you would be right. However, we can reflect on the model of data collection which this concern implies.

If we believe that the diary sheets are more-or-less accurate snapshot representations of everyday life (the experimentalist view), then it makes methodological sense to restrict participants' access to previous sheets since the researcher wants each day's sheet to reflect *only* that day's events directly and 'without prejudice'. This is because the diary sheets are seen as essentially a technical instrument, recording participants' perceptions and experiences.

If, on the other hand, we believe that the diary sheets are essentially means of helping the participant construct a personal account of their experience over time (the social constructionist view), then there is no reason in principle why participants should *not* have access to earlier sheets. The participant might wish to build cumulatively on previous accounts – possibly qualifying, amending and elaborating on earlier statements, indeed possibly actively distancing herself from statements made previously. In this instance, the researcher is interested in identifying ways in which the participant's account is constructed over time and would want to allow the participant to draw on whatever 'texts' and documents the participant wishes.

In your project you will want to consider which of these two approaches you wish to pursue. However, while it is perfectly possible to adopt the social constructionist approach (options 1 or 2) and decide *either* to allow participants to refer to previous sheets or direct them to set the sheets aside, if you wish to adopt a more traditionally nomothetic quantitative approach (options 3 or 4) then you need to insist that participants do not refer to earlier sheets – otherwise it would be difficult to interpret the data within a traditional nomothetic scientific paradigm.

If you decide to take a quantitative approach to the project (options 3 or 4), then as well as summarizing the overall patterns in your data you will be expected to test some basic hypotheses regarding the *correlations between* pairs of key variables, such as satisfaction and intimacy in relationships, using standard statistical tests. Details on the kinds of statistical calculations you will be required to carry out are given in section 4 of this guide.

2.3 Formulating your research question(s)

So far you have considered the diary method, some of the background to the use of diaries in social psychology, and the options that are open to you in this project. It is now necessary to consider the specific research questions you will be attempting to answer in the project.

The first point to make, as mentioned in section 1.4 above, is the importance of sticking to a manageable number of questions. The diaries will generate a great deal of data and you always have to remember that you are in no way expected to analyse anywhere near all of it. The only data you need to analyse are the data relevant to your research questions.

The next issue to bear in mind is that, while there is nothing inherently wrong with simple comparisons such as, say, comparing the kinds of interaction you have over the recording period with males compared to females, you do need to recognize that such simple comparisons often do not provide much scope for detailed analytical interpretations. They can, nevertheless, be done well if approached in an imaginative and reflective manner.

Research questions with diary techniques typically involve descriptive or correlational research questions.

Descriptive research questions

Let us consider descriptive approaches first. These involve research questions which ask, 'What is the range of ... ?', or 'What are the different types of ... ?', or 'What are the patterns of ... ?', and which in *quantitative* or *nomothetic* research try to describe the various forms of social interactions and experiences which participants undergo in relationships. These questions involve collecting data which allow the researcher to classify different types of reported activities. The key here is to go beyond a simple listing of social interactions or experiences and to try to *classify* activities, ideally linking them to some sort of theoretical framework.

Another kind of descriptive research question which can be formulated for the qualitative or hermeneutic options focuses not so much on the reported social experiences as such, but rather on the way in which such experiences are articulated. Thus, questions under this heading might include, 'What are the different ways in which people express X?', 'How is X described in relationships?', 'How do people construct arguments about X in relationships?', 'How do people make their point about X in relationships?'

This kind of approach, which focuses on the *discursive* aspects of relationship accounts as produced through diaries, draws heavily on social constructionist approaches (see Wetherell and Maybin, 1996). From this perspective, we are trying to formulate questions which relate to the way in which accounts of relationships and interaction are constructed, rather than the events and actions which they appear to describe *per se*.

The issues to be dealt with here include the images, metaphors, contrasts, justifications, contradictions and ambiguities which are characteristic of relationship accounts and the interpretative resources people draw upon in making sense of their world.

In traditional experimental social psychology, research questions are typically formulated in *advance* of collecting data, with data being used to identify answers to those questions. This is referred to as a deductive approach. By contrast, discourse analysis and associated social constructionist approaches are more flexible, allowing the data to pose new and unexpected questions. Nevertheless, even the most inductively orientated researcher will have a clear idea about *why* they are collecting the data and what the general focus of enquiry is. In the context of this project it is important that you do not lose yourself in the rich data set that you will be collecting. Therefore, it is worth spending some time thinking through some ways of constructing a research question for your project.

Let us consider first what kind of social constructionist research question might work here in the context of this project (most relevant to options 1 and 2). Consider the following possible research question:

'What are the different words people use to describe relationships?'

What do you think of this as a possible research question for this project?

Is it too narrow? Too broad?

This question, in its present form, is too *broad*. It is also too vague. It is also not a question which particularly needs a diary methodology to answer. A better version might be:

'What are the *forms of metaphors* and *semantic themes* used to describe the *functions* of a range of ongoing relationships (considered as personal constructions)?'

This is a different question, but it is now more focused (it specifies the functions of relationships rather than relationships in general), it is also more specific ('metaphors' and 'semantic themes' rather than 'words'), and it attempts to exploit the distinctive opportunities of the diary approach ('range of ongoing relationships').

As it now stands, this question is satisfactory. However, it can still be improved. The question has no explicit theoretical rationale. That is, although the answer to the question might be of some intrinsic interest, it does not look likely to shed any light on any theory or general account of anything to do with relationships. In particular, no matter how we finished up answering this question we would be none the wiser about theories or perspectives in social psychology. To make this question a better one we need to link it to a theoretical position or perspective in social psychology.

(Ideally, we should begin with a theoretical perspective and then work out questions which we can collect data on and then answer, allowing us to offer some sort of evaluation or reinterpretation of that perspective in the light of attempting to answer that question. In practice, formulating research questions is a mixture of both approaches – we derive questions that are important to ask about particular theories, all the time thinking about what kinds of question our available methodologies are and are not able to answer.)

One way of improving this sample research question would be to reformulate it as follows:

> 'What are the implications of the forms of metaphors and semantic themes used to describe the functions of a range of ongoing relationships (considered as personal constructions) *for Weiss's (1974) model of relationship provisions?*'

This question is now set to shed some light on Weiss's account of social networks and their functions. If the patterning in people's accounts is consistent with Weiss's functional analysis then that would help us expand our understanding of his theoretical framework. If, on the other hand, the accounts are not consistent, then that might lead us to question whether different relationships really do serve the functions that Weiss says they do (though we would hardly reject his model out of hand on this evidence alone).

Correlational research questions

So far we have discussed descriptive research questions for both quantitative and qualitative work. In contrast to such descriptive questions, *correlational* questions typically involve testing a hypothesized relationship between two variables which are measured in the diary sheets. Correlational questions are appropriate for quantitative research. Each scale on the diary sheets for options 3 and 4 (see Appendix) provides the data for a variable. The variables which you are able to measure in the project are either *relationship* variables or *interaction* variables. The former relate to the nature of the relationship between you and the other person with whom you have had the most significant interaction of the day, and the latter refer to aspects of the specific interaction episode. The relationship and interaction variables to be used in the project are listed in Table 1.

Table 1 List of variables to be measured for the quantitative options

Relationship variables

Satisfaction with the relationship

Intimacy of the relationship

Similarity (between you and the other)

Empathy

Liking for other

Commitment to relationship

Interaction variables

Satisfaction (with interaction)

Intimacy (of interaction)

Similarity on topics of conversation

Empathy

Feelings towards other

Significance of interaction

You might want to hypothesize that your interactions are such that similarity and feelings towards other are related in some way. A research hypothesis here might be:

> 'Similarity of topics of conversation will be positively correlated with feelings towards the other person.'

Again, as in the formulation of descriptive questions, it is important that you link your research questions to some aspect of theory. For example, you might be motivated to explore Byrne's (1961) contention that, everything else being equal, similarity leads to attraction (see Dallos, 1996b). Of course, you have to be careful not to imply in your write-up of the project that a correlation between two variables suggests a *causal* relationship. (For example, reading ability and shoe size are strongly correlated amongst children but one does not cause the other. Rather, as children get *older* their feet get bigger and they learn more about reading.)

The variables in Table 1 are the variables which previous researchers have used and which have been found in the past to be most useful. However, it is possible for you to *add* additional variables if you have a specific research question you want to explore. You might, for example, consider *trust* to be a key aspect of personal relationships and social interaction, and might like to explore how trust relates to the other variables which are being examined. However, it is worth bearing in mind that the most interesting variables are those on which individuals score different ratings; that is, variables which *discriminate* between the things that you are measuring. It is, for example, more interesting to measure a variable along which people vary (such as 'extraversion') than a variable on which almost everyone is the same (such as 'enjoys leisure').

As with the qualitative descriptive research questions it is important that you avoid trying to analyse all the data from all the variables. *You should focus first and foremost on those variables which you actually mention explicitly in your research questions.*

In summary then, research questions need to be clear, concise, narrowly focused and linked to some kind of theoretical perspective. Ideally, they should be formulated in such a way that different answers to the research question would lead us to different kinds of evaluations of the theories to which they are linked. A research question which leads us to the same interpretation of its theoretical background no matter what answer to that question we arrive at, having assessed the data, has very little point to it indeed.

3 Data collection

3.1 All options

Your task for this phase of the project is to collect 28 days of data on 28 diary sheets. Make sure you use the correct diary sheet for the option you have selected (see Appendix). Make sure if you are doing option 2 or 4 that the other diarist is fully briefed on what is expected of them. You will be able to brief them only after reading the relevant guidance notes in this section for the option.

Before collecting any data, you should reflect upon whether you have followed ethical guidelines in relation to the other diarist (in options 2 and 4). Have you received informed consent? Have you taken steps to establish confidentiality, and reassured the participant to that effect? Have you made clear their right to withdraw at any time? You should make sure you have addressed these thoroughly before continuing. If you have not dealt with these issues, you must address them now *before* collecting any data.

A further consideration here is what to do if your co-diarist drops out of the exercise halfway through. If the other person drops out and has completed 15 or more of the sheets, you will have enough data to continue as planned albeit on a more modest basis. If the other person has completed 14 or less (that is half or less) of the sheets, you should continue your data collection and subsequent analysis as though you were doing option 1 (if your partner drops out of option 2), or as though you were doing option 3 (if your partner drops out of option 4). This strategy is also an option open to you even if the other drops out having completed 15 or more diary sheets.

3.2 Additional note for qualitative options (1 and 2) only

There is, in principle, no word limit on the number of words you write on the diary sheets, but there is probably no need to write more than 100 words – and you probably need at least 30 words a day as an absolute minimum. There may be days when you feel you have nothing to say – this might be for a number of reasons – nevertheless try to write down what you can. If you have not been in contact with anyone that day, then write down your thoughts about that fact. Your diary entries need to describe what interactions you have in different relationships (option 1) or in a particular relationship (option 2), and to some extent state what you think about those interactions. You want to achieve some middle ground between superficial minimalist comments that will give you no scope for analysis and interpretation when you come to write the project up, on the one hand, and engaging in extensive detailed analysis each day on the other. It would be inappropriate here to give advice on exactly *how* you should express yourself in the diary. This is by definition a matter of personal style and inclination. The whole point of diary studies and the discourse analysis that will follow is that there are no constraints on how you choose to describe your experience. All that can be said is that you should *not* feel that you have to adopt a literary style of any kind or that you should be worried about grammar or spelling – these considerations are completely irrelevant here. All that is necessary is that your entries are legible enough to be clear when you come to read them at the end of the data-collection period.

3.3 Additional note for quantitative options (3 and 4) only

The diary sheets for options 3 and 4 have two parts. Part 1 asks you to rate on a number of scales the most significant dyadic interaction you have had that day – you need to rate the interaction and the relationship. You will find it helpful to write down a *brief* definition of how you will interpret the rating scale words (empathy, liking, etc.) and what they mean to you. If you are doing option 4, you can either instruct your co-diarist to use your definitions, or agree upon a general understanding between you. In social psychological research, participants are not given extended definitions of such terms and it is unnecessary to do so here.

Whatever your definitions you should try to be consistent from day to day. In Part 2 you are asked to record up to a maximum of 10 other dyadic interactions you have in any one day. For all of these ratings, you need to focus only on dyadic interactions: that is, *interactions where only you and one other person are involved*. Others may be present, but not involved. Interactions do not have to be face-to-face, so telephone calls can count (but make a note in your diary that this was the case).

3.4 Specific guidance for option 1: qualitative/individual

Make sure you use the 'Diary sheet for option 1' (see Appendix). On the sheets you are required to write down an open-ended account of the 'three most significant interactions' of the day. The meaning of 'significant interactions' is difficult to define but one practical way is as follows: *significant interactions are ones which, at the end of the day, are most memorable*. Significant interactions could be significant for a number of reasons. It might be because important matters were discussed or because the interaction influenced the relationship between you and the other person. You are asked to write about the three *most* significant – even if they are in an absolute sense not very significant at all. If you have difficulty with the idea of 'significant', simply consider those interaction which are meaningful, interesting or thought-provoking. If you do not have three interactions of any kind in a day, then describe those that you do have. On a practical note, make sure that you make enough copies of the diary sheet and make sure you have a convenient envelope to put the sheet into when it is completed for that day. Obviously, keep the envelope and its contents secure until you are ready to do the analysis.

The theme of this option is the personal construction of relationships. When describing the significant interactions you have had, you should attempt to make some reference to:

● what *you* 'got out' of the interaction;

● what you think the *other person* 'got out' of the interaction.

In this option you are recommended to look at the ways in which the different interactions you experience reflect the functions of relationships. Weiss (1974) contends that each relationship offers some or all of the following 'relational provisions': attachment, social integration, opportunity for nurturance, reassurance of worth, sense of reliable alliance, obtaining of guidance. Weiss points out that these issues raise questions we puzzle over throughout our lives. He states that his hope is 'that it is possible to pursue their study systematically' (*ibid*., page 26). Essentially, your brief in option 1 is to explore whether the diary technique offers a means of meeting that hope.

3.5 Specific notes for option 2: qualitative/ dyadic

You will have to advise your partner, friend or colleague (hereafter 'co-diarist') on how to construct an account of their day. They will probably not have participated in this kind of exercise before, but the instructions should be largely self-explanatory. You will need to advise them that it is really important that they complete the sheets on a day-by-day basis. You should be clear with them that as each diary sheet is completed it needs to be kept secure in an A4 envelope (which you will have to provide them with). You should really see this as an exercise in *negotiation* – not simply because they are more likely to understand what to do if they have had a role in drawing up what is to be done, but also because it underlines the joint participation in the exercise which should help allay any concerns the co-diarist might have about the project.

It is important that you advise the partner not to discuss the sheets or their completion with you during the 28-day period, unless it is to check a procedural matter (but be wary of such discussions on minor clarifications turning into full blown discussions of what 'opinions to give').

Boundaries:

You will need to be clear with your partner, friend or colleague about what boundaries you both want to establish around the exercise. You will want, for example, to agree on whether there are issues which will not be discussed in the diary, or whether there are issues which will only be discussed in a limited way. This is obviously an aspect of the project which would not be typical of a full research exercise, but a degree of perspective is necessary. If you feel that you or your co-diarist might be uncomfortable in keeping notes on significant interactions and the relationship over 28 days, initially privately and then sharing them, then you should address that at the outset, rather than retrospectively.

3.6 Specific notes for option 3: quantitative/ individual

In this option you are collecting quantitative data (though you are encouraged to collect a very small amount of 'back-up' qualitative material data on each diary sheet). The theme of this option is *relationship networks*. The data that you collect are designed to enable you to address research questions related to the networks of social and personal relations you engage with in your everyday life.

Make sure you use the 'Diary sheet for option 3' (see Appendix – NB each sheet comprises two sides for this option). On the sheets, you are required to complete the rating scales for the one 'most significant interaction' of the day. The meaning of 'significant interaction' is difficult to define but one practical way is as follows: *significant interactions are ones which, at the end of the day, are most memorable.* Significant interactions could be significant for a number of reasons. It might be because important matters were discussed or because the interaction influenced the relationship between you and the other person. You are asked to write about the *most* significant – even if it is in an absolute sense not very significant at all. If you have difficulty with the idea of 'significant', simply consider those interactions which are meaningful, interesting or thought-provoking. On a practical note, make sure that you make enough copies of the diary sheet and make sure you have an envelope convenient to put it into when it is completed for that day. Obviously, keep the envelope and its contents secure until you are ready to do the analysis.

Scale 9 has been left open for you to select a dimension to measure of your own choosing. You can choose to measure any aspect of interaction and relationships which you may have come across in your reading or which intrigues you. It is important that you make sure that the small qualitative section of the diary sheet is completed separately from the quantitative ratings. For example, the qualitative section should not refer to the ratings given for that day (though similar issues could be addressed). The qualitative account given day-by-day in the diary is a statement about each significant social interaction in its own right, *it is not meant to be merely a running commentary on the rating scales. Remember each day you will need to complete both Part 1 (the 'Relationship', 'Interaction' and 'Description' sections), and the Part 2 section of the diary sheets.*

3.7 Specific notes for option 4: quantitative/ dyadic

In this option you are collecting quantitative data and a partner, friend or colleague (a co-diarist) is doing likewise over the same period on the interactions between you both. The data that you collect are designed to enable you to address research questions related to the significant (and other) social interactions you engage with your partner/friend/colleague (hereafter 'co-diarist'). Make sure you use the 'Diary sheet for option 4' (see Appendix).

On the diary sheets you are required to complete the rating scales for the one most 'significant interaction' of the day which you have had *with your co-diarist.* That is, even if you have a more significant interaction with someone else, you should still record your impressions of the most significant social interaction you had with the co-diarist. They should be instructed to do the same. The meaning of 'significant interaction' is difficult to define but one practical way is as follows: *significant interactions are ones which, at the end of the day, are most memorable.* Significant interactions could be significant for a number of reasons. It might be because important matters were discussed or because the interaction influenced the relationship between you and your co-diarist. You are asked to write about the *most* significant – even if it is in an absolute sense not very significant at all. If you have difficulty with the idea of 'significant', simply consider those interactions which are meaningful, interesting or thought-provoking.

On a practical note, make sure that you make enough copies of the diary sheet and make sure you have an envelope convenient to put it into when it is completed for that day. Obviously, keep the envelope and its contents secure until you are ready to do the analysis.

It is important that you make sure that the small qualitative section of the diary sheet is completed separately from the quantitative ratings. For example, the qualitative section should not refer to the ratings given for that day (though similar issues could be addressed). The qualitative account given day-by-day in the diary is a statement about each significant social interaction in its own right, *it is not meant to be merely a running commentary on the rating scales. Remember each day you will need to complete both Part 1 (the 'Relationship', 'Interaction' and 'Description' sections), and the Part 2 section of the diary sheets.* Make sure your co-diarist understands this too.

Option 4 gives you the chance to model the social interactions that occur within ongoing relationships. Some of the most interesting findings are likely to be in relation to the precise ratings of significant interactions over time that each *individual* makes and the degree of *agreement* on perceptions between these two individuals on their key interactions.

4 Analysis of the data

By now you should have completed four full weeks of data gathering. You will hopefully have found this enjoyable and intriguing. The focus now turns to the analysis of the data.

You will find, whichever option you have pursued, that you will have collected a great deal of data and you may find that you are feeling a little overwhelmed by it all. This is a common feeling – even for rather experienced researchers. You should bear in mind the fact that you are not required to say something about *all* the data you have collected. In particular you are expected to offer summaries of your information, and even then data should only be discussed to the extent that it bears upon the research questions you identified at the outset. Having said this, if you are doing one of the qualitative options (option 1 or 2) then it is likely that the data will itself suggest new and additional questions that you will want to explore. You should be cautious, however, about pursuing *every* 'interesting lead' and should try to keep the theme of the option in focus.

How to analyse the data

If you are doing options 1 or 2 then your data is exclusively qualitative. If you are doing options 3 or 4 then your data will be partly quantitative and partly qualitative. However, the qualitative analysis required for options 3 and 4 is much less intense than for 1 and 2.

4.1 Analysing the qualitative options (1 and 2)

In analysing the data in option 1 or 2 you will using the approach of discourse analysis, as described by Potter (1996, section 4). As you do your analysis, what you need to bear in mind is that the accounts recorded in your diary need to be treated as *constructions* not as objective records. Discourse analysis rejects 'the idea that language is simply a neutral means of reflecting or describing the world' and replaces this with a 'conviction of the central importance of discourse in constructing social life' (Gill, 1996, p.141). Potter (1996) uses political interviews to indicate what this means in practice, and we probably have little difficulty in seeing how a politician's words are not simply reflections of the world. But what about the situation where we are analysing our own words – as you are being asked to do here? This reflexive exercise, where you are applying a research technique to your own social activity, poses many interesting questions, though for the moment we will note that in the first instance you have to cast yourself in the role of researcher rather than participant. Before going through a procedure for the analysis of the diary accounts step-by-step, we will consider some central theoretical principles of discourse analysis which provide the rationale for that procedure.

Six theoretical principles for discourse analysis

Potter and Wetherell (1995) provide a useful summary of some of the main theoretical principles of discourse analysis which offers a context for the practical analysis of texts such as your diary accounts. These principles will be briefly reviewed and some illustrative examples given of what to look for in your data.

1 Discourse practices are drawn from discourse resources

Discourse analysts are interested in the things people say and write (discourse practices) and the cultural resources they are drawing on (the discourse resources). Discourse resources might include such things as category systems, narrative forms, imagery and generally the language scripts, metaphors and even clichés that are available within a culture.

For example, in a diary account you might come across a statement saying:

> 'My boss was late again today. He isn't concentrating on the job – he is letting his private life spill over into the workplace. He needs someone to give him a good shake and tell him to pull himself together. He can't go on like this – I wonder whether it is all going to turn out OK in the end?'

Here the *discourse practice* is the statement itself as a diary entry. The *discourse resources* involved include: (i) the *categories* of 'boss' and 'worker' (that the person referred to was referred to as 'boss' rather than his name constructs his role as the boss in this account – he could have been described otherwise); (ii) a general *narrative form* of things in 'crisis' being resolved one way or another for good or bad (is it all going to turn out OK in the end?); and (iii) *metaphors* of physical agitation to describe some kind of enforced social and moral realignment ('give him a good shake and tell him to pull himself together').

Obviously, these interpretations are not the only possible ones but they are designed to illustrate the two interrelated aspects discourse analysts focus on: discourse practices (e.g. diary entries) and discourse resources (e.g. specific categories, narratives or metaphors).

2 Description is construction

Discourse analysis does not treat linguistic accounts as simply factual statements of what really happened. Rather it considers how 'objects' in accounts (be they people, actions, feelings, incidents, etc.) are actively constructed in discourse through selective presentations and phrasings, even though presented in a way which implies that they are nevertheless 'solid, real and independent of the speaker' (Potter and Wetherell, 1995, p.81). In other words, discourse analysis tries to show how the versions of the world and experience presented in discourse are (i) *presented* as matter-of-fact descriptions, when in fact they are (ii) discursive *constructions*.

For example, in your diary accounts you might find a statement along the lines of:

> My friend John is in his mid forties and looking for a career move. He is doing this because he is stuck in a rut in his present post. His partner has mixed feelings because she likes her job and wouldn't want to move from the area if he found something in another part of the country. She told me this last week in the pub.

Again, we might speculate here that the description of John's career crisis is presented as more or less matter of fact – as a true and solid account of the way things are for him. But the active construction of it can be discerned (perhaps) in the way the 'stuck in a rut' cliché/metaphor is used as an unproblematic shorthand for what is possibly quite a complex set of multiple circumstances surrounding the experience of work for John, his career aspirations and possibly his self-identity.

Can you think of other possible versions and constructions of John and his situation which might be offered?

Note that it is not being suggested that the writer is *deliberately* and *consciously* attempting to manufacture an unjustifiedly simplistic account of John's situation, but simply that the discourse works this way. Social life would be in some ways impossible without exploiting the summarizing effects of clichés, metaphors, narratives and so on. What discourse analysis is trying to do is show how this process of construction operates.

3 The content of discourse should be taken seriously

Much social psychology in the traditional mainstream experimentalist mode seeks to discover the general underlying cognitive *processes* which operate independently of content. An example would be attribution theory where social psychologists have sought to discover whether observers attribute the behaviour of others to 'internal' or 'external' causes, irrespective of the relationship between actor and observer, the nature of the behaviour, or the specific causes identified. By contrast, discourse analysis looks closely at the specific content of what people say. This is linked to the issue of identifying the discourse resources mentioned above in the notes on principle 1 ('Discourse practices are drawn from discourse resources'). To be able to link a statement to a potential resource the precise content needs to be examined carefully. This emphasis on content in analysis also presupposes a familiarity with the cultural experience of the speaker/writer whose discourse is being analysed and with the cultural context in which it is produced. Discourse analysis therefore cannot easily be done at a distance from the circumstances of the participants. In this project the discourse is generated by yourself, so you are attempting to consider reflexively the content of your own language and the cultural discursive resources on which you are drawing.

4 Discourse is rhetorical

This principle means that the statements made can be usefully treated as attempts to deal with real or imagined disputes, dilemmas and conflicts, as attempts to persuasively present one's own version of events in order to win 'hearts and minds'. In other words, 'people's versions of actions, features of the world, of their own mental life are designed to counter real or potential alternatives' (Potter and Wetherell, 1995, p.82). Social life is replete with conflicts of interests and competing accounts. Almost everything we say and write is directly or indirectly influenced by these tensions and oppositions. In the case of politicians the disputes are foregrounded and explicit. In relationships, the tensions may be more subtle. The constructive aspect of discourse in accounts discussed earlier under principle 2 is clearly linked to this fact. The account of John's career crisis could possibly reflect a dispute over competing interpretations (between you and your partner as co-diarists) about whether John is a reasonable man or not. Making sense of this piece of text is almost impossible without reference to such disputes – where they exist. You should be on the alert for rhetoric over specific individuals, actions or relationships which reflect broader *ideological* tensions linked perhaps to gender, class, age or role. Quite often, rhetorical features are signalled by explicit or implicit references to *right* and *wrong*. Where a speaker or writer feels moved to comment on the appropriateness of behaviour, this can be motivated by an awareness that the behaviour is not self-evidently or unequivocally wrong, and that there is a debate.

5   Stake and accountability are central to discourse

This principle refers to the fact that accounts often contain attempts by the writer to show themselves to be separate from the claims they are making and hence disinterested, while the claims made by others are presented as motivated by self-interest or other form of bias. In other words, people don't want to appear to be accountable for what they claim – they are seeking to make their claims appear to be natural and to almost have a life of their own.

In the brief account of John above, the final sentence ('She told me this last week in the pub') could be seen as an attempt to distance the writer from the claims being made about John, by attributing the analysis to someone else.

It is possible, however, that the issues of stake and accountability are rather different in the arena of personal relationships. In the analysis of political speeches and interviews, it is commonly found that speakers present their personal positions as facts or self-evident common-sense truths, and not typically as personal opinions. This, however, may not be the case in relationship accounts. Rather than *distancing* themselves from their analyses (in order to show impartiality), individuals may seek to *construct ownership* of their relationship analyses (in order, for example, to show *involvement* and the *authenticity* of the analyses). You may find that you or your partner (for option 2) have made statements such as '... but that's only my opinion', or 'I should know, it's my relationship', or 'The way I see it ...', and so on. In this context, you might want to consider whether your data suggest that in discourse some opinions tend to be presented as objective (e.g. politics and scientific theories) but others as subjective (e.g. relationship understandings) and consider the different contexts in which this might happen.

6   Relocate cognition and emotion to the public arena

Discourse analysis attempts to demonstrate that many of the entities and processes which traditional psychology locates in the *private* internal psychological arena are actually more validly located in *public* interpersonal and cultural arenas. Potter (1996) describes how the concept 'attitude', understood as 'enduring evaluations of the world', is profoundly problematic. Discourse looks instead at the *production of evaluative situated accounts*. In the context of your diary you might want to explore how emotions, reasoning, attitudes and other psychological processes typically located intrapsychically can be interpreted as existing *between* people, jointly performed in action and constructed in accounts. For example, you might find that your diary contains statements such as:

> 'She hasn't come home yet. She is meant to be here now. How annoying. She might be working late and not had a chance to call me. Or she might have gone for a drink after work and forgotten that we had a date. Maybe I'm overpossessive but I think I have a right to be angry. But maybe she has an excuse.'

Subsequent diary entries might refer to this non-appearance of the partner and a justification for being late. There might be a dispute over whether anger is justified and so on. All of this would be written in the diary and so would be constructed in a particular way (notwithstanding the fact that you would have your own recollections of the events). You should examine your data to see whether there is evidence of accounts showing jointly constructed emotions. There is also the possibility of retrospective labelling of emotions, behaviours or arguments. For example, you might find that a diary account describes what happened earlier that day or on a previous day in such a way that indicates that intervening interpersonal transactions between the incident and the time of the diary entry have influenced the categorization of the incident. You might begin to wonder which of the various different accounts of your emotional state is the 'real' experience and from there begin to question the idea of emotion or memories as simply records of private and 'real' internal events. This would be an example of one of the ways in which apparently personal activities can be seen to be fundamentally interpersonal.

Practical steps in carrying out the discourse analysis

Several writers have remarked upon the fact that discourse analysis does not lend itself to a recipe-book approach. Nevertheless, some basic steps can be followed which will enable you to carry out the analyses you need to do for this project.

Step 1   Consider the aims of the analysis

Ask yourself: what are the research questions I am trying to address? Your research questions and the themes of *personal construction of relationships* (option 1) or *intersubjectivity* (option 2) should be foremost in your mind as you approach your diary sheets.

Step 2   Recognize and describe the discursive context

You need to think about the context of the accounts. You should ask yourself: What are the circumstances surrounding the production of the account under consideration? Who is writing? Who is the audience? What are the conventions of the diary genre? Although this is a key consideration, there is no need at this stage to do anything more than write down a few notes on this for future reference.

Step 3 Familiarize yourself with the accounts

You need to read through *all* of the written accounts (including those of your partner if you did option 2) and become almost *immersed* in the data. The thing to remember here is that you are not reading for 'gist' – the overall general picture of what the individual is trying to convey. Rather, you should try to be sensitive to the subtle nuances and connotations of specific words used, particular turns of phrase and idiomatic vocabularies.

One of the features which you should look out for in your accounts is that of narratives (stories). These will not be explicitly announced, as in the traditional 'Once upon a time ...', but will be brief accounts of how things developed over time or how a sequence of events unfolded. Discourse analysts and personal relationship researchers agree that stories have a powerful role in relationships.

Narratives in relationship accounts   One way of approaching the analysis of narratives in your diary accounts is to consider some of the claims made by LaRossa (1995), who emphasizes the symbolic interaction, meanings and differentiations achieved through stories. Is there evidence in your accounts of stories which implicitly suggest that the diarists are saying '... This is how I see myself ... this is how I see you ... this is how I see you seeing me ...' (Watzlawick *et al.*, 1967), as suggested by LaRossa?

Step 4   (i) Identify organizing topics and themes; (ii) Establish categories for coding

These two steps go hand in hand and you may well find yourself switching between them as you go through your data. Identifying *organizing topics* and *themes* involves drawing out repeated references to key aspects of relationships which help interpret the accounts overall. You might want to begin your analyses here by looking for the themes discussed by Miell and Dallos (1996) such as *power, meanings, time, autonomy, interaction patterns, functions, norms and emergent properties of relationships*. Further key themes might be identified through consideration of Weiss's (1974) functions (option 1) and the idea of interaction and impressions (Radley, 1996).

Establishing *categories for coding* involves identifying a number of categories which relate to the research questions you formulated and the themes of the option. These categories will help you identify the main themes and discursive resources/interpretative repertories on which the diarists were drawing. For example, if you were interested in the personal discursive constructions of the functions served by relationships, you might initially establish a categorization system which enabled you to classify the way each different type of function is articulated in the data. A category system in this sense might be no more than a set of blank pieces of A4 paper or large index cards with the category written in the top centre of the sheet. As you read through the diary accounts you would simply make a brief quote from the diary (or even just an entry code: e.g. 'Person 1, day 18, para 4') of the statement of interest. The piece of discourse which gets categorized could be of any length. It could be an entire entry, or it could (in an extreme case) be just one word. However, it is more likely that you will find that your categorizations will be of short paragraphs of two or three sentences. A piece of discourse can be coded in more than one category and not all pieces of discourse need to be categorized. If in doubt about categorization, err on the side of categorizing a piece of discourse under a heading rather than leaving it out. You may well find that your initial categorization scheme needs revision in the light of the quantity of examples. Too few and the category system is probably covering the wrong area (or you are being too cautious in allocating data to categories); too many and the categories probably need further subdivision. What is being categorized here is the repertoires not the actual functions. In other words, you are trying to identify the different ways in which you have been *describing* functions, rather than trying to identify what the 'real' functions of your relationships are.

Step 5   Search for variability in the accounts given by one person

The most interesting findings in a discourse analytic study come from demonstrations that the same individual appears to be presenting subtly different or even contradictory accounts. This shows that individuals are drawing upon a range of discourse resources (and interpretative repertoires) as they make sense of their experience. You may find, for example in relation to option 1, that on one day an entry seems to suggest that the main function of your relationship with a particular work colleague is the 'provision of mutual professional support'. On a later entry, you might find that you indicate that the main relationship provision (Weiss, 1974) is that of providing a 'sympathetic ear' for personal domestic problems and challenges. At this stage you may want to revise or add to your categorization scheme as you discover examples of discourse which do not fit the system. One example of the kind of variability you might find is in relation to the 'predicates' (essentially adjectives and verbs coupled with a concept) and metaphors which appear in the diaries. When researching the St Paul's riots of 1981, Reicher (1984) found that the category 'community' was predicated with a wide range of terms. For example, adjectives such as 'close-knit', 'integrated' and 'tight' suggested a *spatial* metaphor, whereas 'grows', 'evolves' and 'matures' implied a form of *organic* metaphor, while describing the community as 'acting', 'knowing' and 'feeling' implied a metaphor of agency, suggesting that the community itself had a degree of autonomy. These metaphors are not contradictory but they do convey different images of community and amount to different forms of constructing the category of 'community' in talk.

You will find it useful to identify key categories (reflecting research questions and themes) and search for the predicates of those categories used by each person. This should allow you to identify the explicit and implicit metaphors and images mobilized by the diarists. The range of metaphors so identified should take you some way towards discovering the *discourse resources* and *interpretive repertoires* being employed by the diarists. If you have done option 2, you will be able to take this analysis one step forward and consider whether both you and your partner are employing the same predicates and metaphors in constructing versions of your experiences. Indeed, it is not inconceivable that such misunderstandings between each other that you experience may derive from not sharing the same interpretative repertoire.

Interpretative repertoires   What are 'interpretative repertoires' exactly? These are the topics and to a lesser extent the ways of speaking and writing which are already in the culture and which are available to be drawn on by social actors in their everyday dealings with each other. In their strongest and most extreme forms they might be considered as ideologies. Other forms might involve the clichés of everyday life as they exist in discourses about politics, relationships, technology and so on – in fact, every aspect of human activity that can be talked about. These repertoires are made up of connected images and metaphors which are invoked in conversations or texts and which offer means of classifying and evaluating incidents, problems and ideas in terms of constructions already worked out and publicly available in a culture. The idea of interpretative repertoires is offered by discourse analysts to emphasize and help explore the idea that communication and meaning exists in cultures outside of any individual, or individual conversation or text. Examples of components of interpretative repertoires in the area of personal relationships (in a western culture at this moment of historical time) might be said to include some of the following: 'true love' narratives; 'loyalty at all costs' themes; 'starcrossed lovers' theme; 'only human' justifications; 'Mr Right' themes; 'in this day and age' themes; 'being mature' values; 'young, free and single' roles; 'caught in the middle' metaphors, and so on.

Step 6   Identify the functions of the discourse practices

It is important to remember that, from the point view of discourse analysis, language is functional. In particular, it is *rhetorical* – that is, it seeks to *persuade*. Crucial to this analysis of the persuasive function of discourse is being clear about who the audience of the account is. In this project this needs a little careful thought. In terms of your own diary accounts, the audience is *yourself*. You need to consider yourself both as a writer constructing an account and as a reader and analyst interpreting this account. Beyond this, however, the tutor who is going to be marking this project is an audience. It is inevitable that you have been aware of the fact that your accounts would be read by her or him. You should look through your accounts, and seek to identify any examples of discourse where you appear to be attempting to present a convincing account of your experiences for him or her. Even if you are doing option 2 you may have agreed with your co-diarist that you would share with her or him the contents of your diary. In that case, then, your partner is also an audience. Thus, your account may well have multiple audiences and you will find it interesting to identify constructions in your accounts which address the concerns of each.

Also under this heading are a number of analytic tactics you might want to employ to get at the more subtle aspects of the accounts.

First, *consider what problem the writer is trying to solve* (Widdicombe, 1993). We are thinking here, of course, in terms of a social and communicative problem. The writing of a diary account under the circumstances specified by this project as part of an educational course may not sit easily with what is after all a contemporaneous account of personal experiences and activities. You should look for ways in which this 'social balancing act' is discernible in the accounts.

Second, you can attempt to *be sensitive to what is not written* (Billig, 1991). Rather like the dog that did not bark in the night, the absence of references to certain events or relationships may be significant.

Third, you can *consider the ways in which the written accounts themselves anticipate future readings and interpretations*. Whether in the case of option 2, where the other person is likely to see the account at some point, or in option 1, where you as a diarist participant know that you are going to have to analyse your own data, there may well be features of your written accounts *which betray their status as research data*. In other words, the accounts may explicitly or implicitly reflect the fact that these are not diaries kept spontaneously for their own interest, but as part of a research project. If you *do* find evidence of this, it does not mean that the accounts are invalid – quite the reverse: you will have captured some of the real-world influences on discourse from within research.

Step 7 Assess the validity of the interpretations made

Validity is important to discourse analysts but it takes a very different form from that commonly encountered in traditional social psychology textbooks. Potter and Wetherell (1987) suggest a number of ways of assessing validity, but for the purposes of this project we will focus on just one: *deviant case analysis*.

Deviant case analysis essentially means checking that there are no counter-examples to the general interpretations that you have made. For example, you may conclude that your partner uses only three metaphors to describe the development of your relationship: let's say a spatial metaphor, an organic metaphor and a journey metaphor. However, there might be one reference (and one reference only) by your partner to your relationship with each other as 'battling on'. You might want to categorize this as a part of the 'journey' metaphor, but you may feel that it is really a metaphor of combat and conflict. The original interpretation could be partially validated if you could show that this apparent anomaly (the deviant case) led to some kind of interactional, communicational or other difficulty, as this would suggest that the other metaphors *served some kind of interpersonal or rhetorical function* which the combative metaphor did not. Alternatively, the assessment of the overall validity of your interpretations can be indicated by the number of deviant cases left after the analysis. It is perfectly acceptable in the present context to offer an analysis which still leaves a number of deviant cases uninterpreted *so long as you make it clear that you recognize that this is the case*.

Step 8   Stop!

Discourse analysis is notorious for having no natural endpoint and often even very experienced researchers finding themselves wanting to rework the data over and over for even more subtle nuances of expression and rhetoric. For the purposes of this project it is important that you do draw a line under your analyses in sufficient time to write up your interpretations in the formal report. When you have gone through the above steps at least once, and possibly reorganized your categorization system once, then you almost certainly have enough to start your write-up. More than this is fine if you have the time, but the law of diminishing returns (where each successive hour of effort leads to smaller and smaller improvements in the quality of the end product) applies to all research and probably applies to discourse analysis research more than most.

Extra note for option 2 only (qualitative/dyadic)

In this option the key theme is *intersubjectivity*: that is, the extent to which you and your partner (or colleague or friend) inhabit the same 'discursive universe', as it were. There is thus more to this analysis than simply checking the number of times you and your partner agree or disagree (though this is important too). The analysis here operates on two levels: first, the degree of agreement and convergence on any given day; and second the overall similarity of accounting style evident across the full diary period. This latter idea concerns the examination of whether or not you and your partner are drawing upon the same interpretative repertoires.

For example, you will want to check whether you and your partner use the same 'predicates' for describing your relationship with each other, and whether or not you also share common metaphors for relationships with common acquaintances or relatives.

4.2 Analysing option 3: quantitative/individual

Overview of the analysis for option 3

In this option your aim is to analyse aspects of your social network based on a 28-day sample of your significant and routine social interactions within it. On this basis there are several types of questions you will be using your data to answer. For example, to what extent are satisfaction, intimacy and similarity in interactions connected in terms of your involvement in your network? You might, for example, find from your ratings that where there was a high level of intimacy experienced, there was also a high level of similarity, and where intimacy was low, similarity was low also. In other words, you will be exploring how different aspects of interactions are *correlated* with each other as far as you and *your* network are concerned.

It is very easy to lose sight of the hypotheses being tested when faced with a large data set, so an example might be useful here.

Let us suppose that you have hypothesized that 'similarity' (in interactions) will be positively correlated with 'empathy' (in interactions). We can assume that you came to this hypothesis on the reasoning that within your network you anticipate that those individuals who share the same interests, problems, time demands and values as yourself will have a much better basis on which to identify with you than when those shared contexts are missing. You want to test this hypothesis by examining the data you have collected.

We can go through this process step-by-step.

Step 1 Calculate basic descriptive statistics

The first thing you should do is calculate the means for all the variables which appear in your hypotheses (and any other variables you feel might be interesting to explore). In terms of the relationship variables, you will probably want to calculate the means for 'satisfaction' and 'liking' even if they do not appear in your hypotheses, as they will provide useful information for interpreting your relation with your social network overall. For the interaction variables, 'satisfaction' and 'feeling towards other' are likely to be informative, but you may want to consider 'significance' also. These averages will be useful later in Step 6 when we come to consider how expected or unexpected your findings are.

Step 2 Construct your data table for correlations

First of all draw up a simple table with columns and rows to put the data into.

This table will have 5 *columns*. The first two will be headed 'Similarity' and 'Empathy' (in this example) and the third, fourth and fifth columns will be used for calculations to be described later.

The table needs to have as many *rows* as you have interactions where you were able to rate *both* 'Similarity' *and* 'Empathy'. This should normally be 28, of course, but there is not a problem if you have less than this.

Step 3 Work out the correlations between your key variables

Full details of the calculation of the appropriate correlation (either Pearson product moment or Spearman rank) can be found in any basic statistics textbook. On the basis of your calculations you will have worked out the *correlation* between your two variables (in our example, the two variables are 'similarity' and 'empathy'). This correlation will be a number between +1.0 and –1.0 (make sure that you make a note of the positive or negative sign at the end of your calculations). You will also need to determine from the significance tables of your statistical texts whether or not the correlation is statistically *significant*. If the correlation *is* significant (that is to say, if the correlation is unlikely to have been brought about by chance), then you are able to conclude that the two variables are related in some way. If the correlation is greater than zero (e.g. +0.3) and significant, then you can conclude that the two variables are *positively* correlated (meaning that when one is high the other is too). If the correlation is less than zero, that is, if the correlation is *negative* (e.g. –0.3) and significant, then you can conclude that the two variables are *negatively* correlated (meaning that when one is high the other is low, and vice versa). You need to go through the correlation calculation procedure for all the variables mentioned in your hypotheses.

Step 4 Interpret correlations one-by-one in relation to your hypotheses

Now you have to make sense of the correlations. The first thing to note is that a significant positive or negative correlation does not necessarily prove that a *causal* relationship exists between the two variables. All that it means is that the two variables are related in some way. If in our example the correlation between 'similarity' and 'empathy' *was* positive and significant, this implies that 'similarity' is influencing 'empathy', *or* that 'empathy' is influencing 'similarity', *or* that some third variable is influencing them both in similar ways. If the correlation is *not* significant, this suggests that there is no relation between the variables. You need to consider whether these *observed* correlations correspond to the *hypothesized* correlations you specified before data collection.

Step 5 Interpret correlation results as a whole

You now need to consider the correlation results *as a whole*. This will include observed correlations calculated in order to test your hypotheses (see Step 4) and other correlations calculated which might shed some light on these. For example, in our example you might have found that 'similarity' and 'empathy' did *not* correlate significantly. You might then check the correlation between 'similarity' and 'intimacy'. If *this* correlation was found to be positive and significant it would suggest that higher levels of similarity were associated with higher levels of intimacy *but not associated with higher degrees of empathy*. It is in this way that *patterns of results* (in this case a set of correlations) can help you get a better overall picture of the psychological processes at work in your study.

Tip for interpreting correlations

A good technique for interpreting the role of a variable in a correlational study is to reserve judgment until you have found at least one variable which correlates with it significantly (positively or negatively) *and* one variable with which it does not correlate significantly. This will allow you to state that variables X and Y are related – but almost certainly not because of the influence of variable Z. (This interpretational technique can be expanded by looking at the three correlations that exist between three variables.)

A word of caution is appropriate at this stage. It is very tempting to calculate the correlation of every variable with every other variable. You should avoid this since it is very time consuming and adds unnecessarily to your workload. Your tutor will be looking at the *quality* of correlational analysis, not the *quantity*. Additionally, there is the danger that in calculating so many correlations spurious 'significant' results will appear by chance.

Step 6 Consider how the set of correlation results fits into your expectations about your social network

Having identified the connections between variables and made some attempt to interpret the psychological significance of the results obtained, you can now turn to considering whether or not the results are what you expected given your knowledge of your social network and your involvement in it. You may not have written down any of these expectations but you are quite likely to find some of your results suprising. It might have been the case, for example, that you have generally felt rather detached and uninvolved with those you come into contact with at work or around your community (for whatever reason). However, your results might suggest that, contrary to this view, your interactions (as indicated by, say, the mean rating of 'satisfaction' and 'liking') are actually quite positive (with, say, an average rating of 5 or above). The reverse might be the case for some people, of course. Your expectations about your social network and your interactions within it might have generally been quite positive, and yet the mean ratings might be relatively negative (with, say, an average of 3 or less). In making sense of the overall ratings you might want to consider whether your general expectations are largely influenced by just one or two individuals within your network, or by just one or two locations where you have social interactions. Looking at these aspects in more detail may help clarify some of the reasons for any unexpected findings you come across.

The correlational results are also of relevance here in making sense of overall mean ratings. For example, if your ratings of 'satisfaction' in interactions were unexpectedly negative then you might want to identify which variable correlates best with 'satisfaction' in interactions. If it turns out that, say, 'similarity' is the most significant and positively correlated variable with 'satisfaction', this might suggest that when you normally think about your network you base your thoughts only on the degree of satisfaction you experience in interactions with *similar* others. That is to say, you may have not have been taking into account the fact that you do not really find interactions with dissimilar others very satisfying at all.

Of course, there are other reasons why your results generally might not correspond to your overall perceptions of your network prior to the study. It is possible, for example, that the sample of interactions observed (and the roles of the participants that go with them) might only cover a part of what you consider to be your overall network. You need to consider in the 'Discussion' section of your report whether or not your data is *representative* of the fuller networks in which you are involved. It might be the case, for example, that your employment is seasonal and that at the time when you collected the data you were not in contact with people you would normally consider to be part of your network.

Step 7 Consider how your results can be interpreted in relation to previous work on social networks

One of the most interesting and exciting aspects of psychological research is the opportunity to compare your results with the results and theories of other researchers. It is also worth considering whether or not any anomalies or 'puzzles' in your data can be explained by reference to psychological theory in related areas. It is important that you attempt to provide a *theoretically-informed* interpretation of your data, as distinct from the more personal and reflective analyses described in Step 6 above.

Some theoretical issues which you may want to consider on the basis of the descriptive and correlational results you have found include the following:

1   Do the interactions recorded in your diary appear to reflect networks of *significant others*, *exchange* networks or *interactional* networks, or some combination of all three? (Milardo, 1992)

2   Are any aspects of the differences between your expectations and your results interpretable in terms of *actual versus perceived* social support? (Miell and Croghan, 1996)

3   Does the pattern of satisfaction in roles or interactions lend itself to interpretation in terms of the *costs and benefits* of social relationships? (For example, see Walster *et al.*, 1978.)

4   To what extent do the concepts of *investment* and *comparison level* help explain any of the aspects of your network which appear to have low satisfaction or significance ratings? (Rusbult *et al.*, 1986)

NB: Other questions are equally valid. This set is meant to be illustrative and may not be the one most directly relevant to your data.

4.3 Analysing option 4: quantitative/dyadic

Overview of the analysis for option 4

The aim of your analysis in this option is to determine the extent to which you and your co-diarist have had similar or dissimilar experiences of significant social interactions between you. You will be doing this by correlating the ratings made by your co-diarist and yourself on the same aspect of the same social interaction. Taking 'satisfaction' (of interaction) as an example, we can consider how different types of correlations can be interpreted. If your ratings and those of your co-diarist correlated positively and significantly then you can conclude that your perspectives on the degree of satisfaction are related. If the ratings are negatively correlated – that is, when you rated an interaction as high on satisfaction, your co-diarist rated it as low on satisfaction (and vice versa) – then that might suggest that you and your co-diarist are getting very different things from the social interactions between you. Your interpretation of this kind of result will depend upon whether your co-diarist is your partner, co-worker or friend, of course. If the correlation between you and your co-diarist is not significant then this means that there is no systematic relation between the two experiences of the social interaction. It should be very interesting to carry out the correlation analysis for a set of variables in order to identify which aspects of social interactions you are both experiencing similarly, which areas you are experiencing in diametrically opposing ways, and which areas you are experiencing in independent and unconnected ways.

Analysis tip

Make sure when correlating ratings on significant interactions that you and your co-diarist have identified the *same* interaction episode as the most significant. If you and your co-diarist have been selecting different interactions as the most significant then you cannot correlate the ratings (as they are ratings of different episodes). However, this discrepancy is informative in itself and you may well want to reflect upon it in your 'Discussion' section. You will be assessed in terms of the interpretation you make of the discrepancies. You will be expected in this situation to consider what the correlations are between your own ratings of different aspects of the significant interactions (as described in option 3).

It is important to recognize that a significant correlation between your ratings and those of your co-diarist only implies that the relation between them is *not random* – it does not mean that you and your co-diarist are experiencing the *same* perceptions of the interaction episodes. As a general guide, correlations between co-diarists should be somewhere around or above 0.75 before you could start to claim that you were both 'in agreement' in any meaningful sense.

Having identified the extent to which and the ways in which you and your co-diarist have similar or dissimilar ratings, you can interpret these in terms of your hypotheses and the relevant literature on perspectives in relationships as discussed in section 2.3. Remember it is the quality and depth of analysis that are important, not the quantity, and you should concentrate your efforts on addressing the issues directly raised by your hypotheses.

In this option, you are exploring aspects of *significant social interactions* as perceived by you and your co-diarist. You will need to analyse the data in terms of the extent to which you and your co-diarist appear to have similar or dissimilar perceptions of the significant interactions between you.

Your analysis will be in two parts. The first part will be a preliminary *summary of the main aspects of the data as they pertain to similarities and differences between you and your co-diarist.* This need only involve a summary of the main features of the data you have collected on the rating scales, possibly using bar charts and means to compare data on each variable (notes for option 3 provide some basic information on what is expected here – you simply need to set the data for both diarists side-by-side). One interesting aspect here is the percentage of times you and your co-diarist identified the *same* interaction as being the 'most significant'. One feature of your data which you will want to analyse is *what were the characteristics of the significant interactions*? In other words, what were the mean ratings of the interaction variables across the 28 days for each diarist?

The second part of your analysis should be based on the degree of agreement between you and the other diarist. In order to calculate the correlation you will need to arrange the data so that one variable (x) in the correlation equation is *your* rating on a specific interaction scale (e.g. satisfaction) and the other variable (y) is your co-diarist's rating. You will have to check that you and your co-diarist are referring to the *same* event, so you will only be including data where you both have identified the same specific encounter as the 'most significant'.

The specific *interpretations* that you will be able to make of your results here depend on the degree of agreement between the diarists (as reflected in the correlations). However, there are different types of interpretations possible whether the agreement is high or low. If agreement is high then this might suggest openness, transparency and a shared vision of what is significant in interactions and relationships – or it might mean that one of the diarists has imposed their frame of reference on the relationship. If the level of agreement is low then there might be an issue of reliability – that is, you and your co-diarist might, despite your attempts to the contrary, have been using *different* subjective definitions of the terms on the rating scales. It might mean that you see relationships differently or it might indicate that the relationship is in a period of transition. You must consider each of these possibilities (and others as appropriate) when making sense of your results. Be sure to link your results to the questions you identified at the outset.

5 Writing the report

Your report should should consist of the following sections. Check with your module or course tutor on word length or any other special requirements.

Title page

This should contain the title of the study and your name. This should be on a page of its own.

Abstract

The abstract is meant to be a self-contained summary of the entire study. It should indicate the general area of the work, the main method used and a brief statement of whether or not the hypothesis or research questions being addressed were supported/answered or not. It should be about 100–200 words long. The abstract should be presented on its own page at the very beginning of the report, immediately after the title page.

Introduction

This is where you provide the general rationale for the study and some of the background. You will want to review briefly work on diaries and some of the general issues involved around the notion of 'personal relationships', from your reading. It is important that you discuss the rationale for the research questions you explored.

Method

This part falls into a number of different subsections:

Participants

Give the number, sex and age of your participants as appropriate.

Materials

This section should describe the diary sheets and any other equipment used.

Procedure

This is essentially a blow-by-blow account of how you actually carried out the data collection. The general idea is that anyone reading this section should be able to repeat what you did fairly closely, so it is a good idea to get someone to read this section and then tell you what they think you did. If they can't tell you then you have not been clear enough – rewrite the section. You should be very clear here about any in-structions you gave to the co-diarist or any negotiations you entered into with them (if you did option 2 or 4). Full details of ethical procedures and considerations should be discussed here.

Results

This should be a straightforward summary of your statistical or discourse analyses. Actual computations and diary sheets should be put in a separate appendix. You should present all the relevant statistical information (options 3 and 4 only) in this section. For options 1 and 2 (discourse analysis) this section will contain a full account of your analyses – including any provisional analyses/interpretations which you eventually rejected. For options 1 and 2 you are permitted to draw out subtleties and nuances of the discourse you have been analysing at some length. For the quantitative options (3 and 4) you are expected to be rather more concise and matter-of-fact. *For options 1 and 2 only, you could combine the 'Results' and the 'Discussion' sections into one section if you find it useful.*

Discussion

In many respects this is the most important part of your report (and probably the most enjoyable part to write). Here you need to interpret the relevant psychological theories in the light of your results. You should also be critical of any aspect of the study and indicate how it could be done better if sufficient time and resources were available. In particular, you might want to comment on the internal and external validity of the study and consider the study as an example of social psy-chology in general. What aspects of personal relationships would this method help us understand better? What aspects of personal relation-ships would this method not be able to help us understand? You have been referred to various suggestions for reading for the various options and you should make sure that you incorporate discussion of those here.

It is important that you include as part of the 'Discussion' section a fairly detailed critique of the method you have used. You should indicate what alterations should be made to the study to improve it if it were being run again. You should also discuss the underlying assumptions of the social psychological approach to studying personal relationships.

References

Here you should cite each study that you refer to in your write-up. Remember this is not a bibliography (which is a list of books you have read) but a list of all the sources and studies to which you *explicitly* refer. These should be in alphabetical order and in the standard format. You should include appendices in your write-up. These will be your computations for the correlational tests and any additional materials you have used.

References

Argyle, M. (1996) 'The experimental study of relationships', Reading C in Miell, D. and Dallos, R. (eds) (1996).

Billig, M. (1991) *Ideology and Opinions: Studies in Rhetorical Psychology*, Cambridge, Cambridge University Press.

Burnett, R., McGhee, P. and Clarke, D.D. (eds) (1987) *Accounting for Relationships: Explanation, Representation and Knowledge*, London, Methuen.

Byrne, D. (1961) 'Interpersonal attraction and attitude similarity', *Journal of Abnormal Social Psychology*, vol.62, pp.713–15.

Byrne, D. (1971) *The Attraction Paradigm*, New York, Academic Press.

Dallos, R. (1996a) 'Creating relationships', in Miell, D. and Dallos, R. (eds) (1996).

Dallos, R. (1996b) 'Change and transformations of relationships', in Miell, D. and Dallos, R. (eds) (1996).

Duck, S. (1994) *Meaningful Relationships: Talking, Sense, and Relating*, Thousand Oaks, CA, Sage Publications Inc.

Duck, S.W. and Miell, D. (1982) 'Charting the development of personal relationship research', paper presented to the International Conference on Personal Relationships, Madison, July.

Duck, S.W. and Sants, H. (1983) 'On the origins of the specious: are interpersonal relationships really interpersonal states?', *Journal of Social and Clinical Psychology*, vol.1, pp.27–41.

Gill, R. (1996) 'Discourse analysis: practical implementation', in Richardson J.T. (ed.) *Handbook of Qualitative Research Methods for Psychology and the Social Sciences*, Leicester, British Psychological Society.

Lalljee, M. (1996) 'The interpreting self: an experimentalist perspective', in Stevens, R. (ed.) (1996).

LaRossa, R. (1995) 'Stories and relationships', *Journal of Social and Personal Relationships*, vol.12, no.4, pp.553–8.

Miell, D. (1987) 'Remembering relationship development: constructing a context for interactions', in Burnett, R., McGhee, P. and Clarke, D.D. (eds) (1987).

Miell, D. and Croghan, R. (1996) 'Examining the wider contexts of social relationships', in Miell, D. and Dallos, R. (eds) (1996).

Miell, D. and Dallos, R. (1996) 'Introduction: exploring interactions and relationships', in Miell, D. and Dallos, R. (eds) (1996).

Miell, D. and Dallos, R. (eds) (1996) *Social Interaction and Personal Relationships*, London, Sage/The Open University.

Milardo, R. (1992) 'Comparative methods for delineating social networks', *Journal of Social and Personal Relationships*, vol.9, pp.447–61.

Potter, J. (1996) 'Attitudes, social representations and discursive psychology', in Wetherell, M. (ed.) *Identities, Groups and Social Issues*, London, Sage/The Open University.

Potter, J. and Wetherell, M. (1987) *Discourse and Social Psychology: Beyond Attitudes and Behaviour*, London, Sage.

Potter, J. and Wetherell, M. (1995) 'Discourse analysis', in Smith, J.A., Harré, R., and Van Langenhove, L.V. (eds) *Rethinking Methods in Psychology*, London, Sage.

Radley, A. (1996) 'Relationships in detail: the study of social interaction', in Miell, D. and Dallos, R. (eds) (1996).

Reicher, S. (1984) 'St Pauls: a study in the limits of crowd behaviour', in Murphy, J., John, M. and Brown, H. (eds) *Dialogues and Debates in Social Psychology*, London, Lawrence Erlbaum.

Rusbult, C.E., Johnson, D.J. and Morrow, G. (1986) 'Predicting satisfaction and commitment in adult romantic involvements: an assessment of the generalizability of the investment model', *Social Psychology Quarterly*, vol.49, pp.81–9.

Sapsford, R. (1988) 'Evidence', in Sapsford, R. *et al.* (eds) (1998).

Sapsford, R., Still, A., Wetherell, M., Miell, D. and Stevens, R. (eds) (1998) *Theory and Social Psychology*, London, Sage/The Open University.

Stevens, R. (1998) 'Trimodal theory as a model for interrelating perspectives in psychology', in Sapsford, R. *et al.* (eds) (1998).

Stevens, R. (ed.) (1996) *Understanding the Self*, London, Sage/The Open University.

Walster, E., Walster, G.W., and Berscheid, E. (1978) *Equity: Theory and Research*, Boston, MA, Allyn and Bacon.

Watzlawick, P., Beavin, J.H. and Jackson, D.D. (1967) *Pragmatics of Human Communication: A Study of Interactional Patterns, Pathology and Paradoxes*, New York, Norton.

Weiss, R.S. (1974) 'The provisions of social relationships', in Rubin, Z. (ed.) *Doing Unto Others*, Englewood Cliffs, NJ, Prentice Hall.

Wetherell, M. and Maybin, J. (1996) 'The distributed self: a social constructionist perspective', in Stevens, R. (ed.) (1996).

Wheeler, L. and Nezleck, J. (1977) 'Sex differences in social participation', *Journal of Personality and Social Psychology*, vol.35, pp.742–54.

Widdicombe, S. (1993) 'Autobiography and change: rhetoric and authenticity of "Gothic" style', in Burman, E. and Parker, I. (eds) *Discourse Analytic Research: Readings and Repertoires of Texts in Action*, London, Routledge.

Wilkinson, S. (1987) 'Explorations of self and other in a developing relationship', in Burnett, R., McGhee, P. and Clarke, D.D. (eds) (1987).

Further reading

The following articles demonstrate how a diary technique can address issues in the study of personal relationships that are not generally amenable to empirical analysis through more traditional methods.

Goldsmith, D.J. and Baxter, L.A. (1996) 'Constituting relationships in talk: a taxonomy of speech events in social and personal relationships', *Human Communication Research*, vol.23, pp.87–114.

Nezlek, J.B. (1995) 'Social construction, gender/sex similarity and social interaction in close personal relationships', *Journal of Social and Personal Relationships*, vol.12, pp.503–20.

Kashy, D.A. and DePaulo, B.M. (1996) 'Who lies?', *Journal of Personality and Social Psychology*, vol.7, pp.1037–51.

Acknowledgement

I would like to thank Margaret Wetherell for her extremely useful comments given on earlier drafts of this chapter.

Appendix: Diary sheets for options 1, 2, 3 and 4

Diary sheets for Options 1 to 4 are to be found on the following pages.

Diary sheet for option 1

Diary sheet no. ...

Describe below the three most significant interactions of today in your own words (continue on extra sheets if necessary).

Diary sheet for option 2

Diary sheet no. ...

Describe below the three most significant interactions of today between you and your 'co-diarist' in your own words (continue on extra sheets if necessary).

Diary sheet for option 3
Part 1

You are required to complete the rating scales for the one most significant interaction of the day.

Diary sheet no. ...

Other person: Initials ...   Sex ...   Age ...

The relationship

1 *Role* relationship: ...
2 *Duration* of relationship: ...
3 *Satisfaction* with relationship: Completely satisfied   7 6 5 4 3 2 1   Not at all satisfied
4 *Intimacy* of relationship: Deeply intimate   7 6 5 4 3 2 1   Not at all intimate
5 *Similarity* between us: Deep similarity   7 6 5 4 3 2 1   Not at all similar
6 *Empathy* between us: Deep empathy   7 6 5 4 3 2 1   Not at all empathic
7 *Liking* for other: Like very much   7 6 5 4 3 2 1   Do not like at all
8 *Commitment* to relationship   Deeply committed   7 6 5 4 3 2 1   Not at all committed
9   7 6 5 4 3 2 1

The interaction

1 *Location* of the interaction: ...
2 *Time* of interaction: From ... a.m./p.m. to ... a.m./p.m. Total: ...
3 *Satisfaction* with interaction: Completely satisfied   7 6 5 4 3 2 1   Not at all satisfied
4 *Intimacy* of interaction: Deeply intimate   7 6 5 4 3 2 1   Not at all intimate
5 *Similarity* on topics of conversation: Deep similarity   7 6 5 4 3 2 1   Not at all similar
6 *Empathy* on these topics: Deep empathy   7 6 5 4 3 2 1   Not at all empathic
7 *Feeling* towards other today: Highly positive   7 6 5 4 3 2 1   Highly negative
8 *Significance* of interaction: Deeply significant   7 6 5 4 3 2 1   Not at all significant
9   7 6 5 4 3 2 1

Description

Now describe this same interaction in your own words as fully as possible. You should say what it was about the interaction that made it so significant for the relationship between you and your partner.

Part 2

Record below information about all other dyadic interactions lasting more than 5 minutes in which you have participated today. If you have a large number of interactions, you may wish to restrict your records to, say, 10 of the interactions.

Initials of other person	Role relationship	Duration of relationship	Location of interaction	Time of interaction	Significance of interaction
				From ... to ... *Total: ...*	
					7 6 5 4 3 2 1
					7 6 5 4 3 2 1
					7 6 5 4 3 2 1
					7 6 5 4 3 2 1
					7 6 5 4 3 2 1
					7 6 5 4 3 2 1
					7 6 5 4 3 2 1
					7 6 5 4 3 2 1
					7 6 5 4 3 2 1
					7 6 5 4 3 2 1
					7 6 5 4 3 2 1

Diary sheet for option 4
Part 1

You are required to complete the rating scales for the one most significant interaction of the day with your co-diarist.

Diary sheet no. ...

Other person: Initials ...   Sex ...   Age ...

The relationship

1	*Role* relationship: ...			
2	*Duration* of relationship: ...			
3	*Satisfaction* with relationship:	Completely satisfied	7 6 5 4 3 2 1	Not at all satisfied
4	*Intimacy* of relationship:	Deeply intimate	7 6 5 4 3 2 1	Not at all intimate
5	*Similarity* between us:	Deep similarity	7 6 5 4 3 2 1	Not at all similar
6	*Empathy* between us:	Deep empathy	7 6 5 4 3 2 1	Not at all empathic
7	*Liking* for other:	Like very much	7 6 5 4 3 2 1	Do not like at all
8	*Commitment* to relationship	Deeply committed	7 6 5 4 3 2 1	Not at all committed
9			7 6 5 4 3 2 1	

The interaction

1	*Location* of the interaction: ...			
2	*Time* of interaction: From ... a.m./p.m. to ... a.m./p.m. Total: ...			
3	*Satisfaction* with interaction:	Completely satisfied	7 6 5 4 3 2 1	Not at all satisfied
4	*Intimacy* of interaction:	Deeply intimate	7 6 5 4 3 2 1	Not at all intimate
5	*Similarity* on topics of conversation:	Deep similarity	7 6 5 4 3 2 1	Not at all similar
6	*Empathy* on these topics:	Deep empathy	7 6 5 4 3 2 1	Not at all empathic
7	*Feeling* towards other today:	Highly positive	7 6 5 4 3 2 1	Highly negative
8	*Significance* of interaction:	Deeply significant	7 6 5 4 3 2 1	Not at all significant
9			7 6 5 4 3 2 1	

Description

Now describe this same interaction in your own words as fully as possible. You should say what it was about the interaction that made it so significant for the relationship between you and your partner.

Part 2

Record below information about all other dyadic interactions with your co-diarist lasting more than 5 minutes in which you have participated today. If you have a large number of interactions, you may wish to restrict your records to, say, 10 of the interactions.

Initials of other person	Role relationship	Duration of relationship	Location of interaction	Time of interaction	Significance of interaction
				From ... to ... *Total: ...*	
					7 6 5 4 3 2 1
					7 6 5 4 3 2 1
					7 6 5 4 3 2 1
					7 6 5 4 3 2 1
					7 6 5 4 3 2 1
					7 6 5 4 3 2 1
					7 6 5 4 3 2 1
					7 6 5 4 3 2 1
					7 6 5 4 3 2 1
					7 6 5 4 3 2 1
					7 6 5 4 3 2 1

CHAPTER 3

STRUCTURED OBSERVATION AND THE INVESTIGATION OF GROUP INTERACTION

by Carol Tindall and Peter Banister

Contents

1 Introduction

Observation is a very widely used method in psychology: for an account of how to carry out unstructured observation see Banister *et al.* (1994), Chapter 2. In contrast, this project offers you the opportunity to carry out a *structured* observation.

Structured observation can occur in many settings, including the field and laboratories, and usually comprises the detailed examination of interactions, concentrating on specific behaviour and recording the number of instances that occur during the observation of items of particular concern. It is often used to test specific hypotheses, and has been used in a great variety of settings. Examples of recent research using structured observational methods are listed in Appendix 1 at the end of this chapter.

One of the key features of this structured observation project is that it involves you observing approximately 10-minute interactions of two established groups such as a family or work group in their usual social setting.

1.1 Research focus

You will need to put forward a focus for your project rooted in social psychology which can be examined by means of systematic structured observation. This chapter provides detailed examples of social psychological research from the particular areas of gender and power, which you could draw upon, although you may, of course, use material from any area of social psychology.

You then examine your focus by comparing *one* of the following pairs of material:

- Observation of two groups known to you (for example, either two family groups or two work groups or two groups of friends).

- Observation of the interactions of one person in different contexts, such as in their work and family groups, or in their work group and friendship group etc.

You will need to negotiate permission to observe your chosen groups for at least 30 minutes (see section 2.2 below for details). We also advise you to interview two of the participants briefly about their experiences as a group member and their interpretations of the situation. If you choose the second of the above options, make sure that one of your interviewees is the person who appears in both contexts. You may also want to make use of a video camera and/or an audio recorder. If this is the case, you again need to gain the permission of your participants.

This project is a small-scale, ideographic study of established group inter-actions involving the collection, via structured observation, of quanti-tative data, plus some qualitative comment. Structured observation requires you to work with a particular focus, which you select, based on your reading of social psychology, in advance of carrying out the obser-vations. Your observations are then guided, as it were, by your particular focus.

Your project will involve a number of different stages. The first stage is to observe the interactive *content*, to note the frequency of occurrence within the interactions of those naturally occurring behaviours and actions, both verbal and non-verbal, that you have selected as being relevant to your focus. To do this, you will need to draw up a simple observational checklist (see Appendix 2 for an example). You will also be asked to track the interactive flow, to focus on relevant *interactive sequences* and patterns observed. As you will be aware from your reading, the observer has much to do with what is observed. You are therefore also required to make explicit the *inferences* you draw from your obser-vations, and also to comment on the links or otherwise between your view as one *outside observer* and the participants' *insider perspectives*. These last two stages are made easier if you jot down your thoughts and feel-ings about both what you have observed and yourself as observer im-mediately you finish each observation.

Finally, precise write-up details of the report format are give in section 6.

2 Background

It is important to state at the outset that this project involves observing established groups of people, discussing very usual issues within their natural environment, and thus behaving as naturally as you might ex-pect given the presence of an observer with maybe a video camera or audio recorder. Our intention in these background notes is to highlight issues that you need to think about at each of the stages in the process of data collection.

Your first task is to select a pathway through the wealth of potential material by formulating a research focus. *You need to think carefully about this as your focus forms the core of the project*. It may be useful at this point to read Miell and Dallos (1996) or Wetherell (1996) or Stevens (1996) for ideas as to what you might focus on. It is essential that you are able to provide a theoretical rationale for your focus. Also, as this is an obser-vation project, the observational method must provide you with suitable material with which to explore your focus.

Your next task is to choose which combination of the contexts listed below interests you. Do note that it is necessary to use two interactions to explore your research focus.

2.1 Options

You should choose *one* of the following options.

1   You might be interested in family interaction, in which case you could compare the interactions of two very similar or two very different families known to you. Examples of different families might be ones from different ethnic backgrounds or differently constituted families.

2   Similarly, you could compare the interactions of two very similar or two very different work groups or friendship groups known to you.

3   You could choose to compare the interactions of one person in very different contexts, such as their work and family setting or their family and friendship setting.

Be aware that you must gain the informed consent of all the participants in the groups you have chosen to observe.

2.2 Informed consent

In order to make an informed choice your potential groups need to know what you require of them and what your intentions are. You must ask them:

•   for their permission to be observed in their natural setting, for about 30 minutes from which you will select 10 minutes to analyse;

•   to discuss something which they would all normally be involved in making a decision about.

We advise you to tell your participants that you will be observing what is going on verbally and non-verbally, as well as trying to track the flow of interaction and note interactive sequences. You might want to tell your participants that your general area of concern is gender differences, power, or whatever. You may be concerned that this information will influence their behaviour, as it will. However, if you do not tell them what your interest is they will not treat you as a neutral observer but will construct their own understanding of what is going on which will equally bias the material gained. If you choose not to tell your participants your general area of interest, then it is important to give them this information, and generally comment on what you have noticed, immediately you finish observing.

ACTIVITY

In preparation for your observations, list how you intend addressing each of the issues detailed in the extract below from Tindall (1994), to gain the informed consent of your participants. Bear in mind their possible need to see your final report and have copies of the audio- and videotapes.

INFORMED CONSENT

Good research is only possible if there is mutual respect and confidence between researcher and participants. This is gained initially by open and honest interaction. All elements of the research need to be fully disclosed, including your position and involvement as researcher in the issue, the purpose of the research, what is involved, how it is to be conducted, the number of participants, the time it is likely to take and, importantly, what is to happen to the material collected. Only when prospective participants are fully informed in advance are they in a position to give informed consent. Positivists claim that such information contaminates the subsequent material gained, but it is inevitable that people will construct their own understanding of what is going on.

It should be clear at the outset that initial consent is just that, and that participants have the right to withdraw at any time, even retrospectively. This rarely happens in my experience, but if it does the material gained from that person must be destroyed.

Prospective participants may be informed in a variety of ways: by letter, an informal chat or group discussion, with the researcher. It is important for a researcher to be available to prospective participants, to provide them with the opportunity to query and comment on any aspect of the research. A group discussion also allows them access to others' interests, anxieties and expectations and may enable them to air their own more freely. It is good practice to remain available and easily contacted by participants right the way through the research to outcome, so that they are fully involved and provided with the opportunity to withdraw consent if they so choose, or more usually to have ongoing queries and comments responded to. This is also part of the democratizing process [...].

Initially people will have been fully informed of the intended uses of the research material. If this changes, or at a later stage the work is published, then participants need to be contacted for their permission and, if it is granted, informed of when and where the research will be published.

(Tindall, 1994, pp.153–4)

2.3 Content

To help you in formulating your own research focus, we have put together some ideas from Miell and Dallos (1996), particularly Chapters 2, 3 and 5 and associated readings, and from Deborah Tannen's (1992) book, *You Just Don't Understand: Women and Men in Conversation*.

For this illustration, we have looked at gender differences, which is something many of you may be concerned with, and at power, which is a key issue in social psychology. Below are just some ideas of previous work in these two areas from which you may like to devise your own research focus and eventually your observational checklist. It is not an exhaustive nor a prescriptive range of ideas, but rather is one which we think represents some of the critical aspects of gender and power issues within relationships.

Gender

Verbal and non-verbal content

Tannen's (1992) work on gender differences in communication suggests that women involved in decision making tend to consult and ask for advice, whereas men decide without consultation, and are more likely to offer advice and problem solve. Women tend to negotiate a collaborative floor (Edelsky, 1993), changing the topic of conversation (interrupting) as often as men in this collaborative context. However, when what to do next appears to be unclear, men tend to initiate topic changes unilaterally, thus holding a single floor (West and Garcia, 1988). We must be cautious, as James and Clarke (1993) rightly point out, about interpreting interruptions as 'attempts to seize the floor', as we as observers have no way of knowing the participants' intentions. Canary and Hause (1993) claim that 'Gender stereotypes indicate that in conversation adult men are more likely to assert, challenge, make statements or ignore than are women, while women tend to use conversation constructively to negotiate or maintain relationships.' The accommodation hypothesis (Rosenthal and DePaulo, 1979), suggests that women are more 'polite', more accommodating of men's conversational demands, smile more, laugh at jokes rather than make them, and listen more and interrupt less than men. Tannen (1992) notes differences in gazing style and body orientation during interaction. Women tend to orient themselves directly towards other interactants, gazing directly at faces with the occasional glance away, whereas men orient themselves much more indirectly and spend more time gazing elsewhere, only occasionally glancing at interactants' faces.

As Radley (1996), Hinde (1984) and Giles and Coupland (1991) make clear, gender differences in conversational style are often quite small. Our individual conversational styles are influenced by many factors, including our role, context and particular social domain. We must be wary, when observing, of identifying only those behaviours and actions which match our expectations, be they gender-specific or otherwise.

Power

You might be interested in focusing on power: who has the power, how it was achieved, how it shifts or fails to shift between the interactants. We have identified some power issues from Miell and Dallos (1996) below. Again, these are merely illustrative, and not exhaustive.

Verbal and non-verbal content

Are any of the gender differences in power bases outlined by Williams and Watson (1988) evident in the verbal content of the group interaction? Are hierarchical norms such as parent/child, manager/team worker in operation? If so, how is the power dealt with? Is it shared via negotiation or given (or maybe taken) by another group member? Who is centre stage and on what do you base your opinion? Who sets the agenda initially, and does this get changed? If so, by whom and with what effect? Who spends longest speaking and what does this imply? Who is asserting and who complying? Cameron *et al.* (1988) distinguish between affective tag questions, which indicate a concern for others (e.g. 'Are you quite comfortable there?'), and modal tag questions which either request or confirm information (e.g. 'You did pass that report on, didn't you?'). Their work suggests that those in powerless positions make use of modal tag questions but do not use affective tags.

What is going on non-verbally? It may be important to pick up on Goffman's (1959) distinction between what is 'given' and what is 'given off'. Be aware of dress, gestures, and the tone and pace of voice. Who looks most relaxed, who is taking up most physical space? Henley (1977) claims that these are often taken as signifiers of power differences. Body orientation and direction of gaze are also likely to be important in achieving, monitoring and shifting power non-verbally.

As you will be observing only one brief interaction in each group, you will only be able to comment on apparent power and power bases within the interaction. Try not to be distracted in your observations of known groups by impressions of power that you have already gained.

As observers so closely focused on the verbal and non-verbal aspects of what is going on, we are in danger of failing to note the group dynamics: how participants are simultaneously influencing and being influenced by others – the mutuality of influence. This is the stage you must move to next.

2.4 Interactive sequences

You now need to widen your focus to observe how the interaction flows between the participants. What are the relative positions of group members through the sequence of interaction? Interactive qualities are emergent; power, for instance, does not necessarily reside within an individual or status position. Children can operate from a position of power with regard to their parents. For example, children may attempt to gain power by playing one parent off against the other. Your aim here is to track the interactive flow, to record and represent the relationship dynamics – what Rudi Dallos, in Miell and Dallos (1996), Chapters 3 and 5, calls 'the recursive spirals of mutual influence'. What you observe will depend on your chosen research focus as well as what you see going on within your specific contextualized interactions. Below is a list of potentially relevant interactive sequences, which you might expect to be concerned with. However, it is important to be open to novel events, so do not let this list constrain you. Note any interactive sequences that seem important.

You should look for evidence of:

- Strategies:
    - Coalitions: who is connecting with whom, and with what effect? Attend here particularly to who is agreeing with and/or dissenting from whom. Non-verbally, coalitions may be apparent from physical proximity, the giving and receiving of smiles, frowns, head nods, touch, etc. Interactants' direction of gaze and body orientation may also be important.

    - Subgroups, factions, in-groups and out-groups.

    - Scapegoating, conflict management, escalation.

    - Hierarchy, power and/or cooperative relationships – are these stable or changing? If changing, how is the shift achieved? For example, less powerful participants may 'gang up' against a more powerful one, or a subservient participant might try to curry favour with a more powerful one in order to gain power.

- Apparent rules or norms, both explicit (conscious) and implicit (unconscious), that are operating. Examples would be participants all speaking at once or politely waiting their turn, and role behaviours, particularly those associated with gender, family, occupation and friendships.

- Overall patterns, cycles of action and interactive sequences. These may not be apparent at all in such a short interaction, in which case you will have no comment to make. However, be aware of them should they appear. For example, maybe all decisions are made through one person who is the hub of attention and activity.

Finally, at this stage, you need to tell the overall story of what you as an observer thought was happening in the group. What was achieved by the observed patterns and strategies? What was the focus of the interaction? What about the apparent intents of the participants and the energy level within the group – was it subdued or excited? What about the emotional tone – was it warm and intimate, argumentative but friendly, hostile, task centred? Try to represent, in as far as it is possible, how the group appeared to you. Remember, too, the constraints set on the interaction by the task.

2.5 Inferences

We now move to a third stage of observation, where you are being asked to attend to the boundary between observation and perception: how you as an outsider make sense of what you have observed; what you perceive to be the underlying beliefs and understandings driving the actions and thus the group dynamics. Be alert to what appear to be interlocking beliefs and actions between the participants which both drive and maintain patterns of interaction within established groups. In Appendix 3, which provides some background on personal construct theory, Dallos (1996) considers Kelly's (1955) notion of sociality and suggests that in order to interact, and certainly to be involved in an established relationship, we need to develop a set of constructs or understandings about each other's constructs: for example, how Janet thinks John sees her and equally how John thinks Janet views him. In other words, interactions are based on our understandings of each other's construing. In turn, as observers, we likewise formulate ideas about how we think people see themselves and each other. As indicated in Figure 1, we can infer from observed behaviours that father and son have these constructs about each other and that this fuels their interaction.

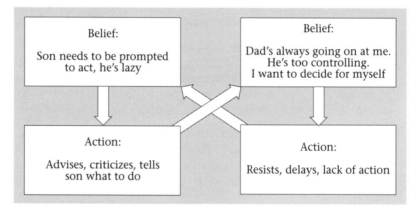

Figure 1

Since making inferences is part of our natural everyday activity, you should find it relatively easy. However, do remember that these are inferences, and they may be wrong. This is something that you can check in the post-interaction interviews and comment on in the reflexive analysis. It is important to bear in mind that we create the meanings; the inferences that we make are our construction of what we perceive to be going on.

Take care not to generalize from your group to other groups, nor to attribute actions that you have observed and given your own meaning to, in social psychological terms, to enduring characteristics within the individual participants. (You may, however, want to speculate about how the observed interaction represents the evolving nature of the interactive flow characterizing the group.) All you have observed is people behaving in particular ways in a specific social context at a particular time – a mere snapshot of the interactive flow.

Clearly, the only way to gain understanding is to imbue actions with meaning. However, Shotter (1987) cautions us against assuming that actions are intentional and complete – they may be otherwise. Yet our analysis based on an outsider's perspective requires us firstly to construct a personal understanding via our own frameworks. In terms of Kelly's (1955) sociality corollary, this is our ability as observers to construe the construction processes of others, to understand their personal reality. Secondly, our analysis requires us to take an additional step away from the group's jointly constructed reality by informing our personal reality with appropriate social psychological theories.

2.6 Reflexivity

Stevens (1996, Chapter 4) considers our capacity to reflect, claiming that reflexive awareness is 'our ability to reflect on the act of experiencing (i.e. to be conscious of being conscious)' (p.183). In Tindall (1994), reflexivity is linked with the researcher role: 'Reflexivity, then, is about acknowledging the central position of the researcher in the construction of knowledge, that [...] all findings are constructions, personal views of reality, open to change and reconstruction' (p.151). There is inevitably a gap both within and between insiders' (participants) and outsiders' (observers) constructions of what is or might be going on. As observers, we are engaged in making sense of what is going on. In terms of Kelly's sociality corollary, this can be seen as our ability to construe the construction processes of others, to understand their personal reality. Mostly, we infer what people might be thinking from how they act towards each other. We must remember, however, that we as outsiders are onlookers, and thus have a more distant as well as a physically different view of the interaction. In addition, when people are known to us, we have our own ideas of their agendas, and of how each participant relates to other group members – ideas which of course will influence our observations.

Similarly, participants' experiences of being actively involved in an observed group interaction are influenced by what they perceive as going on in the group, by their role, by their perceptions and previous experience of other group members, and by the group dynamics and their ideas about the observer's intentions. Each of us, whether participant or observer, is influenced by our current role, personal frameworks and experience, plus our positioning within or outside the group.

It is important to acknowledge that your analysis is inevitably *one* outsider's personal construction, one of many possible interpretations, inevitably constrained by your own frameworks and the societally available realities open to you.

Usually as observers we have no access to participants' accounts, their intentions, or the strategies (if any) they employed to achieve their preferred outcomes. Given that on this occasion you can have access to the reflections of two of the participants, from each interaction, it would be both useful and interesting to comment on the connections and diversities between your outsider's constructions and their insiders' perspectives. Equally, there is often a difference between what people seem to be doing and what they claim their intentions are. How might this difference be accounted for? You might find it useful to read Lalljee (1996, section 3). You might also find Goffman's (1959) distinction between what is 'given' and 'given off' and Kelly's (1955) sociality corollary of use.

Having outlined some of the things you might be looking for within your chosen interactions, we now provide some practical advice on how to operationalize your ideas.

3 Preparation

3.1 Research focus

You are now in a position to decide on a research focus. Remember this needs to be explorable using structured observation, in addition to being grounded in social psychology. Some of the obvious previously mentioned key issues on which you might focus are gender, power, or the influence of context on one person's interactions.

Having selected an observational focus, you now need to consider how you might collect useful observational material with which to explore your focus, at each of the stages (i.e. verbal and non-verbal *content*; the *interactive sequences*, the patterns and strategies within the interactive flow; your *inferences* about beliefs; and *reflexivity*, both yours and that of the participants).

Once you have decided on a focus and selected appropriate groups to observe, you must gain the informed consent of your potential participants (see section 2.2 above for details). If you elect to video your groups' interactions, think carefully about the camera position and the inevitable biases any position introduces.

3.2 Content

Verbal

Having selected a particular focus from within your chosen issue, your next step is to define your focus in terms of a checklist of *observable* characteristics. For instance, if you are interested in the influence of context, your specific focus might be styles of contribution within the two contexts. Next you need to identify a set of observable behaviours which will give you useful information about participants' styles of contribution. In addition, you should observe groups informally, to check if the behaviours you have in mind are actually used by such groups. You then need to develop a coding system or checklist based on your identified behaviours which will allow you to categorize and record the behaviours you observe. This needs to be as clear and straightforward as possible for easy and reliable use.

To give you an idea of how this might be done, an example of a coding system developed by Bales (1950) and still widely used has been included as an Appendix 2. One of the areas Bales focused on was leadership in small groups. His coding system is structured around four general categories of interactions: (i) positive socio-emotional; (ii) task related answers; (iii) task related questions; (iv) negative socio-emotional. Each of the four categories is based on a number of observable behaviours and actions which Bales considered appropriate to the specific categories. This coding system was then used to record the frequency of occurrence of the listed behaviours and actions, for each participant, across a series of small group interactions, and later used to comment on leadership style in terms of 'task leader' and 'socio-emotional leader'. You are similarly required to develop a coding system (simpler than the Bales one) which allows you to record the frequency of specific behaviours relevant to your observational focus.

Non-verbal

In the same way, use your reading of this chapter and other appropriate material to draw up a simple checklist of non-verbal behaviours which relate to your particular observational focus and which allows you to record the frequency of occurrence of the selected non-verbal behaviours.

Pilot

Once the checklists are devised, you must pilot them. Use a group interaction in your own environment, but *not* a group that you intend observing for your project, to pilot the adequacy of your checklists. Analysing a video of a soap opera or a drama documentary from television might also be particularly useful for this purpose. You can then refine your checklist in the light of your experience in carrying out your pilot work.

Your checklists should:

- define your observational focus in terms of observable behaviours and actions (i.e. they should have face validity);
- allow you to record the frequency of observed behaviours and actions;
- provide you with useful material with which you can begin to address your research focus.

If they prove less than adequate you must modify your checklists appropriately and re-pilot them.

Example

Let us take as an example the Bales (1950) structured observation system, which is included as Appendix 2. When you come to look at this in detail, you will realize that it is not as simple as it might originally appear to be; for instance, it contains the sub-category 'shows solidarity', which you might decide to use. What you consider to be 'solidarity', however, may not be the same as what somebody else viewing the same material would necessarily think of as solidarity. Behaviour which one of the participants intends to be helpful may be seen by another as being obstructive, patronizing, sarcastic, etc. It is thus important to be clear as to what you are taking as instances of 'solidarity', so that others could work out what it is that you are doing (even if they might not have done it in this way themselves!).

Your verbal checklist must be tailored to reflect your area of interest; for instance, it could be used for recording the frequency and type of comments made by women and men in the different family and work contexts. It is important to emphasize that this is purely a suggestion, and you may decide to concentrate on other areas of interest. You will need to give a great deal of thought to devising your checklist, whatever your focus. You will soon realize that even the sub-headings will need to be thought about carefully. Let us take as an example 'Time speaking'.

An obvious initial task here is to decide what constitutes 'speaking'. Remember, what you are hoping to achieve is an operational definition which you could use in your project, and which somebody else could reliably use, achieving (ideally) identical results to you if they analysed your videotape. It might be even worth asking somebody else to code the same video material as you independently, and to explore where differences have occurred.

A good starting-point might be to look at 'fly on the wall' programme on television, and just observe people speaking to each other, to get some flavour of the sorts of problem that are likely to arise, and which you will need to take into account. Take notes of your initial observations, jotting down thoughts as they occur to you. One thing you will notice immediately is the difficulty of doing this; the moment you start looking in detail at behaviour in this fashion, you will find that it disappears before you have had a chance to think about it, let alone record it! The physical act of note-taking, you will also find, will interfere with your observations; this does improve with practice, and an obvious advantage of using a videotape (or an audiotape for verbal interactions) is that the same segment can be watched (or listened to) repeatedly until all the appropriate behaviour has been recorded.

You might find, for instance, that some speaking consists of turn-taking in a very orderly fashion (sometimes plays are like this), where it is very easy to record who talks the longest. A lot of talking in real-life settings, however, does not conform to this pattern: you may find instances of overlaps (where one participant starts talking before the other has finished); gaps (where somebody holds the floor but does not actually say very much); interruptions (where someone deliberately attempts to stop another who is holding the floor); or simultaneous talking (where two or more people carry on talking at the same time). We suggest that these may even be separately recorded in your checklist. What constitutes 'talking' may be problematic; how do you code such sounds as 'mmm', 'yeh', 'but' (or other even less verbal sounds)? Some verbal utterances may be very brief, whilst others might take some time; is it worth recording the number of utterances, as well as the length of time talking? You may find marked differences in different settings, with different subjects being discussed; you may find that children behave differently, and that the nature of the power relationships, gender ratio, etc. all make a large difference.

You can check the intra-rater reliability of your checklists (i.e. how reliably you use them on separate occasions) by using the same video interaction at two separate times, which should be at least 24 hours apart. Your checklists need to be reliable; that is, you need to be sufficiently clear about your operationalized terms that whenever you use the checklists you are categorizing and recording the same observed behaviour in the same way, regardless of the specific interaction. Once your research focus is operationalized via your reliable piloted checklists, you are ready to begin data collection. Piloting also enables you to familiarize yourself once again with the observational method and your position as a researcher.

3.3 Interactive sequences

Patterns and strategies

As will be clear to you from your reading, much of importance is left out of the picture by using content checklists alone. In addition to the frequencies of specific behaviours and actions, it is important to observe and note interactive sequences. Given that this is a small-scale study based on brief observations, it is unlikely that extended interactive sequences will be evident. Your main task here is to identify some of the notable, brief interactive sequences relevant to your observational focus. For example, a team leader chairing a discussion may frequently ask if anyone has a comment to make while looking directly at one team member, or a child may invariably look towards one parent before responding to a question. The identification is best done by making field notes and diagrams on blank sheets of paper, either during (if you can manage it) or immediately after observing the interaction. It is difficult to pilot this task, as patterns are often specific to a particular group, and so cannot be validly checked out on other groups. The best idea is to look back at section 2.4 on interactive sequences, and familiarize yourself with those interactive sequences which seem most relevant to your observational focus. However, what is most important is to note those sequences within the observed interaction that seem most relevant, to both the group and your focus, *whether or not* they have been listed in section 2.4. Think also about the best method of note-taking; a combination of words and diagrams is usually most informative. A diagram showing interactants' relative positions and proximity, and the number of times each addresses the other or the group generally, may be useful to gain an overall pattern of observed interaction. A diagram of this sort is known as a sociogram (see Figure 2 for an example).

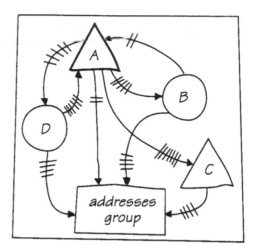

Figure 2 *Sociogram (Source: adapted from Moreno, 1934)*

A circle represents a female participant and a triangle a male participant. When A addresses B, an arrow is drawn from A to B. Each additional time A addresses B, a cross-line is drawn through the main arrow link. Interactions between the other participants are represented similarly. When the whole group is addressed by a participant, an arrow or cross-line is drawn to the square – representing the group.

If your group includes young children, they are likely to change positions during the course of the observation. They will, however, have a favoured position which they return to – this should be obvious to you by the time you start your observations. The best way to represent their interactions on the sociogram is to draw a circle or triangle in their favoured position, with the usual arrows and cross-lines to others. If they move, note their new position on the sociogram using their letter identifier. You are then in a position, at the end of the observation, to map the territory within which they wandered. In addition to the diagram, your observations on the interaction shown in Figure 2 would note:

- Why A speaks often to individuals but rarely addresses the group.

- Why C seems to be relatively quiet or isolated.

- Why D only addresses the group or A.

- Why there is no interaction between B and C, etc.

Remember, the task here is not to record all possibly relevant sequences (otherwise you will be overwhelmed with material) but rather some of those which seem most salient in terms of both the interaction and your observational focus. You need to be in a position to support the claims you make about the interaction with illustrative extracts.

You may choose to record the interaction on video or audiotape (with the participants' permission). This would allow you to explore the non-verbal and verbal content in a more leisurely way later.

Ethics

It is important that you attend to the ethical implications for both the participants and yourself throughout the process of the project. Essentially, the psychological well-being, values and dignity of all need to be maintained from planning through to outcome.

The main concerns here are to:

- treat participants with respect throughout;
- fully inform participants of the process and the purpose of the research in order for them to make an informed decision as to their involvement;
- gain the informed consent of all participants;
- inform participants of the purpose of the observation and what will become of the data;
- ensure participants' anonymity beyond the group;
- be prepared to share your observations and analysis with participants.

At this stage you should have:

- a clearly defined observational focus;
- identified two appropriate interactions to observe;
- drawn up reliable and useful checklists;
- thought about the best way to record apparently relevant sequences;
- negotiated, if necessary, with your known group;
- gained the informed consent of all participants.

If you are in this position, then you are ready to move to fieldwork (i.e. gathering material with which to explore your observational focus).

---

4 Fieldwork

Your initial task is to contextualize the interaction to the extent that you can. A brief description of the setting, the event and the participants involved is required. Begin a sociogram by drawing who is sitting or standing where (see Figure 2). Next, think about where best to position yourself, and talk this over with the group. It is often a good idea, if the situation allows and the group is comfortable with it, to change positions during the observation, in order to reduce positional bias. Clearly, they know that you are present and what your general intentions are, but even so you need to be as unobtrusive as possible during the interaction. Once participants are engaged in the discussion they frequently appear to forget that they are being observed.

It is a good idea to allow the group time to become engaged in the discussion and used to your presence (and the camera if you are videoing the interaction), before you begin observing. (If you are using a video camera, you should video about 30 minutes of interaction from which you will later choose a 10-minute section to analyse.) Remember, interaction is free-flowing with no clear start and stop boundaries; it is the observation which sets the parameters.

Use your verbal and non-verbal checklists to record the frequencies of specific behaviours and actions. Make separate notes of salient interactive sequences either during or immediately after you stop observing. The discussion may well still be in full flow at this time.

Ask two of the participants (which two will depend on your observational focus and what has gone on in the interaction – if you observed the interactions of one person in different contexts, one of your two interviewees should be that person) to reflect on their understanding and experience of the interaction. Give them some questions to talk around, such as:

- What was going on in the group?
- Who were the major contributors?
- How do you feel about the interaction?

You might also want to add some specific questions about your particular focus. Make notes of the main points of their responses.

If you have used a video camera it might be interesting and informative to ask the two participants interviewed to watch the videotape and comment.

Make neutral, non-judgemental notes, as far as it is possible, of what you observe. Try also to distinguish between your observations (what you see), and your own interpretations (what you think).

As soon as possible after the observation, make notes about your own experiences. Note whatever seems relevant to you.

Things to think about here are your:

- role as observer;

- immediate awareness of the strengths and limitations of the observational method;

- immediate awareness of any biases, confusions, anxieties and satisfactions, interpretations.

Having completed your observation, you may want to refine your research focus in the light of material collected. This process of modifying the observational focus via work in the field is a normal part of the research cycle.

5 Analysis

When you have gathered all your material, then you will be in a position to examine the *content* data in terms of your initial observational focus. More details are given below in the write-up section as to how this could be done. Do remember that you are only focusing on a few behaviours and actions relevant to your project; it is not necessary to try to represent all of what you have observed.

You will need to use some descriptive statistics to describe part of what it is that you have found.

These statistics are used to describe what a given example or population is like; they can be used for something as broad as talking about the number of people convicted of a crime in this country during the last year, or for something as narrow as the average length of time during which one of your participants talks. They can be presented in numerical form, or in a variety of other ways, such as by using histograms. Do remember that such statistics only describe, and do not allow you to conclude anything that you have found is generalizable. What you are doing is summarizing your findings in such a way that the reader can understand clearly what it is that you have observed, and can see what your subsequent discussion of the findings is based on.

What precisely you do will depend on what measures you take during your observation; a minimum would be to take two variables, and to summarize them statistically. At a basic level, this can be achieved through simple counting (e.g. number of interruptions), but it is often useful to convert figures to some common form, so that direct comparisons can be made. Differences between numbers of interruptions might, for instance, be related to the differential length of time people talk for; it might be interesting, in these circumstances, to calculate the length of time that each individual spoke for and to divide this by the number of times an individual speaker is interrupted. This will enable you to see at a glance whether somebody is interrupted to a disproportional extent.

In addition, calculations of this nature will give you further information which may be of relevance to the focus of your project. For instance, calculating the mean length of time speaking may give additional information over and above that provided by a simple measure of the total length of time talking.

As well as presenting material in terms of descriptive statistics, it is often useful to present it pictorially, in terms of histograms or pie-charts; it might be easier to show the length of time participants speak in terms of a proportion of a pie-chart, rather than just in terms of numbers.

The important thing is to look at your results systematically, and try to make sense of them; how do they relate to your initial research focus? Depending on your focus, are there marked differences between the different settings or between the participants in terms of gender and power, in terms of age, etc.? Did the inside/outside perspective reveal anything? Were there any unexpected results; if so, how might these unexpected results be accounted for? Remember, what should be done here is a detailed analysis of what you have found. Does it make sense? Was it as expected?

6 Write-up

The conventional major headings are given in this section, but note that it is often useful to subdivide further so that the material is easier to follow. If you do this, then it is often useful to provide an initial outline of the structure of each section, so that the reader can more easily follow the write-up as it unfolds. Banister *et al.* (1994), Chapter 10 provides further detailed advice on writing up projects of this nature, if you would like some more help.

6.1 Title

This should briefly describe your project; thus 'An exploration of gender differences observed in family contexts' might be appropriate, whilst 'The observation project' would not be acceptable.

6.2 Abstract

This should provide a succinct summary of what you did, what you found, and what conclusions you came to.

6.3 Contents

Provide a brief contents list, and paginate your project.

6.4 Introduction

Often project write ups have been described as an 'hour-glass', going from the general to the specific and ultimately back to the general; so here start from the general, and go to the specific. The introduction is often best subsectioned, beginning with its own brief introduction. You will need to review fully the relevant literature which provides the background for your observational focus, and you must include a section giving reasons why you feel that structured observation is the most appropriate way of exploring your focus. Evidence must always be provided to support assertions, and all references must be fully listed, using the conventional format, at the end of the project. What you are going to examine must be clear, and rooted in the literature. Remember, what you are doing here is almost 'selling' your project; at the end of this section, the reader should be convinced of the worth of your project, which relates to the literature, and has a carefully worked out justification for the methodology used.

6.5 Method

Do remember in your write-up that you are an observer or a researcher, and the people taking part are best referred to as 'participants' (not as 'subjects'!).

Remember that the aim here is to provide replicability, so that the reader can clearly understand what it is that you did, and why, and could repeat what you have done given the same opportunities. The first stage to report on is any pilot work you carried out – for instance, clarifying how you developed your checklist. For each checklist (verbal and non-verbal), you need to describe briefly the piloting process, indicating what changes were thought necessary as a result of this process. Also include the results of any reliability checks which you have carried out (percentage agreement, between yourself and another independent rater, or between yourself on two separate occasions, would be appropriate here). This can be simply calculated in terms of the following example:

$$\frac{\text{Agreed number of interruptions}}{\text{Total number of interruptions}} \times 100$$

A percentage agreement in the range 80–100 per cent is worth aiming for; if the agreement is less than this, then it suggests that you need to think through and refine your criteria further. The checklists themselves should be put in the appendices.

Having described the process of developing the checklists, the next stage is to indicate clearly which types of group interactions you chose. For instance, you will need to explain to the reader your choice of a known family, how you approached them initially, what pre-existing relationships and knowledge you had of them, what you told them you were doing, what feedback you agreed, etc.

Ethical considerations are important and need to be included here. Ethical guidelines (e.g. British Psychological Society, 1993) often suggest that observation in general is seen as having less in the way of ethical problems than other approaches in social psychology, but none the less this needs to be carefully considered, and may even be regarded as debatable.

You need to say a little bit about yourself, as you may wish to discuss later the possible impact of yourself on the situation, and to consider whether any of your biases might have influenced the analysis and your interpretation.

You will need to provide a full description of the context of the interactions (a sketch-map of the setting might be useful if you think that this will make it easier for the reader to visualize this): the room layout, the time of day, the location of the video camera (if used), etc.

The participants will also need to be briefly described.

If you interviewed your participants after the observation, spell out how precisely this interview was carried out (e.g. where and when it took place, whether you took notes, etc.).

6.6 Analysis

This is probably best presented in four sections, corresponding to the four stages outlined in these project notes. You could start off with the two stages of *content* and *interactive sequences* (which are both observations), and then move into interpretation, with the two stages of *inferences* and *reflexivity*.

(i) Content

This section needs to be succinct, clear and unambiguous; start off by systematically examining your observational focus, looking in detail at the evidence you have found in the observation. Present the data in tabular form, labelling it clearly so that the reader can make sense of it without having to resort to elsewhere in the write-up. Unlike a conventional 'results' section, you should talk here about what you have found. If you have found what you have expected, then say so. If there are unexpected findings, then again these will need to be included here, and thought through.

Possibilities here have been outlined in some detail in section 5 above on analysis. Do be aware, however, that, even if your analysis supports your research focus, without an appropriate test of their level of statistical significance you can do no more than state what your findings are, and consider in the discussion section how they relate to the literature.

The rationale for this is partly related to the need to get you to actually look at what you have found, and to attempt to make sense of your findings; all too often, students tend to incant statistical formulae which usually turn out to be non-significant, and the actual data obtained are not even examined.

It is important to stress at the outset that what matters is not whether the evidence you find is what you expected to find, but rather that you demonstrate your competence in carrying out the process and systematically consider your observations.

(ii) Interactive sequences

Moving on from describing the content of what you have observed, you should next concentrate on outlining the interactive sequences which you have observed; were any patterns evident? What strategies did people adopt during the observation? Were there any rules or norms that you thought were in operation (these may be explicit or implicit)? End with an overall summary of what you thought was going on in the group.

(iii) Inferences

Include a section on what inferences you made about the interaction from your outside perspective, clearly putting forward the reasons for your conclusions (do acknowledge the basis of your insights, which may even have unconscious links). Note, for instance, any patterns of behaviour you noticed, any differences across the two observation sessions, any other age or gender differences in behaviour, etc.

(iv) Reflexivity

The final section should contrast your outsider perspective with the material gained from your interviews with your participants. Were their views different from yours? What was added by the inclusion of participants' accounts? Note (as has been emphasized above) that people may not always be aware of their behaviour, their reasons for it and their impact on others.

6.7 Discussion

Again, subsectioning is often useful here; if this is done, it should again be clearly labelled, with linking sections.

The discussion offers the opportunity to take a wider perspective, leading back to general issues at the bottom of the 'hour-glass'. You will need to comment on what you have found, whether it is as expected or unexpected, or difficult to interpret, or just inconclusive. The possible reasons for what you have found need to be explored. These could include all sorts of problems, including a faulty checklist, the intrusion of the observer, the particular group or setting chosen, etc. It could be that your expectations were based on previous work which used people from different backgrounds (US rather than UK, for instance) or took place at a different historical time. Do remember that this is a very limited, in-depth, ideographic study, using a very small amount of material (though it is fascinating to note how rich even such a small-scale set of observations are), and thus do acknowledge that it is not valid to generalize from such a small sample! Your discussion should include consideration of each of the four stages covered in the analysis and provide links, where relevant, to the appropriate literature. Comment too on observations not covered in the literature.

Reflexive analysis

An important part of the discussion is the reflexive analysis, where you think about the observational study which you have just carried out and your part in it. In the light of your experience, how would you evaluate structured observation as a method in social psychological research, how might you change the project if you were to redo it, what future research might it be interesting to carry out in this area, what were your feelings as an observer/researcher/social psychology student in carrying out this research, etc.? It is sometimes said, for instance, that structured observation leads to a concentration on the trivial, and a consequence is that not only is a lot of behaviour missed, but, moreover, the *most* important behaviour is missed; did your experiences in carrying out this project lead you to this conclusion, or did the methodology have sufficient flexibility to capture some of the flavour of the interactions observed? To what extent did your inferences match your participants' reflexive comments? What have you learned from this project about the methods you could employ in carrying out research? Note the concept of domains; social psychology looks at people on many different levels such as the intrapersonal and the interpersonal; is structured observation more useful in one domain rather than another, and how might it be improved?

It might even be worth developing a brief proposal for future research within this section. Based on your observations and your experience of this project, how might you develop from this point? What aims/themes might you want to explore further? Discuss how you might go about doing this.

6.8 References

Provide a full reference list, using the conventional format.

6.9 Appendices

Put copies of your raw data (e.g. completed checklists) in a clearly labelled appendix.

References

Bales, R.F. (1950) 'The analysis of small group interaction', *American Sociological Review*, vol.15, pp.257–64.

Banister, P., Burman, E., Parker, I., Taylor, M. and Tindall, C. (1994) *Qualitative Methods in Psychology: A Research Guide*, Buckingham, Open University Press.

British Psychological Society (1993) 'Ethical principles for conducting research with human participants', *The Psychologist*, vol.6, pp.33–5.

Cameron, D., McAlinden, F. and O'Leary, K. (1988) 'Lakoff in context: the social and linguistic functions of tag questions', in Coates, J. and Cameron, D. (eds) *Women in their Speech Communities: New Perspectives on Language and Sex*, London, Longman.

Canary, D.L. and Hause, K.S. (1993) 'Is there any reason to research sex differences in communication?', *Communication Quarterly*, vol.41, pp.129–44.

Dallos, R. (1996) 'Creating relationships', in Miell, D. and Dallos, R. (eds) (1996).

Edelsky, C. (1993) 'Who's got the floor?', in Tannen, D. (ed.) *Gender and Conversational Interaction*, New York, Oxford University Press.

Giles, H. and Coupland, N. (1991) *Language: Contents and Consequences*, Buckingham, Open University Press.

Goffman, E. (1959) *The Presentation of Self in Everyday Life*, New York, Doubleday Anchor.

Henley, N.M. (1977) *Body Politics: Power, Sex and Nonverbal Communication*, Cambridge, Cambridge University Press.

Hinde, R.A. (1984) 'Why do the sexes behave differently in close relationships?', *Journal of Social and Personal Relationships*, vol.1, pp.471–501.

James, D. and Clarke, S. (1993) 'Women, men and interruptions: a critical review', in Tannen, D. (ed.) *Gender and Conversational Interaction*, New York, Oxford University Press.

Kelly, G.A. (1955) *The Psychology of Personal Constructs*, Vols 1 and 2, New York, Norton.

Lalljee, M. (1996) 'The interpreting self: an experimentalist perspective', in Stevens, R. (ed.) (1996).

Miell, D. and Dallos, R. (eds) (1996) *Social Interaction and Personal Relationships*, London, Sage/The Open University.

Moreno, J.L. (1934) *Who Shall Survive?*, Washington, DC, Nervous and Mental Diseases Publishing Company.

Powell, G.E. and Wilson, S.L. (1994) 'Recovery curves for patients who have suffered very severe brain injury', *Clinical Rehabilitation*, vol.8, pp.54–69.

Radley, A. (1996) 'Relationships in detail: the study of social interaction', in Miell, D. and Dallos, R. (eds) (1996).

Rosenthal, R. and DePaulo, B.M. (1979) 'Sex differences in accommodation in nonverbal communication', in Rosenthal, R. (ed.) *Skill in Nonverbal Communication: Individual Differences*, Cambridge, MA, Oelgeschlager, Gunn and Hain.

Shotter, J. (1987) 'The social construction of an "us": problems of accountability and narratology', in Burnett, R., McGhee, P. and Clarke, D. (eds) *Accounting for Relationships: Explanation, Representation and Knowledge*, London, Methuen.

Stevens, R. (ed.) (1996) *Understanding the Self*, London, Sage/The Open University.

Tannen, D. (1992) *You Just Don't Understand: Women and Men in Conversation*, London, Virago.

Tedder, N.E., Warden, K. and Sikka, A. (1993) 'Prelanguage communication of students who are deaf-blind and have other severe impairments', *Journal of Visual Impairment and Blindness*, vol.87, pp.302–7.

Tindall, C. (1994) 'Issues of evaluation', in Banister, P., Burman, E., Parker, I., Taylor, M. and Tindall, C. (1994).

West, C. and Garcia, A. (1988) 'Conversational shift work: a study of topical transitions between women and men', *Social Problems*, vol.35, pp.551–73.

Wetherell, M.S. (ed.) (1996) *Identities, Groups and Social Issues*, London, Sage/The Open University.

Williams, J. and Watson, G. (1988) 'Sexual equality, family life and family therapy', in Street, E. and Dryden, W. (eds) *Family Therapy in Britain*, Buckingham, Open University Press.

Further reading

Many books will provide further reading on structured observation, including the following:

Cohen, L. and Manion, L. (1989) *Research Methods in Education* (3rd edn), London, Routledge.

Fassnacht, G. (1982) *Theory and Practice of Observing Behaviour*, London, Academic Press.

Judd, C.M., Smith, E.R. and Kidder, L.H. (1991) *Research Methods in Social Relations* (6th edn), Fort Worth, TX, Holt, Rinehart and Winston.

Pretzlik, U. (1994) 'Observational methods and strategies', *Nurse Researcher*, vol.2, pp.13–21.

Robson, C. (1993) *Real World Research*, Oxford, Blackwell.

Weick, K.E. (1968) 'Systematic observational methods', in Lindzey, G. and Aronson, E. (eds) *Handbook of Social Psychology*, Volume II (2nd edn), Reading, MA, Addison-Wesley.

Weick, K.E. (1985). 'Systematic observational methods', in Lindzey, G. and Aronson, E. (eds) *Handbook of Social Psychology*, Volume I (3rd edn), New York, Random House.

Appendix 1: Published work using this method

Observation permeates all psychological methods, and is a process which we are all using continuously. A lot of these observations are unstructured, and could be where we do not have any specific aims or outcomes in mind; we are observing and recording what is going on in real-life contexts. This project has introduced you to some of the methods of structured observation, where only certain aspects of behaviour are concentrated on; this method has a long history in psychology, one of the most famous early studies being the already cited work of Bales (1950). Bales's original work is still utilized; for instance, Copeland and Straub (1995) used his techniques in a study of cohesion in a sports team. Bales and Cohen (1979) have expanded his original scheme to look at other aspects of small group work, such as dominance/submission and friendliness/unfriendliness; Polley *et al.* (1988) outline many practitioner applications of this work. Structured observations are still used extensively in psychology, and recent examples from a number of diverse fields include the following:

- Tedder *et al.* (1993): This paper outlines the development of an instrument specifically to assess people who are deaf and blind and who also have other severe impairments. These people often function at a prelanguage level of communication, and it is important to try to assess the pragmatic aspects of their communications. Tedder *et al.* have developed the Communication Observation Schedule (COS), which systematically records such communications, in the hope that this will help to facilitate the development of communication.

- Fowlkes *et al.* (1994): This study assessed team performance in military settings using a specifically developed new instrument based on structured observation. As part of an aircrew training exercise, various scenarios were presented and responses were videotaped and subsequently analysed. This analysis was seen as being an effective way of evaluating team members' performances.

- Powell and Wilson (1994): The authors investigated the recovery of patients after severe brain injury in a mixed longitudinal and cross-sectional study. Using structured observation, they systematically recorded changes over a time period of up to 14 months, and found that recovery rates were steepest in the initial three months, but none the less were continuing for some patients after four years. In addition, they noted marked individual differences, and made suggestions for future treatment.

- Persson and Stromberg (1995): In a similar study to the previous one, the authors used a structured observation technique to compare the development of premature infants with that of full term infants, finding (after correcting for preterm birth) few differences in mean level between the groups.

- Bull and Mayer (1988a, 1988b, 1991): The authors conducted some interesting studies using structured observation to investigate interruptions in political interviews, and also the strategies used by Margaret Thatcher, Neil Kinnock and John Major to avoid answering questions in televised political interviews.

References

Bales, R.F. (1950) *Interaction Process Analysis: A Method for the Study of Small Groups*. Chicago, IL, University of Chicago Press.

Bales, R.F. and Cohen, S.P. (1979) *SYMLOG*, New York, Free Press.

Bull, P.E. and Mayer, K. (1988a) 'Interruptions in political interviews: a study of Margaret Thatcher and Neil Kinnock', *Journal of Language and Social Psychology*, vol.7, pp.35–45.

Bull, P.E. and Mayer, K. (1988b) 'How Margaret Thatcher and Neil Kinnock avoid answering questions in political interviews', paper presented to The London Conferences of the British Psychological Society, 20 December.

Bull, P.E. and Mayer, K. (1991) 'Is John Major as unremarkable as he seems? A comparison between three political leaders', paper presented to The London Conferences of the British Psychological Society, 18 December.

Copeland, B.W. and Straub, W.F. (1995) 'Assessment of team cohesion: a Russian approach', *Perceptual and Motor Skills*, vol.81, pp.443–50.

Fowlkes, J.E., Lane, N.E., Salas, E., Franz, T. and Oser, R. (1994) 'Improving the measurement of team performance: the TARGETs methodology', *Military Psychology*, vol.6, pp.47–61.

Persson, K. and Stromberg, B. (1995) 'Structured observation of motor performance applied to preterm and full term infants who needed neonatal intensive care', *Neuroscience and Behavioral Physiology*, vol.42, pp.205–24.

Polley, R.B., Hare, A.P. and Stone, D.J. (1988) *The SYMLOG Practitioner Applications of Small Group Research*, New York, Praeger.

Powell, G.E. and Wilson, S.L. (1994) 'Recovery curves for patients who have suffered very severe brain injury', *Clinical Rehabilitation*, vol.8, pp.54–69.

Tedder, N.E., Warden, K. and Sikka, A. (1993) 'Prelanguage communication of students who are deaf-blind and have other severe impairments', *Journal of Visual Impairment and Blindness*, vol.87, pp.302–7.

Appendix 2: Sample structured observation checklist

		Participant						
		1	2	3	4	5	6	All
Socio-emotional area: positive reactions	1	shows solidarity, raises other's status, gives help, reward						
	2	shows tension release, jokes, laughs, shows satisfaction						
	3	agrees, shows passive acceptance, understands, concurs, complies						
		Total						
Task area: attempted answers	4	gives suggestion, direction, implying autonomy for other						
	5	gives opinion, evaluation, analysis, expresses feeling, wish						
	6	gives orientation, information, repeats, clarifies, confirms						
		Total						

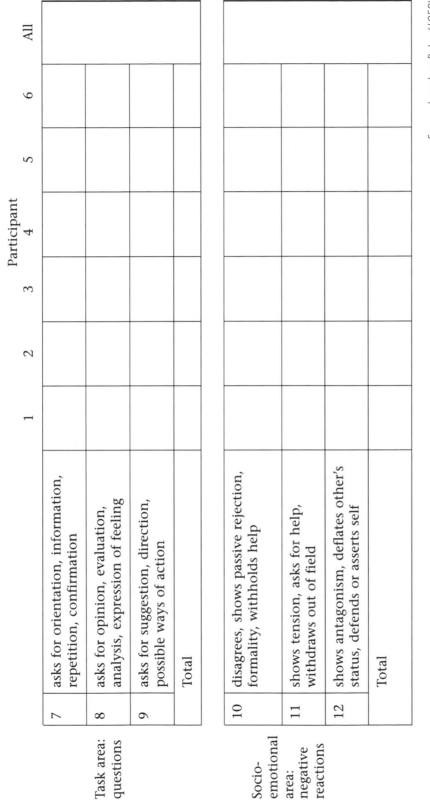

Participant

		1	2	3	4	5	6	All
Task area: questions	7 asks for orientation, information, repetition, confirmation							
	8 asks for opinion, evaluation, analysis, expression of feeling							
	9 asks for suggestion, direction, possible ways of action							
	Total							
Socio-emotional area: negative reactions	10 disagrees, shows passive rejection, formality, withholds help							
	11 shows tension, asks for help, withdraws out of field							
	12 shows antagonism, deflates other's status, defends or asserts self							
	Total							

Source: based on Bales (1950)

Appendix 3: Extract on personal construct theory

3.1 Personal Construct Theory and relationships

George Kelly (1955) suggested that we are all potentially autonomous and capable of actively making choices about events in our lives, including our relationships. Though believing that there is an objective reality 'out there', he proposed that we can only know this through our personal construct system – our idiosyncratic system of interconnected constructs or beliefs which metaphorically is like a lens through which we view the world. Each construct in our system represents a personal set of contrasts – a bipolar division. For example when I use the term 'friendly' the contrast (for *me*) might be 'pushy'. But for someone else the contrasting pole of the construct 'friendly' might be 'aggressive' or 'sullen'. In fact the meaning an individual ascribes to a term such as friendly, Kelly argued, can *only* be gauged if we know its opposite – its contrast – for that individual.

We do not simply see the world and make decisions in our relationships based upon isolated constructs, however. Instead, Kelly argued that constructs are organized in a hierarchical way and linked together to form explanations and predictions. Narratives or stories that we may have about ourselves, and which we offer to others as explanations, may feature a set of constructs connected together. For example, Mary might say, 'I am wary of showing feelings in my relationship because I came from a rather "reserved" family background'. This statement links together a construct about herself – *wary of showing feelings* with a construct that explains her childhood background – *reserved family*. Kelly called these linkages of constructs their 'implications' and regarded people as employing clusters of constructs to explain events. However, he described some constructs as being more central or 'core' than others, for example to think of oneself as 'honest' and 'trustworthy'. In relationships we are concerned that our partners should validate or support our core constructs, and in particular our preferred view of ourselves. Rejection or invalidation of our core views and our preferred view of ourselves is potentially a great source of distress, and a prime reason many people give for terminating a relationship.

Anticipation and replication

ACTIVITY   Think of a relationship that you are currently involved in. What expectations do you have about how your relationship will proceed – how you will both act the next time you see each other? How are your expectations shaped by the way you construe the other person and the relationship with him or her?

Since the world, especially our social world, is continually changing, so also our understandings must be able to adapt and change. Kelly argued that the choice of action taken on the basis of personal constructs influences the interaction that will follow which in turn affects the constructs held by both partners.

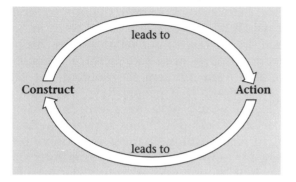

Figure 3.3 *Beliefs and actions are mutually interdependent*

Construct – My parents will be angry that I am using the phone 'all the time' ...

Action – Use the phone in a secret and furtive manner and act apologetically, or alternatively act in a rebellious angry manner ...

Either of these possible courses of action could then start off a self-fulfilling cycle whereby the parents react to the child's actions, triggering further actions from him or her. For example, if he or she acts furtively and apologetically his or her parents might suspect he or she has something to be secretive and apologetic about and start to 'question' or accuse' him or her. Alternatively, if he or she acts rebelliously this might prompt angry counter accusations and criticism.

Kelly suggested that our constructs may not invariably be conscious, so we may have a feeling about someone which is based on construings of which we are not fully aware. He did, however, emphasize our potential for conscious reflexivity – people are seen as able to become aware and to reflect not only on the actions of others but also on their own actions, thoughts and feelings (this aspect of his work is discussed further in Stevens, 1996). Importantly, he also believed that we are capable of reflecting on our relationships, anticipating both the other person's actions and also the outcomes of our own actions. He proposed that gaining insight and awareness of such patterns facilitates change, growth and development in our relationships. This is complicated, however [...], since such unilateral change may be difficult to achieve, especially since the other's continued actions can have a powerful influence in maintaining our constructs and eroding attempts to change. It is also complicated by the fact [...] that some of our actions and feelings in relationships are based upon unconscious processes which are not readily accessible to conscious reflection.

Kelly suggested that all of us are like scientists in the sense that we are concerned with anticipating events in the world. Our constructs help us to make decisions about how to act towards others. We can then test our constructs by seeing how well or badly they help us to anticipate the situations that we enter into. We form hypotheses and build theories about the world which are more or less useful to us in anticipating what is likely to happen. In the case of our relationships this process of anticipation and revision becomes even more critical. People do not usually change unpredictably from moment to moment but certainly they do change. Even if we propose that people have stable personalities which change very little we would have to admit that friendships change, people grow older and take up different interests, relationships develop and disintegrate. In relationships, changes in people's beliefs about each other are required, for example due to changing roles such as becoming a parent, the transition from 'child' to 'adult' status in families, changes in status at work or changes in health. At the same time as allowing us to anticipate and cope with change, our constructs also provide us with a sense of continuity and predictability. We predict the future by expecting a measure of replication of past events. For example we probably expect our friends, our partner and our children to stay 'pretty much' the same, at least over relatively short periods of time – days or a few weeks. Probably most of us expect our interactions with others to be predictable in the sense of being 'like' the interactions we had previously. Constructs therefore provide a bridge and continuity between the past, the present and the future. As we will see, it is more fruitful to think about how our beliefs held about past events construct our future and present behaviour, than it is to think about the past events as 'in themselves' determining what happens.

However, relationships would become extremely chaotic if we did not have any resistance to giving up our constructs in the face of limited samples of evidence. For example if we radically re-evaluate a relationship based upon each shift in the other person's mood we might find it extremely stressful (if not impossible) to plan and organize any activities with them. We might also abandon too readily some useful ways of seeing things. Alternatively, there can be a danger that we become too resistant and try to ignore, discredit or even falsify the evidence available to us. In relationships, a particularly pernicious process can occur (Bateson, 1972; Laing, 1969) when participants falsify evidence so that eventually they may have difficulty in distinguishing 'what is really going on'. Such inability to be able to anticipate, predict and have a sense of control over events and relationships has been linked to serious mental illnesses (Bannister, 1960; Watzlawick *et al.*, 1974).

The commonality and sociality corollaries

As we have seen, Kelly saw relationships as consisting of two or more potentially autonomous and reflexive people trying to make sense of each other and to anticipate not only each other's actions but also each other's thoughts and feelings:

> It would be good to identify two levels of construing. The first would be concerned with events and with [persons] treated as events ... a second ... would be concerned with construing the constructions of other [people]. Instead of making our sense of what others did, we would try to understand what sense they made out of what they did.
>
> *(Kelly, 1955, p.203)*

In order to engage in a relationship it is seen as fundamental that each person has some idea about how the other sees the world, including how the other sees them. Kelly referred to two key processes governing relationships, the first is a recognition of *commonality*: 'To the extent that one person employs a construction of experience which is similar to that employed by another, his psychological processes are similar to those of the other person' (Kelly, 1955).

Commonality has at least two aspects here. Firstly, two people think about the world, and in particular their relationship, in a similar way. One part of such commonality is that we use similar language, for example, a couple who are vegetarians may use terms which they both find familiar, such as 'organic', 'macrobiotic' or 'vegan'. Secondly, their commonality is reflected in their actions (they do not eat meat) and their ways of describing their feelings and experience.

Sociality is the extent to which each person has an understanding or empathy regarding how the other person sees the world: 'To the extent that one person construes the construction processes of another, they, may play a role in a social process involving the other person' (Kelly, 1955).

Sociality involves an ability to predict how the other person uses constructs and this may happen irrespective of the level of commonality. We might understand how someone sees events but totally disagree with them. Likewise, Kelly argues that it is possible to have a high level of commonality with someone but not recognize it, for example if we do not have much communication or discussion with them. The level of sociality, recognition of similarities and differences may fluctuate as a relationship develops.

The idea of commonality suggests that people in relationships evolve some shared ways of construing events, others and each other, Duck (1988, 1994) suggests that in relationships people are continually trying to generate new meanings and explanations and to find more effective ways of understanding each other. An important area of negotiation and potential conflict for any relationship can be the development of a set of understandings and agreements about the relationship itself. A relationship can be seen as a set of ideas or beliefs – a system of meanings. Participants develop a set of constructs about the relationships between each other then establish some agreement or shared way of seeing the relationship; the roles they will play, how they will divide up their time, and issues of obligations, rights, intimacy, dominance and so on. Through participation in a variety of joint activities; cooking, discussions, decorating, physical intimacy and so on people develop a shared set of constructs about each other, including ideas about each other's personalities, but also about how they 'get on together'. Procter (1981) has suggested that a key part of such shared understanding is the agreed allocation of 'roles' within a relationship. For example, one partner may be seen as the practical and unemotional one in contrast to the other who is seen as more emotional, imaginative and spontaneous. In addition to this, there may also be a shared view, accompanied by positive feelings, that this combination 'works well', that they complement each other and so on. Obviously if there is total disagreement about these constructs then the relationship is likely to dissolve into endless arguments, inaction or dissolution. A personal construct theory perspective emphasizes that the important agreement is about the domain of choices seen to be possible, for example, both the roles seen to be necessary and who should fill them. However, both of these may be more or less negotiable – they represent choices seen to be available at any one time in the relationship.

The idea of a shared construct system can be seen in terms of a metaphor of a deck of cards containing an array of options or choices that are seen to he possible by the participants in the relationship. These choices can be presented as bipolar options or constructs. A pair of people may not agree about the choices they should make but there is likely to be more agreement about what choices are possible. Their shared construct system sets out the domain of perceived choices or the 'agenda' for the relationship. The formation of a new relationship can be seen to involve a reshuffling, a synthesis of two decks of options that each partner has brought from their previous experiences. Evolution and changes are possible and prompted by the influences of peers, friends and local community and the wider cultural changes in the attitudes and expectations regarding relationships, for example the implications of changing gender roles within the family.

Emotionality

Relationships are also about sharing emotions, joint experiences of pleasure, joy and sadness. Kelly argued that emotions and constructs were inseparable. We do not simply have emotions but have emotions *based upon* ascribed meanings. Relationships, as we all know, can generate profound and at times intense feelings. From Kelly's perspective these feelings are directly linked to the extent to which we feel a relationship validates our views, and in particular how we would like to be seen, our preferred view of self. Positive emotions: happiness, joy, love, may result from such validation and in contrast negative ones from invalidation. Negative emotions, such as anxiety and anger occur, he suggested, when our constructs are in some way inadequate to help us to predict or exert some influence in a relationship. This may be associated with a sense of inability to be able to influence or persuade another to regard us in a way that we find acceptable or desirable.

[...]

Kelly's definitions emphasize that emotions are fluid and changing as each partner is attempting to deal with the demands and fluctuations of the relationship. He saw problems as associated with an inability to formulate constructs to enable renegotiation and adjustment according to changing circumstances. In any relationship, agreements are seen as to some extent temporary and open to renegotiation. Since these renegotiations will touch central aspects of ourselves it is expected that they will be accompanied by a variety of emotions which may at times result in a relationship becoming volatile, and in some cases the negative emotions may inhibit each person's thinking processes leading in some cases to forms of constrained or 'pre-emptive' construing, a sort of 'tunnel vision' [...]. This is a pattern whereby the constructs operate in a rigid either/or way, revealed by the use of adjectives and adverbs, such as 'every', 'always', 'never' – 'you *always* do that', 'you *never* listen to what I have to say' and so on. In a relationship one person, for example the husband, may see his wife as vindictive and nothing but vindictive, and this feeling may become reciprocated by his wife who may come to see her husband as abusive and nothing but abusive. Typically, the construct will be applied very rigidly to a wide range of actions without any allowance for exceptions or alternative ways of seeing them. Pre-emptive construing has a quality of pushing the other person into a particular role 'whether they like it or not'.

In contrast, the development of relationships, growth, change and more positive emotions seem to be accompanied by a less rigid, propositional style of construing which has a pragmatic quality, rather like a 'working hypothesis' (Kelly, 1955). For example we might see the actions of a work colleague who has been a 'bit short' with us in a number of possible ways, he is tired, is having a hard time at work, is worried about his family etc., rather than just thinking: 'the creep is out to get me, again'. Finally, Kelly also suggested a similar dimension of 'loose versus tight' for describing the person's overall construct system. Overly constricted or tight construing occurs when constructs are used which only cover a very limited range of events, hence the risks of discomfirmation of the constructs are limited. In other words, we can attempt to become more and more certain about fewer and fewer things. In contrast, a construct system can be so loose and vague that it becomes virtually impossible to falsify or test it effectively.

These styles of construing can he seen to be part and parcel of the shared patterns of actions, feelings and beliefs in a relationship. Kelly was keen to emphasize that we are capable of taking a reflexive stance in which we can become aware of our shared experiences, what type of a relationship we are in, how we want to change it and so on, which can be a basis for a discussion and re-negotiation leading to some agreed changes in roles and expectations.

In conclusion, Kelly's PCT offers a view of people in relationships as potentially autonomous, actively making decisions about how to act with others on the basis of their personal systems of meanings. In turn, this system of meanings is seen as fluid, evolving and changing not only in response to changes in a relationship but also simultaneously shaping the nature of the relationship. One danger can be that this view implies that it is easy to change a relationship simply by seeing it differently. [...] Finally, in emphasizing the personal, or even the shared nature of constructs, PCT tends to minimize the wider societal influences which shape personal systems of meanings and identities.

Source: Dallos (1996), pp.119–25

References

Bannister, D. (1960) 'Conceptual structure in thought disordered schizophrenics', *Acta Psychologica*, vol.20, pp.104–20.

Bateson, G. (1972) *Steps to an Ecology of Mind*, New York, Ballantine.

Dallos, R. (1996) 'Creating relationships', in Miell, D. and Dallos, R. (eds) *Social Interaction and Personal Relationships*, London, Sage/The Open University.

Duck, S. (1988) *Relating to Others*, Buckingham, Open University Press.

Duck, S. (1994) *Meaningful Relationships*, London, Sage.

Kelly, G. (1955) *The Psychology of Personal Constructs*, vols 1 and 2, New York, W.W. Norton.

Laing, R.D. (1969) *The Politics of the Family and Other Essays*, London, Tavistock.

Procter, H.G. (1981) 'Family construct psychology', in Walrond-Skinner, S. (ed.) *Family Therapy and Approaches*, London, Routledge & Kegan Paul.

Stevens, R. (1996) 'The reflexive self: an experiential perspective', in Stevens, R. (ed.) *Understanding the Self*, London, Sage/The Open University.

Watzlawick, P., Weakland, J. and Fisch, R. (1974) *Change: Principles of Problem Formation and Problem Resolution*, New York, W.W. Norton.

CHAPTER 4

DESIGNING A SURVEY AND CONSTRUCTING A QUESTIONNAIRE

by Roger Sapsford

Contents

1 Introduction: what is a survey, and why carry one out?

Surveys involve the systematic collection of data from a sample of the population with the intent of generalizing from the nature of the sample data to the nature of the population. Their origins are in the 'scientific' tradition of social research, and like experiments they are concerned to provide data from which inferences about causes or predetermining circumstances can logically be derived. Unlike experiments, however, they do not set up artificial situations in which variables can be manipulated by researchers, but collect their data 'in the field', in the natural circumstances in which they occur. Often they involve asking people questions, but this is not the only way in which survey methods can be applied, as we shall see.

If you are thinking of undertaking a survey, the first thing you need to consider is what surveys will *not* do.

- They will *not* permit the control of variables or treatments. Surveys accept what is there, rather than seeking to change it; any 'control' which is to be exerted is mobilized at the stage of analysis. (However, it is possible to build some degree of prior control into the design by the careful selection of samples for comparisons. It is even possible to combine methods by running a field experiment in which data from those who have received a treatment are contrasted with data from those who have not. Both these possibilities are discussed later in the chapter.)

- They will not provide the richness and individuality of detail which is afforded by more open or qualitative methods of interviewing. Standardization lies at the core of survey work: asking predetermined questions in a predetermined order and asking everyone the same question in the same way. There are ways of getting more individual responses – discussed below – but collecting large quantities of essentially qualitative data works against the survey's main advantage, that it produces easily analysable figures for substantial numbers of respondents.

- Mostly, they will not produce holistic accounts of phenomena. Survey research works in the same scientific tradition as experiments, by isolating and measuring variables whose effects on each other can then be ascertained; in other words, most survey research is reductionist.

- By and large, surveys will not tell you anything you did not already know or guess – or at least, they will not provide explanations cast in different theoretical terms from those with which you started. The only questions that will be answered are those which it occurred to you to ask, and so the *kind* of answer that can be given will have been predetermined by the design of the data-collection instrument. Surveys are very good for exploring researchers' ideas and theories but not always good for collecting the ideas and conceptual frameworks of the respondents.

The great strength of the survey method, when well carried out, lies in its power to handle large numbers, to reach the situations that other methods cannot reach, and to capitalize on the natural variation between people in the social world. The well-designed survey can produce a large amount of data, coded for easy analysis, on a large number of people. If the samples are properly drawn it will allow generalization from the traits of the sample to the probable traits of the population. It can be used in situations where it would not be ethical, or practical, to use other means of exploration. It can help us explore the effects of variables which are not open to manipulation – gender, ethnic group and social class, for example – and it can allow us to capitalize on real-world changes which we would not have had the power to produce (for example, between grammar-school and comprehensive education, or between mothers and those who have never given birth).

2 What you can use surveys for

Survey research is applicable to most research problems in social psychology.

1   It can be used, first, for gathering factual information about people – age, job, gender, physical attributes such as height or weight, behaviours such as smoking and drinking, diet, exercise taken, visits made to the doctor in the last year, usual mode of transport to work, behavioural traits such as tendency to become angry or depressed, self-perceived state of health or health problems as diagnosed by experts, 'history' variables such as details of schooling, past jobs, past friendships and relationships, recent or more remote life events, and so on.

2   A very common use is for the collection of attitudes, beliefs, opinions etc. – verbal responses to questions about what people think about a circumstance or event or future policy, or what they think they might do under various circumstances.

3   A third use, very common in psychology, is the psychometric measurement of enduring traits of personality, or current emotional or motivational states, or the diagnostic measurement of mental health and mental stability.

4   Surveys may be used for assessing ability – in general (e.g. through intelligence tests) or with reference to specific tasks or problems (most often through setting such a task and recording answers or by observing the person carrying out the task).

Survey work often involves lists of questions to ask people, but it is not confined to this. Systematic observation across a sample of locations or instances may also constitute a survey – observing in a hospital accident and emergency department at different times of the day or night to record aspects of nurse and doctor behaviour, for example, or observing in the playgrounds of a range of schools to measure degree of violence in play and who initiates it or is a victim of it. Counting aspects of texts – printed material – can also be regarded as a variety of survey work. Several good projects have been carried out on newspapers, for example, comparing the amount of space accorded to different kinds of story and/ or the kind of language by which the actors are categorized.

Survey work has most often been used in social psychology to look at attitudes or personality, or by sociological social psychologists wanting to explore the correlates of social (work) position or gender or age or ethnic group membership. It has also been used by educational researchers to look at the range of abilities and their social or behavioural correlates, or the origins of aggression or gender identity, or the dynamics of classroom behaviour. It *may* be used by researchers operating within most perspectives, however.

BOX I   Caution

Having said this, there are some surveys which you *ought not* to carry out – particularly if you are a student of psychology whose main interest is in completing a project or dissertation. Some topics are painful for the respondents, some are embarrassing, and many might reasonably be seen as intrusive. Purely 'academic' work should not put respondents to any kind of trouble or distress. Topics such as sexual abuse, AIDS, experiences of bereavement, feelings of acute depression, job failure, painfully disrupted relationships ... this kind of thing is not a fit subject for idle curiosity aimed only at gaining academic credit. Unless you have a legitimate personal interest in the topic area or are part of a team working to make people's lives better within it, they are better avoided. Even if your interest is legitimate, you will want to do everything you can to minimize the impact and the distress that might be caused and to be sensitive to cases where the process of interviewing is doing more harm than the information warrants. Some survey interviews need to be carried out by trained counsellors, because of the risks they involve for respondents. Indeed, all survey researchers need to be alert to the rare and unforeseen chance that someone has been disturbed by the research and might need help.

---

3 Technical questions

Four aspects of design are of paramount importance in survey research (as, indeed, in other kinds of research): representation, measurement, the selection of variables, and the reality of relationships.

3.1 Representation

We carry out surveys on samples, but we intend them to be microcosms of the populations from which they come. That is, we want to treat the sample as representing the population in all respects, so that what we discover to be true about the sample can be taken as true of the population. Under certain restrictive circumstances this is possible in survey research.

The major restrictive circumstance is that the sample should be randomly drawn from the population. Even with a random sample there is a chance of drawing one which is untypical of the population: drawing a sample of four from a pack of playing cards, there is a small but calculable and non-zero chance of drawing four twos or four aces. The point is, though, that if the deal is random then the chance of four aces *is* calculable. Similarly, if you draw a sample of, say, a hundred people, randomly, from a very large population (the population of the British Isles, say), the most likely outcome is that your hundred people will be fairly typical of the population, but there is a small but non-zero chance that it will be very untypical. If the sample is random and reasonably large, however, and the population from which it is drawn is very large, then this chance can be calculated; this is what the branch of mathematics called *statistics* is about. It can be demonstrated that your best chance of typicality is to draw large samples at random.

You should note, however, that a 'random sample' means one where every case in the population has a chance of being selected for the sample, and no case has more chance than any other. The first hundred people you meet when you go out for a walk do *not* form a random sample of the British Isles; if you live down south the sample will have too few people from Scotland, Wales and Northern Ireland, it will contain no people who are housebound or claustrophobic, it will under-represent those who are busy elsewhere at the time when you go out (at work, or feeding the children), and it will probably under-represent the rich (who may be presumed to travel by car rather than on foot). I shall discuss the drawing of random samples in more detail in the next section.

Another way of looking at the problem is to start with the sample and ask 'What population can this represent?' It may to some extent represent the population of Esher, if it is Esher where you took your walk, but it excludes the categories indicated above, and probably others. It *may*, therefore, give us some idea of what things are like among the non-housebound population of Esher (or wherever) who are free to go for a walk at the time when the sample was picked, but we need greater and greater degrees of caution as we generalize beyond this to the population of Esher as whole, the southern counties, England, the British Isles and the whole human race – at each stage of greater generalization we should be less and less surprised if it turns out that our sample is unrepresentative.

3.2 Measurement

However good the sampling, the survey can only be as good as the questions you ask. It is obviously necessary to aim for maximum clarity. You need to be sure that what you are asking is understood by the respondent, and understood in precisely the way that you want it to be understood. This is even more important where the questionnaire is to be filled in personally by the respondent rather than administered by an interviewer, because you have no chance to explain or question the answers.

Technical questions to be considered revolve around the extent to which the questions, conceived of as measuring instruments, do indeed measure what you intend them to measure and do so precisely and accurately. You need to show that the measuring instruments are *reliable* – where the thing being measured is seen as something relatively stable and enduring, that the measuring instruments give reasonably consistent readings of it. Beyond this you have to show – or at least be in a position to argue – the *validity* of the measures: that what is being reliably measured *is* what you say it is. For example, if an intelligence test is not 'culture fair' it may reliably produce lower average results for desert nomads than for Londoners, but this is probably not because of their relative intelligence; what you are probably measuring is familiarity with the English language and with western cultural norms and expectations. Your measures need at least *face validity* – they should look plausible for the purpose for which they are being used. Better would be *concurrent validity* – validation against an already validated measure – or *predictive validity* – validation by showing the results predict a measure (e.g. final examination scores correctly predicted by tests of ability).

3.3 Selection of variables

As well as *how* we measure, we have also of course to determine *what* we measure. Survey variables can be classified, loosely, into four kinds:

1   *dependent variables* – the characteristics whose variability we are likely to want to explain;

2   *independent variables* – those by which we expect to explain this variation;

3   *alternative explanatory variables* – those which might negate our explanation by providing an unwanted but equally plausible explanation; and

4   *descriptive variables* – those which play no part in the explanation but just tell us something interesting about the sample.

For example, in a survey of health variation, the dependent variable is health status – we want to be able to predict which people will have poor health. The independent variables we choose would depend on our theoretical model of how health status is achieved. Suppose we were exploring the possibility that people are more responsible for their own health than many sociological theorists would have us suppose: then the independent variables would be choices made about diet and exercise, occupational choice, risk-taking, use of preventive medicine and health checks, and so on. However, we would know if we had been 'reading up' in the area that income and social deprivation are major predictive factors – there is a gradient of poor health between social classes such that the poor are noticeably less healthy than the rich. We may also have noted that gender is a predictive factor – although women live longer on average than men, they report more illness and disability at every stage of adult life. Gender and some measure of income or material deprivation would therefore have to be collected, because we would probably find that these would explain a great deal of the health variation; the research question might well be: 'To what extent does individual behaviour affect health status *after social variables have been taken into account?*'

We would also measure the age of the respondents, because age is an obvious determinant of health status – we all get less healthy in old age. Beyond this there are variables in which we might be interested for purposes of description – family structure, ethnic origin, aspects of personality perhaps – which might help us 'flesh out' our account of health but would not particularly help us to explain it.

I call this classification of survey variables 'loose' because there is no hard and fast assignment of variables to one category or another. Alternative explanations may turn out to be what best explains the variation and so become the independent variables when we come to present the results. Variables which we collected for purposes of description may also turn out to have explanatory power. We may even find ourselves wanting to explain some of the independent variables in terms of others – looking for behavioural or temperamental explanations for poverty, for example.

The degree of 'pretheorization' makes a difference here. Some surveys are conducted like experiments, with clear preselected independent variables used to explain the variation in the dependent variable. Others are more like fishing expeditions – we have a vague feeling that one or more of a wide range of different kinds of variable may help us to explain the variation in the dependent variable(s), but we have no clearly formulated hypotheses to be tested. While it is clearly advisable to keep the schedule of questions as short as possible, for the convenience of the respondent and to improve response-rate, it is axiomatic that you cannot obtain answers to questions you have not asked, so we generally try to include anything which might prove useful or interesting in the way of questions.

3.4 Mode of delivery

If you are asking questions (as opposed to observing behaviour) you have an important choice to make about how the questions are delivered. On the one hand you can ask them yourself, face to face (or on the telephone – but this has its own problems). Interviewer-administered questionnaires have a lower refusal rate, if the interviewer is reasonably pleasant and competent; people are often not inclined to refuse to deal with someone who is actually present physically. You also have more control (see Section 4.4 below) over precisely how the questions are asked and can soften the impact of questions which might otherwise be thought intrusive. You can also control *how much* is said, prompting the informant for more information if necessary, and you can check that the informant has understood the questions in the same way as everyone else and given a valid answer to them. Interviewer administration is labour-intensive, however – you can only carry out so many surveys in a day – and if you have a randomly selected sample of addresses you may have to do a fair amount of travelling (with some returning at different times of the day to make contact with people who were out when you first called). On the other hand you can deliver the questionnaires (by post or other means) for completion by the respondents themselves. This will enable you to cover a much larger sample, limited by the amount of postage you can afford. However, you have no control over how the questionnaire is filled in (or even by whom!), and refusal rates tend to be high – it is very easy to throw a postal questionnaire away.

3.5 The reality of relationships

The final technical question is whether the findings from the sample can be taken seriously as representing a truth about the population, or whether we have just succeeded in picking a very odd sample. As we saw above, it is perfectly possible to finish up with four aces on a random poker deal; a hand with four aces has a calculable probability of occurring, given a fair system of dealing. Similarly, however good your sampling method, it can be *guaranteed* that you will sometimes pick a sample which is very untypical of the population. If your population consists of 1,000 men and 10 women, if you draw enough random samples from it you will get one which is entirely female. Similarly, although on average men are taller than women in the UK population, there is a calculable (but small) probability of drawing a random sample in which the women are taller than the men. The chance becomes smaller the bigger the sample, but it does not become zero until the sample is very nearly as big as the population.

Given random sampling, however, the odds of picking a very untypical sample are *calculable*. We can specify the probability of getting a sample which shows a difference or correlation of a given size, or larger, by sampling a population in which no such difference or correlation exists. When the odds become so large as to be unbelievable – a probability of 5 per cent (one chance in twenty) or, better, a probability of 1 per cent (one in a hundred) – then we feel confident in rejecting the 'null hypothesis' that the sample result is an anomaly and therefore in believing that what is observed in the sample is also true of the population. This is called 'a test of *statistical significance*'.

4 Practicalities

Now, you have a project to plan and carry out. Let us go through the stages of the work.

4.1 Theories and questions

The first stage, of course, is to have a research question to explore. This may follow from a branch of psychology which you have been studying:

- 'How does attribution theory help to explain people's accounts of how they and others behave when drunk?'

- 'Are women more likely to take domestic ideology for granted as true without question, or men?'

- 'How much of their lives before the age of 5 do people remember, and in what form do the memories present themselves?'

It may come from a problem of practice:

- 'How do clients perceive us when we are interacting with them as social workers (nurses, teachers, bus-drivers)?'

It may emanate from nothing more than vague curiosity:

- 'What images do teenagers have of themselves and how do these relate to how they dress?'

- 'Are "white" children more aggressive than "black" ones?'

A first stage is to go back to the books and/or down to the library to sharpen up the question and see what other people have done with it or similar questions. You would look in the index for relevant books (a keyword subject index is useful here), you might scan abstracts for relevant articles, and/or you might go through recent relevant journals to see what has been published in the last couple of years. This should give you an outline of how the research question – or others in the same general area – has been tackled by other people, what methods they used and what results they obtained. It may identify a gap in our knowledge, or a line worth replicating with a different kind of sample or using different methods.

Now we go on to plan the project itself.

4.2 Selecting the sample

Who are you going to ask, or observe? This depends first, obviously, on the kind of project you intend to undertake and the kind of data you intend to collect.

Are you asking questions or undertaking systematic observation?

If you are observing, your sample is likely to be of settings rather than individuals. If you decided to look at ethnic group membership and aggression in children, for example, the first thing would be to narrow down your age-group – perhaps to primary-school age – and then to do some analysis of the places where such children might be found. You would come up with primary schools (of course), and parks, and the cinema, and around the town on Saturdays, and youth clubs, and the swimming baths, and .... Ideally, you might wish to sample all of these, but resources would not permit. Moreover, in many of them it would be difficult to pick out the target group – how do you tell some 10-year-olds from some 13-year-olds, particularly among the boys? – and they would be mixed with other age groups. To simplify (you cannot tackle everything in one project), you might want to stick to those locations where only primary-school children are to be found, and to simplify even further you might want to stick to the primary schools themselves. (Note the consequent limitation on generality – you are now asking whether some children are more aggressive than others *at school*.) Having selected schools as your focus, you might want to limit yourself even further, to observable activity in the school playground and when entering and leaving the school, unless you have easy access to classrooms. Note the further limitation on generality: classroom behaviour has now been excluded. So you want to sample playgrounds (and the entrances to the school, at arrival and going-home times).

Now we can begin sampling. The best procedure would be to make a complete list of all the primary schools in your area. (Note a limitation on generality which I have so far taken for granted: you are going to be looking at the children of London, or Glasgow, or Wolverhampton, or Southend on Sea, and the generalization from one place to the country as a whole, let alone to other countries, is a leap of faith.) Such a list could be prepared from *Yellow Pages* or some other public directory which listed schools, but you might need to supplement the list if you wanted to be sure to include 'special' schools and some religious schools and some private schools which do not have their numbers in *Yellow*

Pages. Having prepared such a list, you can select a suitable size of sample at random, using a computer-generated random number list or with the aid of random number tables (see Box 2).

BOX 2   Using random number tables

You can find a table of random numbers in the back of most statistics textbooks. It consists of strings of numbers which have no discernible pattern. You can use these to select a sample from a list without the intrusion of personal bias.

- Pick a starting-point in the table by any means you like – the seventeenth number if today's date is the seventeenth, perhaps.

- Count the number of cases in your 'population list' of schools (known technically as a 'sampling frame') and assign each a three-digit number from zero onwards – so if there are 327 schools on your list, the numbers will run from 000, 001, 002 to 324, 325 and 326. Now, working from your starting-point in the random number table, take the first three digits and select the case which corresponds to that number to be a member of your sample. Now take the next three digits and use them to pick the next member, and so on until you have as many cases in the sample as you want.

- If the same number crops up more than once you will have to discard it and go on to the next number.

- Any number which does not correspond to a case in your sampling frame will also have to be discarded. (To save time, however, you could assign more than one number to each case. If you numbered them 000 to 326 and also 300 to 626, for example, you would find yourself using more numbers from the table and discarding fewer.)

If you are asking questions (or taking measurements of individuals, or getting them to do 'tests') then your sampling frame will ultimately be of individuals. Ideally you get a complete list of the relevant population and select cases randomly by the method outlined in Box 2. With a very large list it is more efficient to draw a *systematic* sample rather than a true random one, which means taking every *n*th individual, where *n* is the fraction needed to draw a sample of the right size. If you want a sample of 100 out of a population of 1,000, you would draw every tenth case (from a randomly chosen starting-point, and starting again at the top of the list when you reach the bottom). If you want a sample of 200, you would take every fifth case, and so on. A systematic sample behaves like a random one for most purposes provided the list itself has no obvious pattern or system. (If the list alternates male and female names and you take every fourth or sixth or eighth name, you will miss one gender altogether!)

For some research it may be relatively easy to get such a list; for research in a school, for example, you might use the school role, and for research in a hospital or a prison you might use admission records. For the population as a whole there are also lists, but they all have their problems. The Electoral Register, for example, may be out of date at the time when you use it – people may have died, or moved – and some people fail to register. Telephone directories list only those people with a telephone – i.e. they exclude poorer people and those in temporary accommodation, and also those who choose not to be listed (often the more affluent and those in sensitive occupations, plus some women who do not fall into either category).

Where no such list exists, or none is adequate, you may be able to sample by using geographical locations which correspond to unique individuals. In hospitals, for example, you could sample wards at random and then beds within wards. Looking for school-children, you could sample schools randomly, and within them classes, and within them individual pupils. (In both cases you would have to work out the number to take at the final stage – the number of beds in a given ward or pupils in a given class – to take account of the relative size of the ward or class; otherwise people in the smaller wards or classes would each stand a proportionately higher chance of being selected than people in the larger wards or classes.) Houses could be sampled in this way by selecting postcodes at random and then (using the *Postcode Directory*) individual houses within them, and then individuals within houses. Here it would be quite crucial to correct for size, because postcode areas contain very different numbers of houses; if one postcode contains twice as many houses as another in the population, the sample of houses drawn from it it should be twice as large as the sample drawn from the postcode containing half as many houses.

Where it is not possible to enumerate even the locations systematically, you can still use this kind of principle to pick a *cluster sample*, which will have some similarity to a random sample. This is particularly useful where you need to minimize travelling, or where it is not feasible to select some individuals and reject others. What you do is to stop one stage short of the sampling procedure discussed above, and sample whole classes or whole wards or whole streets. You then have your 'cases' clumped into a relatively small number of geographical clusters, rather than widely and thinly scattered, and you are never faced with interviewing one person while ignoring the next-door neighbour or the person in the next bed. What you pay for these advantages is that a cluster sample shows less variability than a true random one; people in a given class or ward are more similar to each other than to randomly chosen people elsewhere. Thus you tend to underestimate the variability of the population as a whole.

Where it is necessary to work more quickly and cheaply than this, *quota* procedures are often used. Here the interviewer sets out to get a predetermined number of people in each cell of a set of overlapping categories – so many men under 50, for example, so many women under 50, so many men over 50 and so many women over 50 – the numbers having been picked to give a good match to the population with respect to these variables. The interviewer is free to use whatever people he or she can conveniently get hold of to fill these quotas. This kind of sample is very definitely inferior to a random one, because those who can conveniently be got hold of are not necessarily representative of the population as a whole – they may be the interviewer's friends (and therefore resemble the interviewer), or people who have no employment and so can be found at home, or people who happen to be on the street at a particular time of day, and they will almost certainly over-represent the kind, the courteous and the cooperative at the expense of the rough, rude, belligerent and uncooperative.

The worst sample of all from the point of view of assessing representation is the 'sample of opportunity' – the class you happen to be teaching, the area you happen to live in, the conference you happen to be attending, the school or hospital at which you happen to be working. However, this is no doubt what you will use if your survey is small-scale and/or access has to be negotiated, because this is the place you can easily get to, in which you can get cooperation. None of the statistical methods for assessing the significance of results (their real existence in the population) will work for these samples (or for quota samples) because all the key requirements for their use are broken. Undoubtedly you will use them anyway, and you will be quite right to do so; they represent a 'best case' estimate of the likelihood of being in error. However, you will also need to think very carefully about who is favoured and who excluded by your method of sampling – what sort of school yours is, for example, and how it differs from other kinds of school – and point this out to the reader of the results as a further limitation on the credibility of the conclusions.

4.3 Selecting variables and framing questions

What you ask in your questionnaire will depend on what you need to know, and how wide you cast your net depends on how tight your hypothesizing is, how wide your imagination for alternative possible explanations and how much description you need and want to include in this or subsequent reports. If you have a clear hypothesis which follows from a branch of theory you will need relatively few variables to test it – the dependent variables, the posited independent variables, and such alternative possible explanations as occur to you. All things being equal and if it does not make the questionnaire too tedious or time-consuming for the informant, it is always better to collect more rather than less; you cannot control for variables you did not collect and your design probably does not allow for more than one 'pass' at a given informant. Remember to think of the different *levels* or *domains* of explanation that might be involved; consider whether you need to ask questions about the person's attitudes/beliefs, behaviour, intentions, history, interactions, social location and ideological/discursive understanding of the social world. Bear in mind what past researchers have done and consider whether there is some element of their work you wish to replicate exactly in your questions. If you have a preformed hypothesis to test, think what descriptive information will also be useful, but do not let the descriptive questions proliferate unduly – the material is being collected, in a sense, more for its entertainment value than for serious use. (If you are 'fishing' in an area, with no very definite question to answer, you will want to spread your descriptive net more widely.)

Questions must be asked as precisely as possible, to capture *precisely* the meaning you want. Simple questions such as 'Do you have a television?' or 'Do you go to work by car?', for example, can prove very much more complex to answer than you would suppose:

> Do you travel in a car to work?
>
> Do you travel in a car or taxi to work?
>
> Do you own or have the use of a car and use it to go to work?
>
> Do you always (or generally) use a car to go to work? (When do you not do so?)
>
> Do you ever use a car to go to work? (Under what circumstances?)
>
> Do you use a car to travel as part of your work? (e.g. as a travelling salesman, or a domestic cleaner travelling to people's houses)
>
> Do you yourself drive a car to work?

Each of these formulations requires a different kind of answer.

Questions should not be framed in such a way that a respondent can simply go down a column ticking 'yes' to everything; vary the 'polarity' of the question from time to time. Questions should also not be phrased in such a way that the 'correct' answer is obvious – that we are all, in principle, in favour of honour, virtue, motherhood, industry and the like, that we think people should be kind to cats and children, that education is a good thing and that we should like our views to be seen as socially acceptable – none of this is news. These strictures matter most of all when asking for beliefs, opinions and attitudes. Here it is usual and useful to ask the same question twice in the course of the questionnaire (not too obviously!), changing the sense from positive to negative but phrasing it to be just as socially acceptable. Sneakier still is to ask a list of innocuous questions which together add up to an attitude or personality trait; attitude and personality scaling is beyond the scope of this chapter, but you will have no difficulty finding textbooks which tell you how to construct and validate such scales; some are suggested at the end of this chapter.

If your questionnaire is likely to ask about views, behaviours or experiences which are sensitive, intrusive, embarrassing, distressing, illegal, immoral or otherwise socially unacceptable, you will need to think very carefully indeed about how you ask the questions (or whether you ask them at all – if you don't definitely *need* the information, don't ask the question!). To embarrass or upset informants is not acceptable behaviour for a researcher, it breaches the implicit research contract which calls on researchers to act responsibly to safeguard their respondents, and it will probably lead to people refusing to complete the questionnaire. You should have believable assurances of confidentiality in the questionnaire (or anonymity – that even you will not be able to identify the informant) and you should ensure the promises are kept. The questions should be phrased so as not to take a moral stance on any view or behaviour, however strong your own beliefs, nor to invalidate any belief or behaviour, however much you feel it is incoherent or misguided. At the same time you should not patronize your respondents but recognize their intelligence and ability to make their own judgments and decisions. It is good practice, where a questionnaire contains any material of a difficult or sensitive nature, to pilot it on a handful of people, similar to your potential respondents, whom you can trust to tell you if any of the questions are potentially embarrassing or offensive.

4.4 Designing the questionnaire

Once you have your questions, you need to lay them out so that the ordering looks as though it makes sense and each question appears to follow sensibly after the last. Where there is a break in the order and you are 'changing the subject' you will want to do this explicitly, with a sentence or so of explanation: 'Now I'd like to ask you about your health.' At the same time you need to get the questions in an order which prevents one pre-empting the next one: if you want to see whether people spontaneously mention diet or exercise as important for health, or whether they are more likely to come up with factors such as tension, stress or depression, then you do *not* want to ask direct questions about any of these, for fear of putting them into the respondent's mind; if you did, the fact that they mentioned them would be due to questionnaire design, not the normal thoughts of the respondent. Instead, you ask a much more general question first – 'What aspects of your life do you think are important for maintaining your health?' – and only *afterwards* probe for the factors you have yourself identified and wish to follow up.

The physical lay-out and the routing from one question to the next must be very clear. If someone says that exercise is *not* a factor in health, for example, you do not then want to ask her a list of questions about *why* it is important; you would need to skip these and go on to the next substantive topic. This should appear on the questionnaire as an explicit instruction – 'If NO, go to Question 7'. Otherwise, there is a risk that some questions will be missed out accidentally which ought not to have been skipped.

At the beginning of the questionnaire you will need to introduce yourself, say something about what the research is about, ask for their participation and promise confidentiality:

> 'I am a third-year student – my name is Joan Smith – and I'm doing a survey on people's health and lifestyle for my undergraduate research project. Could you spare 20 minutes to talk to me about it? I'd be very grateful. Anything you said would be entirely confidential – I won't use the results in such a way that anyone can be identified from what I write.'

At the end of the questionnaire you need to 'get off stage' with thanks and an expression of gratitude, rather than leaving the respondent waiting for the next question.

Precisely how you lay out the questionnaire, and precisely what questions you can ask, depends on whether you intend to administer it via an interviewer or have the respondents complete it themselves. Figure 1 shows how a block of questions might be laid out for an interviewer-administered questionnaire. The problem is to ask questions about depressive self-identification without causing undue distress and without putting words into the mouths of the informants. We start with a general 'how is life' question which gives people a chance to mention depression 'under their own steam' if this is a very central and salient concept for them. The researcher has made a note to explore the response if it uses the word depression but not unambiguously with a clinical meaning. The next question asks whether the respondent has mood problems, still without using the word 'depression'. The next, finally, asks straight out whether the respondent suffers from depression. Finally, for those who deny depression, a list of common symptoms is presented, and the respondent is classed as potentially depressive if he or she admits to a majority of them. At each stage there are reminders to the researcher to probe where needed and to skip questions which are not needed or are rendered redundant by an earlier response. In a self-completion questionnaire it would not be possible to be so neat, because the 'workings' of the stream of questions cannot be concealed from the respondent. It is also not possible to probe for the meaning of what is said in response to the first two questions.

Q12   Please describe here how you usually feel when you wake up in the morning.

      [If 'depression' mentioned, probe to see whether clinical depression is   17 ☐
      meant or just sadness. If the former, Code 1 here and go to Q16. If any of
      the items in Q15 are mentioned, probe for the others. If four or more are
      given, Code 2 here and go to Q16. Else continue.]

Q13   Do you have trouble with how you are feeling at times?

      [If YES, ask for description and then follow instructions for previous   18 ☐
      question. (Codes for this question also go opposite Q12) If NO, go to Q14.]

Q14   Do you sometimes suffer from depression?

      [If NO, go to Q15]. [If YES, probe for whether clinical depression. If YES,   19 ☐
      code 1 opposite Q12. If not, probe for whether four or more of items in
      Q15. If YES, code 2 opposite Q12. Go to Q16.]

Q15   (a) Do you have periods when you feel worthless and ineffectual? Yes   No
      (b) Do you sometimes find yourself crying for no reason?   Yes   No
      (c) When you look to the future, does it seem full of promise?   Yes   No
      (d) Do you find that other people generally like being with you? Yes   No
      (e) Do you generally feel active and in control of your life?   Yes   No
      (f) Do you find that you often can't be bothered with other
          people?   Yes   No

      [If four or more answers are in the first column, code 2 opposite Q12]

Q16   How often have you been to the doctor's in the last twelve months?

      [Enter number opposite (2 digits – 99 = don't know – but probe for   20 ☐ ☐
      approximate number of times)]

Figure 1 *An example of part of an interviewer-administered questionnaire*

You will notice that there are two types of questions in Figure 1. The last two are *closed* questions, with the permissible replies already determined by the researcher. It is desirable to 'close' as many questions as is possible without distorting answers. This greatly speeds up the analysis, and it makes the questionnaire a shorter task for the respondent. It also has the more 'theoretical' advantage of setting absolutely standardized questions for the respondents, who can choose only one of a determinate range of responses. The other questions are *open,* asking the respondents to report in their own words. These have to be coded up afterwards (see next section), which can be time-consuming, and they will vary in length according to the fluency with which the respondent replies, a possibly confounded source of extraneous variation. On the other hand, open questions are the only way to proceed if you do not wish to put words in the respondents' mouths or if you genuinely cannot anticipate what the answers will be. A possible compromise, often used, is to have a predetermined list of responses but also an 'Other' category where the researcher writes an answer which will not fit into any of the existing categories.

The numbered boxes on the right-hand side of Figure 1 are for recording the coded information. I shall discuss this topic further in Section 5.

4.5 Conducting the interviews

The first essential is that the interviewer be thoroughly familiar with the questionnaire, the routing between questions and any 'processing' which takes place during data collection (for example, the coding of the answer to the depression question in Figure 1). You should normally have tried the questionnaire out on a few people (*piloted* it) to see how it handles and where the awkward places are. Some people get a friend to act the part of the uncooperative or hostile interviewee, to identify where problems may occur.

The ideal interviewer is an impossibility – a self-contradictory goal to both elements of which we have to aspire.

He or she acts as a standardized data-collection instrument, introduces the task in an absolutely standardized way, always asks all the questions in exactly the same manner, minimizes non-verbal manipulation and in general introduces no extraneous between-subject variance which could be ascribed to the procedures of data collection rather than the characteristics of the respondents.

At the same time it is essential that the interviewer be a person of empathy, understanding respondents' points of view and enabling them to express them at their best. He or she should strive to make the interview a pleasant, relaxed and rewarding experience, more like a conversation than a formal interview session. However, it is necessary to keep the interviewer's personal opinions out of the conversation – which in fact makes for a very unnatural exchange – and above all never to express a judgment of the respondent's views or behaviour even non-verbally – as beggars for information it is not our place to sit in judgment.

Thus the ideal interviewer is unlimitedly empathic and interactive while perfectly standardized in the administration of the questionnaire. This is impossible even in theory; you just have to do the best you can to achieve both aims.

The paradox extends into the behaviour of the interviewer 'beyond the confines of the schedule' – to probing for information and the offer of explanation:

1   One of the main points of having the schedule (i.e. questionnaire) administered by an interviewer, face to face, is that he or she can answer the respondents' queries and stop them from misunderstanding questions. To the extent that the respondents do not all understand the question in the same way, they are in essence asking themselves different questions and so their responses cannot validly be compared. On the other hand, to the extent that the interviewer gives different amounts of explanation to different people he or she is asking different questions, and the same problem occurs. In practice we try to avoid explanation – when asked 'What does this mean?' we say something like 'Well, what do *you* think?' In this way we avoid the natural tendency of respondents to probe for 'the right answer' – to try to give us the answer we expect and want. However, obvious misunderstandings need to be corrected, informants often have to be given a modicum of explanation when they look blankly at a question and cannot imagine what we are after, and blatant contradictions (such as describing the children after saying you do not have any) need to be explored and corrected.

2   Probing for more information is an activity faced with the same paradox. If you do not try to get people to say about the same amount when faced with an open question, or do not probe for more information where an answer is thin or feels as though there is more to come, then differences between groups may be due to relative loquacity. If you do probe, however, the questionnaire ceases to that extent to be a standardized instrument. Some probing is necessary but it should be kept to a minimum and preferably confined to generalities such as 'Can you tell me more about that?'; it should never in any way help the informant to decide which answer to give or put words into his or her mouth.

There is always a risk, with interviewer-administered questionnaires, that your prior ideas and hypotheses will be communicated to the respondent, if only unconsciously and via non-verbal signals. Sometimes it is a good idea to use someone else as the interviewer who was not involved in designing the questionnaire and has no particular stake in the outcome. It is then necessary to brief them, telling them enough in order to feel they know what the research is about, but you do not have to share the precise nature of the ideas you are testing.

Many of the same considerations hold for systematic observation surveys as for questionnaire surveys. The observer is not interacting directly with the observed, but he or she is present, and so the behaviour must be controlled. The observer has to be unobtrusive and to behave in as standardized a way as possible in different locations, for example, so that differences are not ascribable to researcher behaviour.

5 Data preparation and analysis

5.1 Preparing the data

The end-product of your questionnaires or observations must be a string of numbers for each respondent or observation setting which records the variables you will use to answer your original question(s) or to explore the relationship of traits or factors. This is what the boxes on the right-hand side of Figure 1 were for – to record the values of the variables on each questionnaire in an easily accessible form – probably for computer entry, unless you have very few cases and/or very few variables. For Question 12 and Question 16 it is clear what these numbers should be. For the latter it is the exact number of visits as a two-digit number (with 00 for none, 99 for a 'don't know' response or a refusal to answer, and 98 meaning 98+ in the unlikely case of the respondent having been to the doctor twice a week almost *every* week for the last year). Question 12 was coded as we went along – 1, as you will see, means 'clinical depression', 2 means 'symptoms but no diagnosis', and you would enter zero where neither of these was the appropriate code. A collection of the meaning of the numbers used for each variable is called a *coding frame*, and you should have prepared one, insofar as you can, before you start the coding process. Additions and amendments should be marked on systematically, so in the end you have a complete record of what every number in the string of variables means for every subject. (You should have as many of these 'precoded' variables as possible in your questionnaire, to save yourself a lot of time preparing the data.)

Where the question is open-ended (as with Questions 12–14) you will need to do more work. Mostly we have used these questions, on this particular questionnaire, to amplify the response in Question 12 and so amend its code, but we have also left space below the questions for recording other pieces of information which came up and might be important. (One code box per question on the right might not be enough – suppose you wanted to record both information about the informant's past and anything he or she said about the effects of his/her mood on other people. If you know you are going to have to do this, it would be tidier if you have the number of boxes you think you will need. If not, and the data turn out to be unexpectedly rich, you can always add extra ones at the end of the record.)

What you tend to do with open-ended questions is to decide what you want to record (possibly after inspecting the first 50 or 100 questionnaires to see the likely range of response) and decide what shall carry what code in the box. For example, you might want to record 'history' responses, so you would go through 50 or 100 questionnaires to see what was said about this. You might get:

28 who made no comment

10 who said they had always felt like this, or for a long time,

3 who said the problems had started only recently

7 who gave you an approximate date when they started

1 who said the problems worked to a timetable determined by God, and

1 who said they came and went in no particular pattern.

A useful pattern might be to code the 28 as 0 or 9 – no response – and the 10 who said they always felt like this (or something equivalent) as 1. The 3 who said they were recent might be coded as 2, and the 7 who gave a rough date could be allocated to codes 1 or 2 according to the date – you would have to decide what constituted 'recent' or 'for a long while'. The other two might be coded with the 'no report' as saying neither 'recent' nor 'old' – or you might look at more questionnaires to see if this is going to be a reasonably common response and, if so, create a code 3 for 'cyclical, irregular, unpredictable' to which both of these cases might be coded. You would then go through the rest of the questionnaires, coding the responses to this question using this frame. The general idea is to build categories which have neither very few nor very many people in them. If the whole point of the exercise is to show that something or other is very rare or very common, then having a code category with very few or very many informants in it will be useful for you. If, on the other hand, you are trying to show differences by age or place of birth or current residence or job or whatever, you should be warned that there will not *be* any differences, for a given code, if your coding frame has virtually all or virtually none of the sample clustered under it. We generally try for categories with no more than half the sample in them and no less than 5 per cent (10 per cent would be better).

If you have allowed questions with precoded categories plus an 'other – write in' response, then you will have to go through coding the 'others'. Some of them, you will decide, belong in one of the categories you have already specified – if you asked 'How many children have you?' and the respondent wrote 'A boy and a girl', then the number would be 2. Where a particular kind of response which you have not already covered looks as though it will be reasonably common, on your preliminary inspection, then you can create a new code number for it. Otherwise, responses which do not fit any of your existing categories and appear to be very rare should be coded under an 'other response' code. If a lot of your sample finish up coded as 'other' however, you will need to go back over those so coded and see if it is worth creating another new code to accommodate some of them.

On the whole it is better to stick to single-coded variables – ones where one and only one number is given to each subject. (If you need to record more information, create more new variables – perhaps a series of 'yes/no' variables for the factors of interest.) Some computer packages can handle multicoding (where more than one code is assigned to a given subject on a given variable), but analysing such variables is always a clumsy and difficult process.

5.2 Tabular analysis

Having created your numbers you now need to know what to do with them. *If you are already an experienced survey reporter and/or familiar with statistical analysis, skip the rest of this section. Otherwise read on: what follows is a simple but still surprisingly powerful way of analysing survey results.* Virtually any of the common computer statistical packages will handle these calculations – SPSS is a good one. If the package you are using does not do three-way tables as one operation, you can produce them by selecting the sub-sample who fall in one category of the 'third variable' and doing a two-way table, then doing the same for the other category.

The first thing you will want to do is to lay out the counts of your variables – how many cases there are in each category of the variable. This is information you need for the report, and it also lets you see if any of the cases have been miscoded, in which case you may be able to correct them, or you will need to assign them to a 'don't know' category and lose them from the subsequent analysis. (Most computer packages give you the option of labelling values as 'don't know' or 'missing' and will exclude values so labelled from subsequent tables and statistics.) For example, in a student survey we used to run we coded Male=1 and Female=2, but there were regularly a couple of cases coded 3 or left blank. If this had been a smaller survey, and we'd had respondents' names on the questionnaires, we could have pulled out the offending cases and made a reasonable guess (Mary is female, John is male, not sure about George). As it was, the sample base was large (over 1,000), and the questionnaire was anonymous, so we just had to label these cases as 'missing value'.

For an example, let us take a fictional survey in which a sample of 300 respondents was drawn randomly from the staff of a very large industrial concern – not a perfect sample, but with the advantage that a complete list of possible respondents would be available. The sample is stratified by class (sub-samples of 150 were drawn from the management and office staff on the one hand and the skilled and semi-skilled factory workers, cleaners, drivers and kitchen staff on the other). The other variables we shall be considering are educational level and an attitudinal question about whether conflict or consensus of values is more to be expected in social relations. The research idea is that social location (class) should predict whether society is seen in consensus or conflict terms, but that education might modify this.

Table 1 gives frequency distributions (counts) for the three variables. (Note the use of percentages, which are much easier for the reader to interpret than the raw numbers.) We can see that the division between 'consensus' and 'conflict' answers on the attitude question is close to fifty/fifty. It comes as no surprise that in class terms the sample is fifty/fifty divided into 'middle' and 'working', because this is how the study was designed. A bit more than a third of our sample have a degree (or a degree-level professional qualification), and about 9 per cent have no qualifications whatsoever. These figures are not representative of the general population; if we wanted to generalize and say what percentage of the population held a particular attitude we would have to do some simple arithmetic and weight back to population proportions. This will not matter for the current purposes, however, because what we are after is the relationship *between variables*.

Table 1 Frequency tables of class, education and attitude

Educational level			Social class			Attitude		
	No.	%		No.	%		No.	%
Degree or equiv.	109	36.3	Middle	150	50.0	Consensus	160	53.3
Diploma or higher prof. qual.	17	5.7	Working	150	50.0	Conflict	140	46.7
A level or equiv.	74	24.7						
Intermediate prof. qual. or GCSE only	72	24.0						
None	28	9.3						
Total sample = 300								

At this point you need to think about the analyses you are going to do. Here we shall be drawing up tables of relationships, and for this purpose (as you will see) we want categories with reasonably large numbers in them, and not too many categories to a variable. 'Social class' and 'Attitude' are fine from that point of view, but 'Educational level' is too widely dispersed, with too many small categories. I would therefore recode it into, say, two categories: 'Higher level' (A level or above – other research suggests that the decision to stay on into the sixth form is an important social turning point); and 'Lower level' (below A level). This is also the time to make sure that any 'don't know' values are assigned a category or declared 'missing' (we don't have any in this survey) and, if you intend to do statistics which depend on categories being in an order from higher to lower, that there are no 'other' categories which do not fit the ordering. (If there are, you'll have to label them 'don't know' if you cannot fit them somewhere on the scale.) The machine will do the recoding for you, to your instructions, if you are using a statistical package. It will also let you compute scale totals if you are using a series of attitude questions which are supposed to add together as a measure of something (and it can do arithmetic to reverse the polarity of items coded 'the wrong way'). Sometimes you may also need to use its logical and arithmetical facilities to create a single variable from several different answers ('Code household income here as the sum of husband's wages plus wife's wages plus welfare and other benefits plus income from children', or 'Code "Has income" here if any of the above are a positive number').

Now we are ready to look at the relationship between our dependent variable – the attitude – and our independent variables, class and educational level. Our hypothesis here is that attitude to society is at least partially predictable from social location – here represented by social class and extent to which educational qualifications have been obtained. Table 2 shows the relationship, in raw numbers and percentages by rows. There appears to be a relationship with social class, though only a weak one: 55 per cent of middle-class people in the sample hold a consensus view, and only 45 per cent a conflict view, and roughly the reverse is true for working-class people. There does not, on the face of it, appear to be much relationship with education; the two rows are very similarly distributed.

Table 2 Relationship of class and educational level to attitude

Attitude	Social class		Educational level	
	Middle	**Working**	**High**	**Low**
Raw numbers:				
Consensus	85	69	104	50
Conflict	65	81	96	50
χ^2(1 d.f.)	3.42 (NS)		0.11 (NS)	
Row percentages:				
Consensus	55.2	44.8	67.5	32.5
Conflict	44.5	55.5	65.8	34.2

The question we have to ask, however, is whether the relationship in the left-hand block of the table is a real one – likely to be true of the population – or whether it is small enough that it could be due to aberrant sampling from a population in which there is no such difference. For this we need the middle row of the table and the χ^2 statistic.

The chi-squared (χ^2– the 'ch' is pronounced as a 'k', and the first syllable rhymes with 'cry') is an estimate of how unlikely it is that we would get a table with as extreme a distribution as the observed one (or one which is more extreme) by chance when sampling from a population in which there was no association between the variables. The values we would expect to get if the independent variable did not predict the values of the dependent one can be calculated by distributing the row totals, say, in the same proportions as the column totals; if there is no association, then both rows should have the same percentage distribution and there will be no pattern caused by the independent variable. This is illustrated in the middle block of Table 3. Then we work out a χ^2 statistic for each cell of the table, which is given by the formula $\frac{(O-E)^2}{E}$: the observed value minus the expected value, squared and divided by the expected value, for each cell of the table. Finally, we add up all these cell χ^2s to get an overall χ^2 whose value we can look up in a pre-prepared table of critical values – see Table 4.

Table 3 Calculating χ^2 for the association of class and attitude

Attitude	Observed values			Expected values		Chi-squared values	
	Social class			Social class		Social class	
	Middle	Working	Total	Middle	Working	Middle	Working
Consensus	85	69	154	77	77	0.831	0.831
Conflict	65	81	146	73	73	0.877	0.877
Total	150	150	300				
						χ^2 (1 d.f.) = 3.42	

Table 4 Critical values of chi-squared

d.f.	1	2	3	4	5	6	7	8	9	10	11	12
p< 0.05	3.84	5.99	7.82	9.49	11.07	12.59	14.07	15.51	16.92	18.17	19.68	21.03
p< 0.01	6.64	9.21	11.34	13.28	15.09	16.81	18.48	20.09	21.67	23.21	24.72	26.22
p< 0.001	10.83	13.82	16.27	18.46	20.52	22.46	24.32	26.12	27.88	29.59	31.26	32.91

We need two more pieces of information before we can use Table 4.

1   Because it is made up by adding sums of squared differences for cells, χ^2 obviously has the potential to grow larger, the larger the number of cells in the table. We therefore need to take account of how big the table is. What we use is a figure called the *degrees of freedom.* In a 2×2 table such as the one we have been examining, with two rows and two columns, there are four cells. However, given that we know

the totals in the margins, only one of them can vary in an unknown way; once we have one figure for a cell, and given that the cells have to add up to the marginal totals, we know what the rest of the cell figures have to be. So we say that the table has *one degree of freedom*. In a 3 × 2 table, with three columns and *two* rows, there would be two degrees of freedom; we need to know two of the cell counts before we can work out the rest from the marginal totals. In general, the degrees of freedom are given by (R–1) × (C–1), where R is the number of rows and C is the number of columns.

2   We need to know how unlikely a result has to be before we reject the notion (the *null hypothesis*) that what we have is an aberrant sample from a population in which there is no association between the two variables. This is a matter for us to decide depending on how important it is not to claim a significant result when in reality the apparent result is due to chance, or not to reject a result which is in fact significant. Conventionally, the least we will accept is odds of better than one in twenty ($p<0.05$ – a probability of less than five per cent of being mistaken). Better would be odds of better than one in a hundred ($p<0.01$ – a less than one per cent chance).

Now we can look up the figure in Table 4. The value of χ^2 we obtained was 3.42. Looking it up in Table 4, in the row labelled '$p<0.05$' and the column for 1 degree of freedom (d.f.), we find we need a value of 3.84 or larger for the result to be significant even at the 5 per cent level ($p<0.05$). So we cannot reject the null hypothesis that what we have is an unlikely sample from a population where there is no association between class and this attitude.

This is a disappointing result, and the analysis might well stop there, with another promising idea rejected as not fitting the facts. However, thinking more about the possible effects of education, we might decide to take the analysis one step further, because education's effects might be working to suppress those of class. If conflict is a natural picture for working-class respondents and consensus for middle-class ones, education might work against it by giving working-class people the attitudes and values of the middle classes. On the other hand, the fact is that we expected there to be an association precisely because of our own education; one way of learning about class differences and divisions is by studying sociology. So educated middle-class people might be more aware of class divisions than uneducated ones. We can check this by eliminating (*controlling for*) the effects of class, and we do this in a fairly obvious way – by repeating the analysis separately for each class.

Table 5 gives the results of doing so. Just looking at the figures we can see that they are promising. In the 'middle-class' block, the highly educated people are evenly split between consensus and conflict, but virtually all of the less educated people hold a consensus perspective; among the working-class people, more of the more highly educated hold a consensus perspective and more of the less well educated a conflict perspective. Working out the χ^2 statistics for the two blocks, we get values of 10.85 for the middle class and 5.76 for the working class. Looking these up in Table 4, for 1 degree of freedom, we find that the middle class value is (just) greater than the 10.83 we need for a significance level of 0.1 per cent (p<0.001) – in other words, there is not one chance in a thousand of randomly drawing a sample which will show this large an association from a population in which no such association exists. The statistic is smaller for the working-class block but still larger than the 3.84 needed for significance at the 5 per cent level (p<0.05). What we have, therefore, is an interaction effect. Middle-class people are more likely to show a consensus perspective, but this effect is partly undone by the effects of education. Working-class people are rather more likely to show a consensus perspective if they have stayed on for A levels or above, and rather less likely if they have not. The value of three-way tabular analysis is therefore demonstrated in this example; we came to an understanding of what is going on which we could not have reached from the two-way tables alone.

Table 5 Relationship of education and attitude, controlling for class

Educational level	Social class					
	Middle			Working		
	Attitude			Attitude		
	Consensus	Conflict	Total	Consensus	Conflict	Total
High	60	60	120	44	36	80
Low	25	5	30	25	45	70
Total	85	65	150	69	81	150
χ^2 (1 d.f.)	10.85 (p<0.001)			5.76 (p<0.05)		

Not very often will you come across a case like this, where one variable is suppressing the effects of another. The more common problem is where you have two variables which *are* significantly related to a dependent variable and you want to establish which of them is the more important and how they relate to each other. Again, you would split the sample by the values of one of the variables – probably into two blocks (you can have any number of blocks, but with four or five you will find that the numbers in the cells get very small unless your sample is enormous, and the χ^2 statistic is not valid if any of the *expected* figures falls below 5).

You would then work out the statistic for each of the blocks, and deduce what is going on from the results:

1   If both statistics are significant, and larger than the one for the original table, then the second variable (e.g. education in Table 5) is probably the more important determinant.

2   If both are significant but smaller on the whole than the original and about the same size as each other, then both variables have a determining effect but the first variable (e.g. class in Table 5) is probably the more important.

3   If neither is significant, then the first variable is definitely the one that is having the effect and the second shows an apparent effect only because of its association with the first.

4   If one is much larger than the other, and even more if one is significant and the other is not, then an interaction effect is at work – the second variable has different effects at different levels of the first.

Thus we are able to work out some quite complex ideas about the relationships of variables from an essentially quite simple form of analysis.

6 Presenting the results

Whatever form of presentation you are required to make, your report will be in four broad blocks: introduction, methods, results and discussion. As you will see from the other chapters in this book, these are the sections of *any* report of research, not just one in the survey style, though they may not always carry these headings.

6.1 Introduction

The first thing the reader or listener needs to know is what the problem is – what your hypothesis is, what the area is into which you are going to enquire. He or she will want to know why it is important or interesting – why it is worth his or her time to read about it, and why it was worth your time to investigate it. This will involve you in explaining how you came to the problem and what its implications are – probably referring to library material (academic books, journal articles, government reports) and possibly using published statistics to show how widespread the problem is and what sort of numbers we are talking about. You will need to speak briefly here about what is known already, from past research, and – if your own research methods are different from or improved upon those generally used – you may need to talk about other people's methods and their strengths and shortcomings. The section moves from establishing the general problem or area of enquiry, through deriving and justifying specific testable hypotheses or selecting conceptual areas to be the focus of the research, to a brief outline of what research is to be done and why.

6.2 Methods

Having set out, briefly, what was to be done, you now need to say what you actually did – generally in enough detail that the reader or listener can spot the weaknesses and assess the validity of the work and appreciate the strengths of the design, and ideally so that the work could be replicated by someone else. In survey work there will be two to five main subsections (which may be headed sections or mere pages or paragraphs), depending on the intended length of the final product.

1   You will need to describe your sampling methods and assess their strengths and likely weaknesses. (The assessment can be quite brief – you will probably be saying more about this in the 'Discussion' section.)

2   You will need to describe the questionnaire, how it was constructed and pre-tested (if it was) and what the logic was behind the selection of questions or things to be observed. Preferably you should include a copy of the questionnaire in your report, probably as an appendix.

You will also need to outline how the questionnaire was presented (how the interviews were conducted, or the observations carried out). You may also need to explain how the project was set up and permissions obtained, if this was an issue, and what special or 'ordinary' ethical/political issues were involved. These may be quite brief reports or they may require sections of their own, depending on how much there is to be said.

6.3 Results

Here you give the relevant results of your survey. These will consist of:

1   Tables such as the ones used in Section 5.2 above – kept simple and readable, and preferably in percentages rather than raw figures – with any relevant statistics that have been calculated (but not the 'workings', which were given above only as an aid to understanding how the statistic is calculated). Tables in the text are kept small and readable; if there is a need for larger 'storehouse' tables which present the detailed results for the reader to analyse further, these should be in an appendix.

2   Visual aids to understanding – graphs and diagrams, where appropriate.

3   Your commentary on the tables and graphs – a summary of the pertinent results and some discussion of what they mean, with special reference to the hypotheses or problems which were developed in the 'Introduction'. Figures do not speak for themselves; you *always* describe them in words as well.

6.4 Discussion

Finally, you need to summarize what you have found, relate it back to the questions you asked in the 'Introduction', and assess the extent to which the questions have been answered. As part of the assessment you will need to look at your own research methods – the sampling, the questionnaire, the conduct of the interviews, other pertinent specific factors, the research situation as a whole – in order to assess their weaknesses and the implications of these for the validity of the conclusions. (The weaknesses need not have been 'mistakes' – they may be necessary features of the research, given the setting and the available resource – but they still need to be taken into account.) You will go on from this to discuss the further implications of your research for disciplinary theory, social policy and/or social practice, and possibly what questions remain unanswered (or what new questions the research raises) and what research would be needed to answer them.

Further reading

All of the topics covered in this chapter are discussed in more depth in either:

Sapsford, R.J. and Jupp, V. (eds) (1996) *Data Collection and Analysis*, London, Sage,

or

Sapsford, R.J. (1998) *Survey Research*, London, Sage.

In the former, I would particularly recommend the chapters by Schofield on sampling and Swift on coding data, as going substantially beyond what is discussed here.

For a higher-level introduction, see:

Oppenheim, A.N. (1992) *Questionnaire Design, Interviewing and Attitude Measurement*, London, Pinter.

This is also a good source of information on composite measurement and attitude scaling – on which topic see also:

Romney, D. (1979) 'Evaluation of a data collection method', in *Classification and Measurement*, Block 5 of Open University course DE304, *Research Methods in Education and the Social Sciences*, Milton Keynes, The Open University.

CHAPTER 5

AN EXPERIMENTAL INVESTIGATION OF FRAMING EFFECTS AND DECISION MAKING

by Patrick McGhee

Contents

PART A: INTRODUCTION

1 Dilemmas, framing and experimental social psychology

We all face dilemmas every day – some trivial, some important. Should I choose a psychology or a geography course as part of my degree? Should I buy the expensive new car which is more reliable or the cheaper car which might break down before the end of the summer? Should I accept the dinner invitation from Mike or visit my ageing aunt who is ill? Should I revise Chapter 3 or Chapter 4 the night before the exam? Should we move house nearer work or stay put?

This project will introduce you to how experimental social psychologists investigate the ways in which we approach dilemmas like these. However, before we go any further I would like you to consider the following four dilemmas yourself *and tick the appropriate box to indicate which option you believe you would select if you really were faced with that dilemma*. After you have responded to the four dilemmas I will consider the psychological aspects of each.

1.1 Try the dilemmas yourself

Please attempt each of the dilemmas which follow. There are four of them (adapted from the originals devised by Tversky and Kahneman, 1981). You must choose just one alternative from the two presented, and you cannot query the assumptions of the scenario! Do not spend more than a minute on each dilemma however. It is your first judgement that is of interest here.

Begin by reading Dilemma 1 and indicate which of the two programmes you would favour by ticking the appropriate box.

There are no right or wrong answers – it is simply a case of which you would prefer.

DILEMMA 1   Health programme

Imagine that the UK is preparing for the outbreak of an unusually dangerous virus which is expected to kill 600 people next winter. Two alternative preventative programmes have been proposed. The scientific estimates of the consequences of the programmes are as follows:

Programme A: if adopted 200 people will be saved.

---

or

Programme B: if adopted there is a $\frac{1}{3}$ probability that 600 people will be saved, and a $\frac{2}{3}$ probability that no-one will be saved.

Which of these two programmes would you favour? Programme A ☐ or Programme B ☐

The second dilemma is much more down to earth and indeed is one with which you may actually have been confronted at some point. Again there are no right or wrong answers, it is simply a matter of you indicating your preference.

DILEMMA 2 Money

This dilemma has two parts: 2(a) and 2(b).

2(a) Which of the following two alternatives would you prefer: A or B?

A: a sure gain of £250 ☐

or

B: a 25 per cent chance to gain £1,000 (with a 75 per cent chance of gaining nothing). ☐

2(b) Which of the following two alternatives would you prefer: A or B?

A: a sure loss of £750 ☐

or

B: a 75 per cent chance to lose £1,000 (with a 25 per cent chance to lose nothing). ☐

DILEMMA 3   The theatre ticket

Imagine that you have decided to see a play where admission is £10 per ticket. As you enter the theatre you discover that you have lost a £10 note.

Would you

A: still pay £10 for a ticket for the play? ☐

or

B: not pay £10 for a ticket for the play? ☐

DILEMMA 4 Jacket and camera

Imagine that you are in a large chain store and about to purchase a jacket for £15, and a camera for £125.

When you get to the till with your purchases the assistant informs you that the same camera is on offer at £120 at a different branch of the store twenty minutes drive away.

Would you

A: make the trip to the other branch to buy the reduced-price camera? ☐

or

B: buy the camera at this branch? ☐

When you have completed this dilemma (and have checked that you have completed all the preceding ones) you will have had a chance to get a feel for the kinds of question you will asking your participants in the actual experiments you will be running in this project.

1.2 Understanding the dilemmas

Let's now go through each of the dilemmas one by one comparing your answers to those given by participants in previous experiments and thinking through *why* people seem to prefer some of the options to others.

Dilemma 1 (Health programme)

Most people (in fact 72 per cent of participants in the original study) preferred option A. That is, they would prefer to 'play safe' and definitely save the lives of two hundred people rather than go for the risky option of $\frac{1}{3}$ chance of saving all those at risk. However, and this is the central issue of this project, the *same* options presented in a different way gave a very different result:

Programme A: If adopted 400 people will die

Programme B: If adopted there is a $\frac{1}{3}$ probability that nobody will die, and a $\frac{2}{3}$ probability that 600 people will die.

Which of these two programmes would you favour? Programme A or Programme B?

Here only 22 per cent (rather than 72 per cent) of people opted for Option A. Note that in this version of the alternatives *the basic facts are the same only the wording has changed* – yet the responses of participants were very different. In other words, the way in which the alternatives are *framed* has a substantial impact on people's judgements. When presented as involving *loss* of life rather than the saving of life, people made riskier decisions (that is, they were prepared to run the risk of letting everyone die in order to save 400 people). Later we shall be considering in more detail the different ways people seem to view 'gains' and 'losses'.

Dilemma 2 (Money)

In Dilemma 2(a) most people (84 per cent in the original study) go for the less risky option – namely a guaranteed sum of £250 (Option A). However, in Dilemma 2(b) most people (87 per cent) go for the *risky* option – where *losses* are involved. This clearly shows that people have different views about risk depending on whether they think they are risking gains or losses.

Dilemma 3 (The theatre ticket)

Most people (88 per cent) faced with this imaginary dilemma prefer Option A; that is, they say that they would still go ahead and pay for the ticket.

However, the same loss of £10 framed as below gives different results:

> Imagine that you have decided to see a play and paid the admission price of £10 per ticket. As you enter the theatre you discover that you have lost the ticket. The seat was not marked and the ticket cannot be recovered.
>
> Would you:
>
> A: still pay £10 for a ticket for the play?
>
> B: not pay £10 for a ticket for the play?

In this version only 46 per cent said they would pay for the ticket. Did you? Some people, even when they have seen both versions of the dilemma, still feel they want to go for Option A in the first version and Option B in the second (and even when they accept that in basic financial terms the two dilemmas are indeed identical!).

What seems to be happening here is that people are much more likely to link (in cognitive terms) the lost ticket with the new one (making total 'ticket expenditure' £20) but do not link the £10 cash with the ticket (making total 'ticket expenditure' only £10 – that is, the cost of the original ticket). This is a form of what has been called 'psychological accounting' – putting things which seem to be connected together into the same category when reckoning up what has been spent on what.

Dilemma 4 (Jacket and camera)

If you are like most people you probably chose Option B here – that is you reckoned you *wouldn't* make the 20 minute journey to buy the reduced price camera in the other branch. In the original study (where incidentally a calculator was specified rather than a camera) only 29 per cent of participants said they would make the drive.

However, when an alternative framing was used, people's decisions became quite different:

> Imagine that you are in a large chain store and about to purchase a jacket for £125, and a camera for £15.
>
> When you get to the till the assistant informs you that the same camera is on offer at £10 at a different branch of the store twenty minutes drive away.
>
> Would you
>
> A: make the trip to the other branch to buy the reduced-price camera?; or
>
> B: buy the camera at the branch you are in?

Here 68 per cent of participants in the original study said they would make the drive – a huge difference compared to 29 per cent. The thing to notice here is that the basic dilemma in both versions in strict financial terms is exactly the same: are you prepared to make a 20 minute drive to save £5? In the second version this is seen by participants to be a saving against a purchase price of £15 and hence a 33 per cent saving whereas in the first version it is seen as a saving against a purchase price of £125 and therefore a saving of less than 5 per cent (and so scarcely worth driving 20 minutes to make!).

1.3 Dilemmas in everyday life

Social psychologists are very interested in what makes people choose one option over another when faced with dilemmas such as those above since, clearly, a great deal of our lives is made up of making decisions about such alternatives. Furthermore, these dilemmas often involve deciding between courses of action that, directly or indirectly, *involve other people* and our relationships with them. Indeed, it is difficult to conceive of a social life that does not in some way involve facing up to dilemmas.

Think about two examples of recent episodes in your life where you have been faced with a dilemma involving two alternatives that involved your relationships with others. What courses of action did you adopt? What factors made you choose one option over the other? How were the dilemmas presented to you? How did *you* present the dilemmas to other people (if appropriate)? Were there any similarities in the way in which you made your decisions about the alternatives available in each of the two cases?

A whole range of emotional, intellectual and pragmatic factors influences our decisions when confronted with alternatives. This project will focus however on one subtle but very important aspect of all dilemmas: the way in which the dilemma is *framed*. That is, the way in which the dilemma is presented to the person making the decision. This is an important social psychological topic because it addresses two issues which are central to our understanding of human social reasoning: that our decision-making processes are often neither *consistent* nor *transparent* to ourselves.

One could criticize the dilemmas described earlier, on the basis that they were very 'artificial'. However, an interesting study carried out in an applied setting confirms the generality of the effects. McNeil *et al.* (1982) asked over 1,000 people whether, if they were ever to suffer lung cancer, they would prefer to have surgery or radiation therapy. They found that, of the people who had surgery described to them as involving a 32 per cent chance of dying within 12 months, only 58 per cent preferred it to radiation treatment; whereas of the people who had the same surgical treatment described to them as involving a 68 per cent chance of *surviving beyond* 12 months, 75 per cent preferred surgery to radiation treatment. (Note that a 32 per cent chance of dying within 12 months is *exactly* the same as a 68 per cent chance of surviving 12 months – it is just *framed* differently, but that framing makes all the difference to people's preferences.)

You might think that if ever the participants in the McNeil *et al.* study really did have to face the dilemma of selecting a treatment for lung cancer they should seek advice from a professional radiologist in order to make a sensible informed decision. The problem is that in that study nearly half the participants *were* professional radiologists! No-one is immune from the effects of framing. You can think about this for yourself: How would you feel about enrolling on a psychology course which had a 91 per cent pass rate? How would you feel about enrolling for a course with a 9 per cent failure rate? Given what we have learned so far, it is likely that most people will prefer a '91 per cent pass rate' to a '9 per cent fail rate' even though they amount to the same thing.

A further study which emphasizes the importance of framing in real life is that carried out by Meyerowitz and Chaiken (1987). They were interested in the factors influencing whether or not women would perform a breast self-examination for cancer. This is of immense importance of course because early detection greatly improves treatability and survival chances. They presented women with three versions of a specially constructed health education pamphlet. Pamphlet 1 simply gave directions on how to conduct a simple breast self-examination; Pamphlet 2 emphasized that women who *did* carry out self-examination had an *increased* chance of surviving breast cancer; and Pamphlet 3 emphasized that women who *did not* carry out breast self-examination had *decreased* chances of successful treatment.

Four months later Meyerowitz and Chaiken returned to assess the impact of the different versions of the health education pamphlet.

Which of the three versions of the pamphlet distributed by Meyerowitz and Chaiken do you think had the biggest impact on the behaviour of the women in the study? Why do you think the pamphlets would have different effects on their recipients? What was the purpose of Pamphlet 1, the one which merely described how to do the breast self-examination without saying anything about the consequences of performing, or not performing, the self-examination?

In fact, Meyerowitz and Chaiken (1987) found that Pamphlet 3, which framed the consequences of *not examining* in terms of *decreased* chances of survival, was the most successful in increasing the probability that the women would initiate a programme of breast self-examination. If you think back to the earlier dilemmas you will remember that people appear to be more concerned about the prospect of losing what they already have than by the prospect of gaining.

The purpose of Pamphlet 1, which only gave advice on how to conduct a self-examination, was to construct a *control condition* which gives useful baseline information against which to compare the other two pamphlets (it is conceivable that the two other pamphlets could have led to *less* self-examination than the control group irrespective of framing – and this would need to be ruled out).

A further issue which the whole notion of framing raises is that of the role of language, not only in constructing our social world but also in constructing our experience of specific decisions within it. Language is clearly a key factor in the way in which we come to perceive the choices that are available to us (Wetherell and Maybin, 1996). Language is one of the main ways in which social lives are delineated (often for us by others). This project tries to give some additional concrete empirical foundation to some of those observations. (You might want to consider Potter's (1996, section 4) discussion of variability in evaluations and assessments as another perspective on the way in which our social world is created through language, not just in a general way but in terms of situation-specific constructions.)

You might want to think at this point about the ways in which the media present certain debates as being about selecting between certain options which are 'framed' in particular ways. In whose interests are these particular framings? Are the broadcasters/producers who write the news bulletins necessarily aware of the consequences of their framings?

Whole areas of policy making can be framed in ways which encourage us to 'see' the choices in one way when an alternative framing would encourage us to see them in a different way. For example, debates about euthanasia are framed by one side of the argument as a choice between dying with dignity on the one hand and unnecessary suffering on the other, while the other side of the argument frames the debate as a choice between the sanctity of life and the immorality of suicide. Similarly, one-parent families are discussed in terms of affirming family values vs. welfare dependency, or choice vs. poverty/discrimination. The 'law and order' debate could be reframed as the 'youth and poverty' debate. Cases such as these are very obvious, however, and politicians are only too aware of the importance of imposing one definition (or framing) of the discussions rather than allowing the framings of one's opponents to pre-dominate and structure the perceptions of voters.

Psychologists, however, concentrate on more subtle aspects of framing which happen in specific dilemmas, and experimental social psychology takes a distinctive approach to these issues. Some hermeneutic or social constructionist approaches would perhaps trace the ways in which certain categories of talk are constructed in interpersonal and public discourses over a number of years and in a range of media. Experimentalists by contrast present a sizeable number of people with specially constructed (and therefore sometimes slightly artificial) sets of imaginary dilemmas in which they select the option that they believe they would pursue if they really were in that situation. By manipulating certain pieces of information in the dilemmas so that different groups of participants are presented with slightly different versions of the same dilemma, experimental social psychologists attempt to show how certain key variables influence people's decisions (see Lalljee (1996) for other examples of this approach).

Let us consider some additional pieces of research relevant to this project and the issue of framing generally. A number of researchers have suggested that not everyone is equally influenced by framing in every situation as was originally implied by Tversky and Kahneman in 1981. For example, Fagley and Miller (1990) found some evidence that women were more susceptible to the effects of framing in the classic dilemmas than men, while Woodside and Singer (1994) found that the strength of the framing effect in the 'ticket' dilemma was reduced where the visit to a theatre was with a *friend* who had lost a ticket. This suggests that social interactions may simply override the effects of framing. Further, Takemura (1993) showed that the framing effect was reduced when participants were warned in advance that a justification of their decision would be required. Takemura (1992) has also shown that the more time people are given to think about a dilemma the less likely they are to show a framing effect.

Weinstein *et al.* (1996) found that framing effects were less pronounced when the key data were presented in terms of time-based rather than probability-based outcomes (e.g. data presented as '1 death expected per 3,500 years' rather than as '1 in 100,000 risk of a death this year'). This suggests that framing effects are at least in part a consequence of the kinds of superficial reasoning participants engage in when they are unable to conceptualize the abstract data presented to them.

The effects of framing when they do occur can affect behaviour as well as cognition. O'Connor *et al.* (1996) found that, when they presented the possibility of influenza vaccine side effects to patients in a positively framed manner (e.g. '96 per cent of people experience no side-effects with this vaccine'), they had fewer days off work *and fewer side-effects* than those who had the *same* information framed negatively (e.g. '4 per cent of people experience side-effects with this vaccine').

Wang (1996) found that the health programme dilemma did not show the usual framing effects if 'family members' were referred to rather than the public in general. In particular, it was found that people preferred the risky option (i.e. trying to save everyone at the risk of saving no-one) even when the dilemma was framed in terms of lives lost rather than lives saved. Interestingly, Wang found that Chinese participants still showed a pronounced tendency to prefer the risky option even when fairly distant relations and friends were the (hypothetical) victims, whereas American participants tended to display the usual risk-averse (i.e. 'play-safe') response to 'loss' frames outside their own immediate family. This suggests subtle cross-cultural differences in the way the social content of framed information affects decisions about risk.

PART B: THE FIELDWORK

2 Carrying out the project: overview of options

This project is based around the four classic dilemmas originally reported by Tversky and Kahneman (1981). They capture the main aspects of the psychological dimensions of framing. The ones you will be using here involve slight amendments to the originals (for example, changing dollars to pounds) but they are in every key respect identical. This project does not involve any statistics beyond the simple chi-square.

You have to present a group of people with one of two versions of some or all of the four dilemmas described in Section 1 and obtain their responses. There are two options:

Option 1

For this option you construct your own version of at least two of the four core dilemmas and give them to between 14 and 40 participants. The option requires that you have access to at least 14 people (not necessarily simultaneously) for about 10–15 minutes each. It also requires a little thought and imagination but can be very interesting indeed. In this option you can test hypotheses about the amount of time given to participants or the content of the dilemmas for example.

Option 2

You give a small number of participants the core dilemmas and carry out a detailed analysis of the explanations they give of their decisions in a *verbal protocol*. This requires access to about four to six people for about 20 to 30 minutes each.

2.1 Introduction to Option 1

This option involves designing your own materials and takes a bit of thought, but can be more rewarding when you come to analyse the results afterwards. The easiest way to create your own dilemmas from scratch is given in Box 1 below. You can alter any of the four core dilemmas or you can design one or more from scratch. If you design fewer than four dilemmas, you can use use up to two of the core dilemmas (in their original form) to bring the total up to four. You will need to construct two experimental booklets as follows:

Booklet alpha	**Booklet beta**
Dilemma 1	Dilemma 1
(version 1)	(version 2)
Dilemma 2	Dilemma 2
(version 1)	(version 2)
Dilemma 3	Dilemma 3
(version 1)	(version 2)
Dilemma 4	Dilemma 4
(version 1)	(version 2)

Each participant should receive only one booklet (either alpha or beta) made up of *one* of the two versions of each dilemma. Each participant should also receive one Response Sheet on which they should write down their answers. You will find all the materials you need to run your project in the appendices to this handbook. All you have to do is make the appropriate number of copies.

(Each dilemma needs to be analysed statistically as a separate experiment so don't worry about any possible connections between them. If you wish you may randomize the allocation of version to participants, so that they do some version 1s and some version 2s. Strictly speaking this is good practice, but unneccessary for present purposes.)

Designing your own versions of the dilemmas

You should try to make sure that the new dilemmas you create allow you to test a novel hypothesis about framing. For example, you might want to test the idea that dilemmas about self are more susceptible to framing than dilemmas about others.

In dilemma 1 (health programme) there is scope for manipulating the type of virus, the type of victims, and their precise number (see Wang, 1996). Dilemma 2 (money) is simple to manipulate – all that is required is that you alter (i) the amounts of money involved and/or (ii) the percentage risks involved. Dilemma 3 (the theatre ticket) is related to the idea of 'psychological accounting' where costs and gains are associated with different categories (accounts) rather than combined overall. The results of studies involving this dilemma suggest we have one 'psychological account' for cash and another for goods (such as the ticket). You might want to create a dilemma which tests a hypothesis about what other accounts people hold (for example, do we have one 'account' for ourselves but another for our spouse? That is, supposing our *spouse* lost the ticket money, would we be likely to buy *them* a ticket?) Dilemma 4 (jacket and camera) is based on the idea of the ratio-difference principle (Quattrone and Tversky, 1988). Simply put, this means that the bigger the percentage one figure is of another the more psychological impact it will have on decision making. You might want to try creating new dilemmas which vary this percentage. You might want to try altering the nature of the purchases (for example, product/service) to see whether or not this makes a difference to the outcome. Alternatively, you might want to change the size or nature of the 'hassle factor' in this kind of dilemma. For example, you could consider making the other branch of the shop only five minutes away and so on.

It is possible to design your own dilemma from scratch. The underlying principle is that the situation or the alternative courses of action/outcomes can be presented in two very different ways *and yet the underlying dilemma and alternatives remain the same*. This is not as difficult as it sounds, but it will require just a little bit of thought on your part. The simplest method is given in Box 2, but your starting-point can be the four core dilemmas. Consider Dilemma 1 (health programme): the basic idea here is that 'saved = not dying'. This can be thought of as the 'remainder are the opposite' principle. All you have to do is think of an outcome and then consider its 'remaindered opposite'. For example, in a classroom of 30 pupils, 25 being present is the same as 5 (the remainder) being absent (the opposite), and so on. These are just two framings of the same state or situation or outcome. (This works better if the two possibilities are mutually exclusive: for example, saved/dying, present/absent.)

In my experience, creating new dilemmas is actually easier to do if you do it back to front – that is, if you start with the question you are going to put to the participant about their responses (rather than starting from the details of the situation itself).

Box 2 contains some ideas to get you brainstorming about the possibilities for new dilemmas, through focusing on the alternatives for responses which you could present to the participants.

BOX I   Some ideas for a new dilemma

Would you agree to help someone if they asked you to . . . .

. . . .

. . . . ?

Alternative A: agree   ☐

Alternative B: refuse   ☐

Would you enrol for a psychology course if . . . .

. . . .

. . . . ?

Alternative A: would enrol   ☐

Alternative B: would not enrol ☐

If you saw the following incident would you report it to the police

. . . .

. . . .

. . . . ?

Alternative A: would report it   ☐

Alternative B: would not report it   ☐

Would you hire someone for an odd job if they . . . .

. . . .

. . . . ?

Alternative A: would hire   ☐

Alternative B: would not hire   ☐

Would you consider joining a club or society if they . . . .

. . . .

. . . . ?

Alternative A: would consider joining   ☐

Alternative B: would not consider joining ☐

Would you pay more for house insurance if the insurance company
offered . . . .

. . . .

. . . . ?

Alternative A: would pay more   ☐

Alternative B: would not pay more   ☐

A very simple (but perfectly valid) way of constructing your own dilemmas involves the use of percentages. All you have to do is follow the 'remaining percentage as opposite' rule. (See Box 2.)

BOX 2   Creating your own dilemmas the easy way

The following is a straightforward technique for creating alternative versions of the same dilemma. It works as follows:

Step 1: This step identifies a behaviour
You identify a behavioural dilemma which people might be faced with (for example, selecting a course, buying a house, taking a job, entering a relationship, recommending treatment, and so on). You start the dilemma by saying 'Would you do <behaviour> if ...?'

Step 2: This step creates the first of the two versions for the dilemma
You begin by identifying some *feature* or aspect of the behaviour mentioned above which might be relevant to the decision (for example – with reference to the examples listed above – the pass rate, land subsidence, promotion, breaking up, healing effects).

You then assign a *percentage* probability to this feature or to this feature being present (for example, the percentage pass rate, the percentage chance of subsidence, the percentage chance of the other person leaving the area, the percentage chance of the treatment working, etc.).

You can now continue writing version 1 by adding to the 'Would you do <behaviour> if ...?' part derived from Step 1 the following phrase (with the actual percentage and feature you have selected, of course), 'there were a <percentage> chance of <feature>. Thus you might say:

'Would you
<buy a house> if there were <a 3 per cent chance> of <subsidence>?'
   behaviour   percentage   feature

Step 3: This step creates the second of the two versions of your dilemma
You now simply use the 'remaining percentage as opposite' rule: whatever percentage you have given to the feature or to the feature being present for version 1, you simply take that percentage away from 100 per cent and attach that percentage to the opposite of the feature or to the feature not being present.

For example, if you have said that there is a 3 per cent chance of subsidence for version 1, then you would now create version 2 by simply putting the question:

'Would you buy a house if there were a 97 per cent chance of no subsidence?'

Step 4: This step makes your materials more participant friendly
In order to make the dilemmas clear and meaningful to your participants you will want to elaborate a little on the information you provided.

For example, here you might want to add to the behaviour and feature to end up with the following form of version 1:

'Would you go ahead with the purchase of a house you had set your heart on if the surveyor's report indicated a 97 per cent chance of no subsidence within the next 10 years?'

(Be careful though how you add on information. The way I have done this here would I think perhaps tend to cue participants slightly into thinking that the wise thing to do would be to back out of the purchase – in both versions.)

Now you have two versions of your dilemma which present the exact same choice in different framings, and which you will give to separate groups of people.

Running your experiments and recording your data

How many participants do I need?

This is always a difficult question which psychologists have to face when running an experiment for the first time. Too few participants and it is quite likely that a genuine underlying difference between two groups will be missed (a so-called 'type II' error). Too many participants and time, money and quite possibly your own sanity will be lost. Overall, you should attempt to have a minimum of 20 participants per dilemma, but around 30 if possible with 14 as the absolute minimum.

When you have collected your data, you need to transfer it, person by person, to a data matrix grid (see Appendix 3). The first column is the participant number (this helps you keep track of each person's data). The column headed D1 relates to Dilemma 1, D2 is Dilemma 2 and so on. 'V' in the columns refers to the version of the dilemma that the participant completed. 'R' is for response. Below is an example of a data matrix grid.

Data matrix grid (example):

Participant	D1 V R	D2 V R	D3 V R	D4 V R
1	1 A	1 A	1 B	1 A
2	2 A	2 B	2 A	2 B
3	1 B	1 A	1 B	1 A
4	2 B	2 A	2 A	2 A
.	.	.	.	.
.	.	.	.	.
.	.	.	.	.
.	.	.	.	.
.	.	.	.	.
24	1B	1A	1B	1B

Totals for version 1 (hypothetical)

D1	D2	D3	D4
A = 10	A =	A =	A =
B = 14	B =	B =	B =
N = 24	N =	N =	N =

Totals for version 2 (hypothetical)

D1	D2	D3	D4
A = 18	A =	A =	A =
B = 12	B =	B =	B =
N = 30	N =	N =	N =

(NOTE: totals for Dilemmas 2–4 have not been filled in.)

From this grid we can see that participant 1 was presented with version 1 of Dilemma 1 (D1) and her response was Option A. She was presented with version 1 of Dilemma 2 (D2) and her response was Option A, etc.

At the bottom of each column for each dilemma the total number of A and B responses *totalled separately for each version* has been added up. 'N' is the number of participants who completed each version. Note that these totals are hypothetical in the data example above because not all the data are presented in the grid.

Analysing your data and testing your hypotheses

Each dilemma should yield four figures:

number of participants given version 1 who preferred Option A=	1A
number of participants given version 1 who preferred Option B=	1B
number of participants given version 2 who preferred Option A=	2A
number of participants given version 2 who preferred Option B=	2B

These figures will be the basis used to calculate a chi-square statistic for each dilemma.

Enter the four totals into the following table:

	Option A	Option B
version 1	[1A]	[1B]
version 2	[2A]	[2B]

The data can now be analysed through a chi-square statistic in the normal way. If your obtained chi-square value is greater than the critical value then the chi-square value obtained is significant and you can rule out the possibility that there is *no* association between the version of the dilemma presented (the framing) and responses made by participants. You can conclude that the framing *does* have an effect on the responses made.

2.2 Option 2

The aim of this option is to analyse the thinking participants carry out as they consider each dilemma, by examining the concurrent verbalizations they engage in as they work. You will need an audio recorder to record what people say and you will need to set aside some time later to transcribe their statements. You are recommended to use four to six participants for this option, but it may be possible to do an intensive analysis on a single person.

Steps in the verbal protocol option

Before you begin you need to read through these briefing notes carefully and consider the questions raised below under 'Analysing your protocol data'. You should try to specify a number of *qualitative* hypotheses about the things the participants are going to say during and after the task. The sequence of presentation is as follows:

1   You will need to work with one participant at a time in a reasonably quiet place (nevertheless it might be interesting to do some in a busy noisy area to improve external validity – after all, we do not always have the luxury of solitude and silence when we are faced with a dilemma in real life!).

2   Once you are sure that the participant understands the basic instructions about the dilemmas *per se*, explain to him or her that you would like them to think out loud as they tackle the questions.

3   Let the participant start tackling the dilemmas.

4   Encourage them to vocalize (that is, talk out loud) as they do each dilemma. If they go silent give them about 10 seconds and then say 'please keep talking'. If you are not taping the vocalizations make sure you are writing down what they say as they say it. The best way to do this is in a clear sequential manner. These vocalizations are the 'concurrent verbalizations'.

5   When the participant has completed the four dilemmas, take them through the alternatives they have selected, dilemma by dilemma, and ask them to explain why they have chosen that alternative over the other. You should still be audio recording at this point. Having elicited this information, you should then present them with the *other* framing of the same dilemma and ask them whether they would have chosen a different alternative or not, and why.

Analysing your protocol data

Since you are analysing a small number of people in depth, you will almost certainly not be able to carry out any statistical analysis of your data. However, you will be able to analyse the statements made by your participants as indications of their thinking while tackling the dilemmas.

You might also find the ideas in Green and Gilhooly (1996) useful as a series of orientations towards your data.

Verbal protocol analysis (VPA) is mainly used as a technique for inferring the thought processes of humans tackling difficult problems. There are many critics of VPA however and it is important not to treat verbal reports simply as direct print-outs of thought processes (McGhee, 1987). Nevertheless, they do offer a rich database that would not otherwise be elicited. Box 3 highlights the main categories that will be relevant in this project.

BOX 3   Segmentation and categorization in verbal protocol analysis

In VPA it is often useful to segment and categorize the responses of each participant. For example, you might want to categorize each statement made by a participant as:

Dilemma reading
The person reads aloud part or all of the dilemma.

Elaborating on the dilemma
The person tries to draw inferences from information explicitly given in the dilemma.

Comments on the decision-making process
The person makes a statement about the task itself.

Questions

Exclamations

Self-statement
The person makes descriptive comment about him/herself.

Self-evaluation
The person makes evaluative comment about him/herself.

(Note that there are many other possible additional categories.)

You will have three sets of verbal data from each participant:

1   Their verbalizations during the task ('concurrent verbalizations').

2   Their verbalizations to you *after* the task explaining *why* they chose the option they did ('retrospective verbalizations').

3   Their response to you when you present them with the alternative framing of the dilemma ('response verbalizations').

There are many different ways of segmenting spoken language as it appears in your transcript. The list on categories in Box 3 is not exhaustive and you may want to use others. Green and Gilhooly (1996) and Green (1995) provide detailed guidance on protocol analysis which you may find useful to consult. One key issue is checking the *reliability* of your segmentation (mapping speech into single ideas units) and coding (putting segments into the correct categories). Reliability here means that the transcript is split into the same segments consistently, and that the segments are coded to the same categories consistently. It is useful therefore to work independently with a friend to check the between-coder reliability of the procedures. In terms of segmentation percentage, Green and Gilhooly (1996) suggest that the total number of segments identified by both coders, divided by the total number of segments, gives a ratio which when multiplied by 100 yields a useful 'percentage agreement' figure. If this figure is 85 per cent or greater, then the segmentation is reliable and the analysis can continue. If it is less than 85 per cent, then the criteria for segmentation may need to be reviewed before continuing.

Once the segments have been identified, they have to be coded according to the categorization system established. Establishing reliability here is again the percentage of segments correctly allocated to a category by two coders working independently (85 per cent can be used as an acceptable threshold again). The fewer the categories the easier it is to get higher levels of agreement, but the resulting information may not be as useful. It may be necessary to revise the categories to get useful codings.

There are many ways of analysing this type of data. The fundamental question is: What do the concurrent verbalizations tell us about the thought processes of people tackling dilemmas of the kind used by Tversky and Kahneman? You can approach your data in two ways: the *sequence* of verbalizations and the overall *organization* of the spoken thoughts of the participant. The sequence of verbalizations tells us about the strategies the participant has used, whereas the organization of the verbalizations tells us about their comprehension of the problem. Whichever you focus on you will find it useful to categorize your data (see Box 3).

The following questions will help you get started:

In reference to the type (1) data ('concurrent verbalizations') above:

1   Are there any similar patterns *between* participants in terms of the ways in which they tried to tackle the same dilemma?

2   Are there any similar patterns *within* participants in terms of how they tackled the dilemmas? (That is, did the same person tackle different dilemmas in different or similar ways?)

3   Did participants choose one of the alternatives and then stick to it, or did they vacillate?

4   Did participants engage in verbalizations unconnected or only indirectly connected to the task? Or were all verbalizations relevant?

5   Did participants try to elicit help from you as they did the task or were all verbalizations self-directed?

6   Did participants engage in 'metatalk': that is, did they talk about their own thinking abilities or about the strategies they were using in coming to a decision or about themselves as decision makers, rather than simply talk about the task *per se*?

In relation to type (2) data ('retrospective verbalizations'):

1   Did participants find it easy to articulate why they had chosen the alternatives they had?

2   What general attitude to justification did participants take? Did they try to offer specific logical arguments or did they just indicate that it was a personal preference or style that led them to make that choice?

3   Did participants emphasize the fact that the dilemmas are hypothetical rather than real and that they could be swayed by other factors or considerations if it had been for real?

4   Was the explanation/justification for the choices made in a monologue by the participant or in a dialogue between them and the experimenter?

In relation to type (3) data ('response verbalizations'):

1   Did participants accept that they might have been influenced by the alternative framing or did they feel that it would have made no difference?

2   What kinds of justifications for their view in relation to the above question did participants give?

3   What did participants say about their own thinking styles/abilities generally after discussing whether they would or would not have been influenced by the other framing?

4   What is the overall pattern of the conversation between the experimenter and the participant (is the experimenter putting words or ideas into the participant's mouth)?

Obviously, the more participants you have the more data you will have to draw upon to tackle the above questions and related ones.

PART C: WORKING WITH THE DATA

3 Interpreting your data

3.1 Option 1

If you have been comparing two framings of the same dilemma, then a statistically significant chi-square means that framing *has* affected the responses of the participant. You must however check that the responses have been affected in the predicted direction before claiming support for your hypotheses.

3.2 Option 2

You need to relate your transcripts back to the fundamental question of what the verbalizations tell us about the thinking processes participants engage in when tackling the dilemmas. The *concurrent* verbalizations (that is, the record of what was said during the tasks) should give you some insight into such issues as the stages participants go through as they tackle each dilemma, the differences in thinking style and whether or not participants seem to get more insightful (or more bored) as they do each task. The *retrospective* verbalizations (that is, the discussions that take place after the dilemmas have been answered) provide evidence about participants' awareness of their own thought processes and their understanding of the factors which influence their decision making.

3.3 Writing the project up

Check with your tutor on the precise write-up requirements for your report. This section gives tips, not instructions.

Title page
This should contain the title of the study and your name.

Abstract
The abstract is meant to be a self-contained summary of the entire experiment. It should indicate the general area of the work, the main method used and a brief statement of whether or not the hypothesis being tested was supported. It should be about 100–200 words long. The abstract

should be presented on its own page at the very beginning of the report, immediately after the title page.

Introduction

This is where you provide the general rationale for the study and some of the background. You will want to briefly review the work of Tversky and Kahneman and some of the general issues involved around the notion of 'framing' (see 'Further reading' list). For Option 1 you should explain (i) why you have chosen the hypotheses you have chosen to test and (ii) the reason for choosing the dilemmas that you have used. There should be some sort of link between (i) and (ii). You should indicate very clearly exactly what your hypotheses were. For Option 2 your hypotheses might be less specific but you still have to state what they are.

Method

This part falls into a number of different subsections:

Participants: Give the total number, sex and mean age of your participants (as appropriate). This demographic data is often reported in experimental reports even if age and sex are not part of the hypotheses or the theoretical framework of the study. This information gives the reader a basic idea of who the participants were.

Materials: Give a clear description of which dilemmas you used and the ways in which any new ones were constructed. Someone reading this section should have a fairly clear idea of what your booklets actually contained.

Procedure: This is a blow by blow account of how you actually carried out the testing with the participants. Someone reading this section should be able to repeat what you did fairly closely so it is a good idea to get someone to read through this section and then tell you what they think you did. If they can't tell you then you have not been clear enough – rewrite it. You will want to mention here any forms of randomization which you carried out. Whatever option you are doing you should spell out clearly and precisely what you did.

Results

This should be a straightforward summary of your findings and statistical analyses. Actual computations should be put in a separate appendix. For Option 1 you are required to report on the chi-square values obtained and whether or not they were significant and what that means for your hypotheses. Since each dilemma should be analysed separately (almost as if each were a separate experiment) you will be reporting 4–6 chi-square values here. For Option 2 you will be giving a quantitative and qualitative account of what your participants said. The quantitative element might involve a table listing the number of times the different aspects of each dilemma were explicitly referred to, or the number of questions asked by the participant, or the ratio of completed to uncompleted sentences. You will want to present this information separately for each dilemma so that any differences in verbalizations will come through (it is possible that you will want to present this information separately for each participant if you are exploring different individual styles in tackling dilemmas).

Discussion

In many respects this is the most important part of your report (and probably the most enjoyable part to write). Here for Option 1 you are interpreting the hypotheses in the light of whether or not they were rejected by the statistical analyses. If, for example, you predicted that the health programme dilemma effect would still work even if small numbers of victims were involved, and the statistics supported that hypothesis (that is, the chi-square value was significant), you might want to conclude that the framing effects are more powerful than had been previously thought.

For Option 2 your hypotheses may not be unequivocally supported or rejected in any clear-cut way. However, you do need to address the questions identified in the subsection called 'Steps in the verbal protocol option' (see Section 2.2) and others in order to demonstrate how your perception of the data from the study can help us understand the thought processes involved in framing tasks. Whatever option you are doing you must link your discussions to the hypotheses you were testing and the theories or theoretical considerations you derived them from.

It is important in this section that you also offer a fairly wide-ranging critique of the study that you have just reported on. You should indicate which aspects of your execution of the study you would change if you were to advise someone who wanted to follow up your research. You should also however make a general evaluation of the assumptions, methods and forms of data analysis incorporated in the whole framing paradigm.

Note: Allow yourself sufficient time and words for the discussion, as the quality of your work here will contribute substantially to your final mark.

You should include appendices in your write up. These will be your computations for the chi-square in Option 1 or your transcripts for Option 2. You should also include a copy of any new dilemmas you have constructed.

References

Fagley, N. and Miller, P.M. (1990) 'The effect of framing on choice: interactions with risk-taking propensity, cognitive style, and sex', *Personality and Social Psychology Bulletin,* vol.16, pp.496–510.

Green, A. (1995) 'Verbal protocol analysis', *The Psychologist,* vol.8, pp.126–9.

Green, C. and Gilhooly, K. (1996) 'Protocol analysis: practical implementation', in Richardson, J.T.E. (ed.) *Handbook of Qualitative Research Methods for Psychology and the Social Sciences*, Leicester, BPS Books.

Lalljee, M. (1996) 'The interpreting self: an experimentalist perspective', in Stevens, R. (ed.) (1996).

Meyerowitz, B.E. and Chaiken, S. (1987) *Journal of Personality and Social Psychology*, vol.52, pp.500–10.

McGhee, P. (1987) 'From self-reports to narrative discourse', in Burnett, R., Clarke, D. and McGhee, P. (eds) *Accounting for Relationships*, London, Methuen.

McNeil, B.J., Parker, S.G., Sox, H.C. Jnr, and Tversky, A. (1982) 'On the elicitation of preferences for alternative therapies', *New England Journal of Medicine*, vol.306. pp.1259–62.

O'Connor, A.M., Pennie, R.A. and Dales, R.E. (1996) 'Framing effects on expectations, decisions and side effects experienced: the case of influenza immunization', *Journal of Clinical Epidemiology*, vol.49, pp.1271–76.

Potter, J. (1996) 'Attitudes, social representations and discursive psychology', in Wetherell, M. (ed.) *Identities, Groups and Social Issues*, London, Sage/The Open University.

Stevens, R. (ed.) (1996) *Understanding the Self*, London, Sage/The Open University.

Takemura, K. (1992) 'Effect of decision time on framing of decision: a case of risky choice behavior', *Psychologica*, vol.5, pp.180–5.

Takemura, K. (1993) 'The effect of decision frame and decision justification on risky choice', *Japanese Psychology Research*, vol.35, pp.36–40.

Tversky, A. and Kahneman, D. (1981) 'The framing of decisions and the psychology of choice', *Science*, vol.211, pp.453–8.

Quattrone, G.A. and Tversky, A. (1988) 'Contrasting rational and psychological analyses of political choice', *American Political Science*, vol.82, pp.719–36.

Wang, X.T. (1996) 'Domain-specific rationality in human choices: violations of utility axioms and social contexts', *Cognition*, vol.60, pp.31–63.

Weinstein, N.D., Kolb, K. and Goldstein, B.D. (1996) 'Using time intervals between expected events to communicate risk magnitudes', *Risk Analysis*, vol.16, pp.305–8.

Wetherell, M. and Maybin, J. (1996) 'The distributed self: a social constructionist perspective', in Stevens, R. (ed.) (1996).

Woodside, A. and Singer, A.E. (1994) 'Social interaction effects in the framing of buying decisions', *Psychology and Marketing*, vol.11, pp.27–34.

Further reading

Baron, J. (1994) *Thinking and Deciding* (2nd edn), Cambridge, Cambridge University Press.

Garnham, A. and Oakhill, J. (1994) *Thinking and Reasoning*, Oxford, Basil Blackwell.

Pagano, R.R. (1994) *Understanding Statistics in the Behavioural Sciences* (4th edn), New York, West Publishing Company.

Ranyard, R., Crozier, W.R. and Svenson, O. (1997) *Decision Making: Cognitive Models and Explanations*. London, Routledge.

Schwarz, N. (1994) 'Judgement in a social context: biases, shortcomings and the logic of conversation', in Zanna, M.P. (ed.) *Advances in Experimental Social Psychology*, vol.26, pp.123–62.

World Wide Web

European Association for Decision Making:

http://www.eadm.org/

(An interdisciplinary web site with useful links to psychology materials for decision making.)

Principia Cybernetica Web:

http://pespmc1.vub.ac.be/ASC/DECISI_THEOR.html

(A web dictionary of cybernetics and systems including decision making.)

Appendix 1: The dilemmas

The following dilemmas are based on Tversky and Kahneman (1981).

Dilemma 1 (v.1): health programme

Imagine that the UK is preparing for the outbreak of an unusually dangerous virus which is expected to kill 600 people next winter. Two alternative preventative programmes have been proposed. The scientific estimates of the consequences of the programmes are as follows:

Programme A: If adopted 200 people will be saved.

Programme B: If adopted there is a $\frac{1}{3}$ probability that 600 people will be saved, and a $\frac{2}{3}$ probability that no people will be saved.

Which of these two programmes would you favour? A or B?

Please circle the appropriate letter on the response sheet.

Dilemma 1 (v.2): Health programme

Imagine that the UK is preparing for the outbreak of an unusually dangerous virus which is expected to kill 600 people next winter. Two alternative preventative programmes have been proposed. The scientific estimates of the consequences of the programmes are as follows:

Programme A: If adopted 400 people will die

Programme B: If adopted there is a $\frac{1}{3}$ probability that nobody will die, and a $\frac{2}{3}$ probability that 600 people will die.

Which of these two programmes would you favour? A or B?

Please circle the appropriate letter on the response sheet.

Dilemma 2 (v.1): money

Which of the following two alternatives would you prefer A or B?

Alternative A: A sure gain of £250.

Alternative B: A 25 per cent chance to gain £1,000 and a 75 per cent chance to gain nothing.

Please circle the appropriate letter on the response sheet.

Dilemma 2 (v.2): money

Which of the following two alternatives would you prefer A or B?

Alternative A: A sure loss of £750.

Alternative B: A 75 per cent chance to lose £1,000 and a 25 per cent chance to lose nothing.

Please circle the appropriate letter on the response sheet.

Dilemma 3 (v.1): the theatre ticket

Imagine that you have decided to see a play where admission is £10 per ticket. As you enter the theatre you discover that you have lost a £10 note.

Would you

A: still pay £10 for a ticket for the play?

B: not pay £10 for a ticket for the play?

Please circle the appropriate letter on the response sheet.

Dilemma 3 (v.2): the theatre ticket

Imagine that you have decided to see a play where admission is £10 per ticket. As you enter the theatre you discover that you have lost the ticket. The seat was not marked and the ticket cannot be recovered.

Would you

A: still pay £10 for a ticket for the play?

B: not pay £10 for a ticket for the play?

Please circle the appropriate letter on the response sheet.

Dilemma 4 (v.1): jacket and camera

Imagine that you are in a large chain store and about to purchase a jacket for £15, and a camera for £125.

When you get to the till with your purchases the assistant informs you that the same camera is on offer at £120 at a different branch of the store twenty minutes drive away.

Would you

A: make the trip to the other branch to buy the reduced price camera; or

B: buy the camera at the branch you are in?

Please circle the appropriate letter on the response sheet.

Dilemma 4 (v.2): jacket and camera

Imagine that you are in a large chain store and about to purchase a jacket for £125, and a camera for £15.

When you get to the till with your purchases the assistant informs you that the same camera is on offer at £10 at a different branch of the store twenty minutes drive away.

Would you

A: make the trip to the other branch to buy the reduced price camera; or

B: buy the camera at the branch you are in?

Please circle the appropriate letter on the response sheet.

Appendix 2: Response sheet

Please circle the appropriate letter to indicate your preference for each dilemma.

(Please make sure the number of the dilemma is correct – you may not have been presented with them in numerical sequence.)

Dilemma 1	A	B
Dilemma 2	A	B
Dilemma 3	A	B
Dilemma 4	A	B
Dilemma 5 (if used)	A	B
Dilemma 6 (if used)	A	B

Age: _____

Sex: _____

For researcher's use only:

Participant number _____

Appendix 3: Data matrix grid

Participant	D1		D2		D3		D4	
	V	R	V	R	V	R	V	R
1								
2								
3								
4								
5								
6								
7								
8								
9								
10								
11								
12								
13								
14								
15								
16								
17								
18								
19								

Participant	D1		D2		D3		D4	
	V	R	V	R	V	R	V	R
20								
21								
22								
23								
24								
25								
26								
27								
28								
29								
30								
31								
32								
33								
34								
35								
36								

D = Dilemma number

V = Version

R = Response by participant [A or B]

CHAPTER 6

GLANCES INTO PERSONAL WORLDS: THE CONSTRUCTION AND ANALYSIS OF REPERTORY GRIDS

by Carol Tindall

Contents

1   Introduction

This project, grounded in Kelly's (1955) personal construct theory (PCT) offers you the opportunity to engage in a personal or collaborative exploration of personal constructions of reality, with the general aim of increasing understanding of the reality explored.

To familiarize yourself with Kelly's PCT you are advised to read the extract reproduced in Appendix 1, where Stevens (1996) introduces the key concepts of Kelly's theory. Also relevant is Dallos (1996), particularly section 3.1, which illustrates how Kelly's theory may be used to frame understanding and thus to gain insight into the development of relationships. You might also find it useful to read Tindall (1994), where I offer a theoretical background to what I call Kelly's 'personal construct psychology'.[1]

Having completed the readings, you will be aware that Kelly offers an idiographic approach to the study of subjective experience, an approach which focuses on the unique and idiosyncratic qualities of an individual's experiencing. Interestingly, Kelly's (1955) ideas can currently be construed as connecting experiential, social constructionist and experimental perspectives. The major concern is with personal meanings; that is, with how each of us makes sense of or construes our experiencing. According to Kelly, our construing '... is experiencing at all levels of awareness, thoughts, feelings and actions in appropriate (personal) harmony' (Tindall, 1994, p.72). Our construing, rooted in the meaning we have attached to our experiencing, frames our current understanding (our personal reality) and simultaneously provides an anticipatory basis for future action. However, some meanings can also be seen to be shared and held in common by members of groups, sections of society and cultures.

The remainder of section 1 outlines the three option possibilities, introduces you to the basic tasks involved and highlights the potential for unexpected revelation within this project. Section 2 offers ideas and examples of links between each of the options and issues in social psychology. Section 3 details how to generate the grid(s) for each option while section 4 takes you step by step through the analysis. The final section gives details on writing up the project.

1.1   Options

Each of the three options provides you with the opportunity of constructing a repertory grid, to reveal in part either your own construing of

---

[1] The debate about whether Kelly presents a theory or a complete psychology is not relevant to this project. You are likely to come across references to both personal construct theory and personal construct psychology and you are advised to read them as one and the same.

an aspect of your personal reality or, if you choose to work with someone else, an opportunity to focus on joint or shared understandings.

You should choose *one* of the following options:

Option 1

Focus on yourself, on how you experience an aspect of your world. Such a focus on self is unfortunately a relatively rare opportunity in psychology.

Option 2

Focus on the extent of your understanding of someone you have a need to understand for either personal or professional reasons. This involves your participant constructing a repertory grid to reveal their current understanding of a mutually agreed topic. Their grid is then offered to you in skeleton form to complete 'as if' you were them.

Option 3

Focusing on agreement and disagreement, explore the extent to which your construction of a negotiated aspect of your personal world, which you share either personally or professionally with your participant, agrees with theirs. This involves you both in a process of collaboration to produce the grid elements and constructs which you jointly consider appropriate to the negotiated aspect. Each of you then completes the grid from your own perspective, so revealing your individual current understanding of the chosen aspect.

The process of analysis involves making sense of the data by examining it for patterns and associations relevant to your project focus. During this process you may elect to extend your exploration via conversational elaboration (see sections 4.1, 4.2 and 4.3). If you choose Option 1, the laddering technique outlined in section 4.1 is recommended in addition to the repertory grid and conversational elaboration.

1.2 Project focus

Initially, for all three options, there are two tasks to achieve. First, you need to think of an area within social psychology which is of current interest to you. In this way you are ensuring that your work is personally relevant and grounded in social psychology. Next, you must decide on a project focus within the area, a specific purpose for completing the grid. For example, your area of interest might be as wide as identity, whereas your focus will be narrower and might be to explore your current construing of your sense of personal identity as it has developed over time. You will be given some specific examples of potential areas in the next section.

There are many project focus possibilities within any one area of interest. Consider your focus carefully as it forms the core of your project.

Once you have decided on a focus your next task is to select your grid elements. Elements must represent your focus; they may be people, roles, activities, interests, events – whatever is relevant to your focus. The elements are then used in threes (triads) to externalize how you currently construe your chosen topic. Your final task in generating your grid is to rate each element on each construct using a five-point scale. (Note that terms such as *elements* and *constructs* will be explained in detail as you proceed.)

Aims of this project

The aims of this project are:

- To experience and therefore help you to gain an understanding of the potential of the repertory grid.

- To reflect on your current understandings and their implications, as revealed by the grid.

- To offer the possibility of opening up and changing awareness.

- To increase critical awareness of PCT research methods.

- To increase critical awareness of the process and potential of re-search.

1.3 Caution

There is often the assumption that the repertory grid and other PCT methods only operate at a superficial and already known level. This indeed may be the case. It depends to some extent, although not entirely, on the level at which you and/or your participant (if you elect to work with someone else) choose to work. However, anyone, including yourself, completing the grid needs to be aware of the potential the grid has for making explicit personal links between constructs. As Stevens (1996) states, analysing grids '... can often bring surprises' (p.163), not only in the revelation of constructs of which the person was previously consciously unaware, but also in the idiosyncratic interrelatedness of personal constructs. Such revelation of personal patterns of understanding offers the opportunity for increased awareness via new insights and thus the potential for change, which is indeed one of the purposes of completing the grid. However, such revelations may simultaneously be disturbing. Your participant needs to be fully informed at the outset and both of you need to be aware of the possibility of revelations which may be disturbing.

2 Background to options

The rest of these notes provide you with detailed information on how to complete this project. Section 2 outlines a number of possibilities within each of the three options and provides you with food for thought. However, the final choice of area, project focus and elements is, of course, up to you. Also in this section I locate each of the options within PCT, although you will need to link the content of your project with other relevant theories and research from social psychology. Section 3 gives detailed instructions for carrying out your project. Initially I present general information relevant to all three options, on the selection of elements, how to use element triads to externalize constructs, and how to rate the relationship experienced between elements and constructs. This section then continues with very specific instructions for each of the options on how to generate the appropriate grids. Section 4 addresses the analysis of grids for each of the options – essentially, how to identify patterns of personal meaning revealed via grid completion. Each of the options also has a conversational elaboration sub-section, where techniques beyond the grid (although often triggered by grid completion) are outlined. These offer the potential to extend understanding of the initial analysis. Finally, section 5 details what to include in the various sections of your write-up.

2.1 Option 1

This is the option to choose if you want to work alone, to explore your own construing. This option links directly with the reflexivity aspect of PCT, tapping into your subjective awareness, and your ability and willingness to reflect on your own actions, thoughts and feelings. Stevens (1996) defines reflexive awareness as '... being aware of being aware' (p.149). You are required to reflect on your own experiencing with the intention of gaining insight and thus increasing self-awareness which offers the potential to facilitate change.

You should begin by choosing a current, personally relevant *area of interest* from within social psychology. The project will be more engaging and potentially of more use to you if you have a personal reason for completing the grid. Next, you need to think about a specific *project focus* within your chosen area of interest. When deciding, bear in mind that devising an appropriate project focus, one that opens up rather than limits possibilities, is an inherent part of PCT. Your focus may be on your construing of yourself, other people, significant events, leisure pursuits, anything in fact that interests you.

For example, if you elect to focus on your construing of yourself you may elect identity as a personally relevant area of interest. You may then choose to explore, via your project focus, a specific aspect of identity. Below are just four examples (illustrations only) of the sorts of project foci that identity might give rise to, with the kinds of elements you might use for each of them.

- You may be interested in your construing of your social identities. More specifically your project focus may be to explore your construing of the influence of roles (the various parts you play in life), perhaps you feel some 'fit' more easily than others and that it would be helpful to compare how you construe your significant roles. Your elements in this case would be a sample of your current roles, such as student, colleague, friend, nurse, parent, daughter, partner, sister, relaxed me – whatever is currently appropriate to you and your topic.

- You may wish to explore your construing of your sense of personal development over time, in which case you need to choose significant events or periods in your life as your elements. These must have some personal reality for you. Here, as illustration, are some examples of ways in which you might identify significant periods in your life as elements – time unemployed, childhood, adolescence, time in Cumbria, me in five years time, me now, me with a degree, me without a degree, me with x, me alone, etc.

- Perhaps you would prefer to explore your identity by comparing your construing of yourself with your construing of others. In this case your elements would again be roles, but this time roles that you see others fulfilling for you. Your elements might be those you identified as – someone I admire, someone who makes me anxious, someone significant, someone supportive, someone challenging, someone I dislike – including yourself as an element, of course, in order to make comparisons. Or, if you are interested in who you see yourself as similar to and different from, then you would include a personally appropriate range of elements consisting of friends, relatives, colleagues, acquaintances, etc. – remembering to include yourself as an element.

- Alternatively, to gain new insights you may choose to focus on your construing of other people, events or interests rather than yourself (e.g. people at work, family, the different social settings you participate in regularly and so on). Again, the general aim of the exploration would be to facilitate change, to encourage the adoption of new strategies, to aid decision making, to problem solve – whatever is currently relevant for you. You may be interested, as schoolteacher Barbara Thompson (1975) was, in how to construe children in your class. If so, your elements would be a representative range of children in your class. Similarly, you may wish to explore your construing of fellow-students in a work team, to reveal your personal criteria for choosing to work with them. Or maybe you are concerned, as Alex was (see Tindall, 1994, p.78), to clarify your view of the management style underpinning your work climate, in which case your elements would be a representative range of managers considered responsible for your work climate. (Although I was involved in working up the grid with Alex, he may well, with an understanding of PCT, have achieved this alone.) You may wish to explore your construing of aspects of life other than people. Your elements would, of course, reflect your project focus and may be anything open to construing, including such things as aspects of your job, possible careers, leisure pursuits, sports teams, forms of art, newspaper articles, radio or television programmes, whatever is currently relevant to you and your topic.

2.2 Options 2 and 3

Options 2 and 3 require that you work with one other person. You need to think carefully about your choice of participant. It needs to be someone you have a reasonable amount of contact with and with whom you can work freely around the topic you have chosen, and, of course, someone you believe can equally well work openly with you. There should be no personal barriers to construing.

Your participant needs to be in a position to make an informed choice to generate a grid with you around an agreed topic. You must therefore take responsibility for ensuring that your participant is fully aware of the possibilities outlined in section 1.3 above. In addition it is important to attend to the ethical implications for your participant and yourself throughout the process of the project. The psychological well-being, values and dignity of all involved need to be maintained from initial idea through to outcome.

2.3 Informed consent

It is your responsibility as researcher to give your prospective participants sufficient information about your project to enable them to make an informed decision as to whether or not to participate.

You **must** ensure that you:

1 Fully inform your participant of the purpose and process of completing the grid before you begin.

2 Inform your participant of the possibility of unexpected revelation, detailed in section 1.3 above.

3 Inform your participant of their right to select their level of disclosure.

4 Negotiate a topic of interest.

5 Gain the informed consent of your participant.

6 Ensure your participant's anonymity if possible. If not, make sure that your participant gives permission for their identity to be known.

7   Invite your participant to read and comment on (if they so wish) your finished project.

8   Point out to the participant that as a volunteer they have the right to withdraw from the research at any point.

Taking part in research may be disturbing. You must handle any emerging issues sensitively. Remember that you are not a trained therapist, and it is not your role to act as one with your participant. You must not present yourself as qualified to give psychological advice. Such inappropriate action may, in fact, be harmful to you both. Following such ethical guidelines is part of good research practice.

You have two choices if you elect to work with a participant:

Option 2

To explore the extent to which you can empathize with an aspect of your participant's experience. How much of an understanding do you have of their understanding?

or

Option 3

To explore the areas and the extent of agreement between your view and your participant's view of your jointly selected topic.

Remember that it is your responsibility to ensure that your exploration of understanding or extent of agreement is firmly grounded in appropriate background literature. It would be a good idea to produce a list of potential topics of interest within social psychology to discuss with your participant. Having jointly selected an area of interest you then need together to choose a more specific focus within the area, one which is meaningful to you both.

Some examples of potential areas of interest for both Options 2 and 3 are:

Work

Group experiences

Ethnicity

Family life

Relationships

Social interaction

Your project focus will arise from your discussions and current concerns. Below are some examples of the sorts of participants you may choose to work with and topics from which to devise a project focus.

Option 2

Colleague/
fellow-student

- work-based issue
- college-based issue
- work culture
- your department culture
- management style
- learning and/or teaching styles

Friend/partner/
relative or
housemate

- your relationship
- a personal dilemma
- a social or cultural issue

Sports team
member

- individual member's performance
- team performance

Option 3

Colleague/
fellow-student

- criteria for ensuring work groups operate effectively
- members of work team/study group/class of students, other students
- ward or group of patients or clients/students studying different degrees
- group of managers/members of staff
- different aspects of job (may be particularly useful for mentor and less experienced colleague)/ different aspects of learning or of being a student

Friend/partner/
relative or
housemate

- personal dilemmas
- types of holiday, leisure activities, career choices, radio or television programmes
- friends, relatives, colleagues
- places to live

2.4 Option 2: understanding

Interaction depends to an extent on our ability to connect with the subjectivity of others. The more able we are to understand, although not necessarily agree with, the way an event is experienced by someone else the more effective our interaction is likely to be. Theoretically this is an exploration of Kelly's sociality process, which states: 'To the extent that one person construes the construction processes of another, he [*sic*] may play a role in social process involving the other person' (Kelly, 1955, p.95)

Clearly, as Dallos (1996) highlights, understanding is very important in personal relationships. Partners' construing of themselves, each other and the nature of their relationship serves both to help them make sense of and also to shape the nature of their relationship. Kelly too emphasizes empathy: 'Instead of making our sense of what others did, we would try to understand what sense they made out of what they did' (Kelly, 1955, p.203). Understanding, usually of different aspects of experience from those involved in personal relationships, is equally important in professional relationships.

For the option to be personally useful and engaging, you need to choose someone you believe you already have some understanding of and where you would like to increase that understanding. Your choice of participant is inextricably bound up with your *area of interest* and *project focus*, as our capacity to understand is almost always context bound. That is to say, we may have a good understanding of someone in their professional or sports-team role but know little of them in their other contexts. Your choice of participant is up to you.

2.5 Option 3: agreement

The second possibility is to explore the extent to which your view of an agreed topic of interest matches with your participant's. This option is partially theoretically rooted in Kelly's notion of individuality, which states that, 'persons differ from each other in their construction of events'. However, it would be difficult to interact at all if our views were totally individual, always different from others. As Dallos (1996, section 3) makes clear, over time we may well evolve a shared construct system with those with whom we have close contact. This may be a largely shared system, or in the case of knowing someone well in only one context, such as a work colleague or a member of a sports team, a partially shared system. Similarity of construing also exists, of course, quite independently and may well go unrecognized. Kelly acknowledged such similarity by highlighting the commonality of construing: 'To the extent that one person employs a construction of experience which is similar to that employed by another, his [sic] processes are psychologically similar to the other person' (Kelly, 1955). The commonality process relates to *how* we construe our experiences. This option then partially explores the tension between the individuality and commonality processes.

This option provides you with the opportunity to explore how well your construction agrees with your participant's construction of the same aspect of your shared experience. Areas of agreement and disagreement will be highlighted during the analysis, thus opening up problem-solving potential. Ideally, you would choose to make use of this potential with your choice of both topic and participant. Although you are highly likely to have a topic in mind when inviting your participant to take part in this exploration, part of gaining informed consent is to mutually agree on an acceptable topic. And, remember to think through the relationship between your topic (which becomes your *project focus*) and your broader *area of interest* connected to social psychological issues.

3 Carrying out your project

3.1 Generating a grid

I suggest that as you generate your grid you keep notes of procedural detail, not only what you did but why and any other information which you believe may facilitate you in writing up your report.

At this stage you should have:

- elected to work alone or with a participant;

- selected one of the three options;

- chosen a topic to construe either alone or via negotiation;

- devised a project focus which is firmly grounded in PCT and relevant issues in social psychology.

ACTIVITY

Have another look (if it is still available) at the grid you produced for the activity on 'repertory grid technique' in Appendix 1. If you elected not to complete the activity at the time, it is worth doing so now to get an initial feel for the procedure. Ensure that you understand what Kelly meant by elements, constructs and triads and how triads of elements are used to externalize current constructs.

Examine the elements and constructs included in your grid. Jot down what they might reveal about your current experiencing of the people you have included as elements. If you are looking back at a grid you completed some weeks ago, reflect on this – if you were asked to complete the grid now, using the same elements, would you complete it any differently? Give the reasons for any difference or lack of change. Think also about elements and constructs which you might have included but did not. Why were they excluded? If they had been included, how would your grid be different?

Whichever option you have chosen, the grid is generated in the same way with minor variations and additions which are detailed under the specific option headings below. First, however, there is some general information relevant to all options, on elements, constructs and how to represent the relationship between the two.

3.2 Choice of elements

Your first task in generating the grid is to select a sample of elements appropriate to the chosen topic – about ten is usual, and certainly no fewer than six.

Elements are anything that gives rise to construing, they are in Thomas and Harri-Augstein's (1985) terms 'items of experience' (p.99). Your element sample needs to be as representative as possible of the topic and personally relevant to whoever is completing the grid, either yourself (Option 1), your participant (Option 2), or yourself and your participant (Option 3). Your aim, when choosing your elements, is to allow the most useful grid to be generated. Inadequate elements limit the grid's possibilities. To summarize, elements should be representative of your topic, relevant to your project focus and known reasonably well.

For example, if I'm interested in my construing of my friends, my elements will all be friends of mine, very likely from different arenas of my life. If I am interested in how I construe myself in relation to my friends, then I need to ensure that I also construe myself as an element. If, however, I am interested in my construing of what differentiates those who are my friends from those who are not, my elements will include friends, acquaintances and people well-known to me whom I do not consider friends. (For examples of ranges of elements, see Tindall, 1994, p.75 and also Alex's sample of managers on p.78.)

Other possibilities include:

People	colleagues, friends, relatives, celebrities, politicians, teachers, schoolchildren, clients, patients
Events	radio or television programmes, plays, different learning experiences, life events, work events
Interests	leisure activities, holidays, photography, career possibilities, books
Activities	jobs, job aspects, games, sports, court cases
Social entities	project teams, bands, orchestras, sports teams, schools, organizations

Source: modified from Thomas and Harri-Augstein (1985)

3.3 Eliciting constructs

Having decided on your elements, your next step is to make explicit the current construing which you and/or your participant uses to frame your chosen topic area, as represented by your elements. A construct is a personally relevant, often highly idiosyncratic, bipolar dimension involving thoughts, feelings and actions, which is used to discriminate between elements.

Constructs are most usually generated using the triadic method described in the extract in Box 1.

BOX 1   The triadic method of construct generation

The next task is to identify some of the constructs currently being used within the area of exploration. This is done by choosing any three elements and asking in what way two of the elements are similar and different from the third. I find it more useful to ask participants to identify a *difference* rather than a contrast or opposite, as in my experience these last two terms encourage people to search for some generally accepted contrast and therefore shift the emerging picture away from the personal.

The three elements to be compared can be chosen systematically or randomly. (If you are comparing, say, friends and non-friends, then, to gain the most useful information you must include a friend and non-friend in each triad.) Each element can be allocated a number and then three numbers can be chosen. Or each element can be written on a separate card, with the cards being shuffled and the top three chosen. Used cards are returned to the pack, the pack is reshuffled and the top three are chosen, and so on. This process of choosing three elements and identifying personal similarity and difference continues, ideally until the person runs out of constructs. Ten to fifteen constructs often provide a useful picture.

The similarity, which may be positively or negatively stated, is written on the left and the difference on the right. In the example below it is clear which three elements a friend I will call Nick compared. The ✕s indicate the two elements who were seen similarly, as lacking awareness, when compared with the third element ◯ who was identified as being astute.

	Elements (numbered)									
Similarity pole	**1**	**2**	**3**	**4**	**5**	**6**	**7**	**8**	**9**	**Difference pole**
Lacks awareness	✕	✕			◯					Astute

Figure 1 *Nick's comparison of elements*

In this way one of the constructs used by Nick to understand 'what is going on at work' is externalized. This procedure is repeated until the participant decides that sufficient constructs have been externalized. It is assumed that the constructs are permeable, i.e. they can and will be applied to new elements and that they do indeed represent the participant's understanding of the area. It is also assumed that the language does, to an extent, reflect the personal meaning of the construct. However many constructs are generated, it must be remembered that you are only gaining access to a sample of current constructs

Source: Tindall (1994), pp.75–6

Note also whether you or your participant generate spontaneously or thoughtfully or hesitantly, etc. Try to represent construct meanings as best you can, they do not have to be single word labels, you may find metaphors or phrases useful. Alex (see Tindall, 1994, p.80), occasionally elaborated the meaning of his constructs. For example, 'perceptive' for him at that time, with those elements, was to be 'people aware'. Similarly, 'politically malleable' was someone who 'blows in the wind'.

At this stage you should have a personally meaningful grid with an appropriate range of elements plus at least ten bipolar constructs generated in response to various element triads.

As you will remember from Appendix 1, constructive alternativism is a key feature of PCT. Our current theories (interlinked constructs) are just that, *current*, open to revision and reconstruction in the light of new experiences. Our understanding is always in the process of change. At times this change may be considerable, at others slow, or even relatively non-existent. Grids or any other method of externalizing understanding offer us a single snapshot of the continually changing flow of experience. Be aware too of the problems in representing the richness of construing via a verbal label. Consider, for instance, what assumptions about language and discourse this procedure makes.

3.4 Rating

Your next task is to consider each construct in relation to each element. Take the first construct generated and decide, working through each element in turn, whether the element is more like the similarity pole, in which case it will be allocated an X, or more like the difference pole, in which case it will be allocated an O. Your grid will now look something like Figure 2 overleaf.

It may become apparent at this stage, although it is unlikely, that some of the constructs are not applicable to some of the elements. In Kelly's terms, the constructs are beyond their 'range of convenience'.

Kelly claimed that our constructs have a 'range of convenience' (i.e. those elements for which the particular construct is meaningful) and a 'focus of convenience' (i.e. those elements for which the construct is most appropriate and therefore most useful). The construct friendly–chilly, for instance, has a wide range of convenience; it is applicable to people, places, events but not normally to appliances or novels, which would be beyond its 'range of convenience'. A slightly different construct, friendly–unfriendly, is likely to have a slightly wider range of convenience and may well be used to describe such things as computer software.

Similarity pole	Elements									Difference pole
X	James	Piers	Karen	Sue	Mary	Al	Kris	Frank	Jan	O
Lacks awareness	X	X	O	X	O	X	O	O	O	Astute
Effective	O	O	X	X	X	O	X	X	X	Fails to get things done
Not to be trusted	X	O	O	O	O	X	X	O	O	Professional
Creative, prepared to take risks	O	O	X	O	X	O	X	X	O	Limited – traditionalist
Facilitative	O	O	X	X	X	O	O	X	O	Inhibiter
Rambler	X	X	O	O	O	X	O	O	O	Clear communicator
Challenging	O	O	X	O	X	O	X	X	X	Disinterested
Socially skilled	O	O	X	O	X	O	O	X	O	Socially clumsy
Committed	O	O	X	X	O	O	X	X	X	Just a job

Figure 2 *Nick's current view of a sample of her work colleagues*

In practical terms, if an element is beyond the 'range of convenience' of a particular construct, you are unable to assign an X or O as neither is appropriate. There are two ways to deal with this:

1. You may include NA – not applicable, to highlight such a lack of fit. This gap is part of the personal pattern of meaning and should be incorporated later in the analysis and discussion.

or:

2. You may choose to refine the grid by changing elements, constructs or both. If you do exchange an existing grid element for another, you must of course allocate the new element an X or O depending on whether you experience the element as more like the construct similarity pole (X) or the difference pole (O). Similarly, if you exchange a construct you must locate each element on the new construct by the use of Xs or Os. Do not be concerned about making changes, refinement when necessary is very much part of the process.

However, if changes are made, you either need to bear in mind the original focus of the grid and ensure that any new elements or constructs are appropriate to that focus or, in the light of the experience of doing the project, change the focus of the grid.

You will need to present and discuss in your report any changes such as these which you made, so keep good notes of what you are doing and why.

Next, to gain a slightly richer and more personally relevant picture, a 1–5 ordinal scale should be used to rate each element on each construct. A rating of 1 indicates that the element is experienced as very like the similarity pole (left-hand pole) and a rating of 5 that the element is experienced as very like the difference pole (right-hand pole). A rating of 3 may mean that you experience someone or something as between the poles or fluctuating from pole to pole on the particular construct being considered. The numbers allow whoever is completing the grid to position elements in relative terms on each of the constructs and so expose a slightly more subtle picture. Your grid will now look something like Figure 3.

Construct pole rated - 1	E 1	E 2	E 3	E 4	E 5	E 6	E 7	E 8	E 9	Construct pole rated - 5
Lacks awareness C1	2	2	5	3	5	1	4	4	5	C1 Astute
Effective C2	4	4	1	1	2	5	3	2	2	C2 Fails to get things done
Not to be trusted C3	1	3	5	4	5	1	2	5	5	C3 Professional
Creative, prepared to take risks C4	4	3	1	4	1	4	2	1	5	C4 Limited – traditionalist
Facilitative C5	5	5	1	2	1	5	4	2	5	C5 Inhibiter
Rambler C6	1	1	5	4	5	1	3	4	5	C6 Clear communicator
Challenging C7	4	5	1	3	2	5	4	4	5	C7 Disinterested
Socially skilled C8	4	5	1	3	1	5	3	2	4	C8 Socially clumsy
Committed C9	5	5	1	2	3	5	2	2	2	C9 Just a job

Figure 3 Nick's rated grid

3.5 Option 1

Essentially all that you need to do is to follow the instructions above for generating a grid. As you construct your grid make notes on the following as you may find such commentary of use during analysis and for your discussion write-up:

- how readily you generate constructs;

- your rationale for the elements and constructs you choose to include;

- particular elements and constructs you decide not to include and why;

- your rationale for changes to elements, constructs or both.

3.6 Option 2

It is a good idea initially for each of you to complete a few mini-grids separately, with, say, four elements and four constructs on any topic other than the one selected for the project, in order to familiarize yourself with the process. Once your participant feels comfortable with the process of grid construction s/he needs to follow the instructions above regarding elements, constructs and ratings. If s/he needs help with the process you must be very careful not to impose your own construing on her/him. It is the **participant's** construing of the chosen topic which is required.

While your participant is engaged in completing his/her project grid it may be useful to construct your own grid on the chosen topic, to make explicit your view (current construing) of the topic before attempting to enter your participant's understanding. It would also be useful at this stage to identify and comment on aspects of your participant's view of the project topic which you believe you have an understanding of and those aspects which you do not. For example, you may believe that you understand how a colleague experiences team meetings but know little about how s/he experiences negotiating with clients. When your participant has completed their grid they present you with their grid framework which contains their named elements and constructs but *not* their ratings. You may of course discuss the meaning of any element or construct with your participant but remind them not to give away any idea of their ratings in their explanation. Now it is your turn – taking their grid framework you complete the grid 'as if' you were them. Remember the idea here is to assess the extent to which you understand the way your participant views your chosen topic.

3.7 Option 3

This involves you and your participant working collaboratively to produce a grid with agreed elements and constructs and then individually completing it. First, each of you needs to become familiar with the process by completing one or two mini-grids as suggested in Option 2 above.

The first step, before negotiating a grid, is for each of you to complete your own grid to clarify for yourselves your own view of the chosen topic. It might be interesting for each of you at this stage to also identify the aspects of the topic in which you believe you experience agreement and those in which you believe you are in disagreement. Your next task is to work up a joint skeleton grid via a process of conversation and negotiation. First, decide jointly on a suitable range of elements to represent your agreed topic. Then, following the triadic method detailed in section 3.3 above, use your chosen elements to generate mutually acceptable constructs. It is a good idea for each of you to include some, but no more than four, individual and unshared constructs, particularly if you believe that an important aspect has not been included in the joint grid. This is not essential, rather a voluntary extra which may offer additional insight into your personal views. Before separately including your individual ratings remind yourselves of the purpose of the grid. The focus for each of you is your *own* construing of the chosen topic. The final step is for each of you, working separately, to take the negotiated grid and include your own ratings of each element on each construct. It is the ratings which are compared in the analysis.

It is worth noting that analysis cuts through the fluid quality of understanding. Analysis and writing-up bring the ongoing reflexive process of understanding to a natural pause, thus offering a snapshot of current understanding. All three options offer the possibility of extending understanding beyond the grid analysis by using some of the meanings, understandings or agreements revealed in the grids to trigger further thoughts. The possible ways that such elaboration might be achieved are detailed in the analysis section below, under the heading 'conversational elaboration'.

---

4 Analysis

Your analysis should be guided by your focus. It is very easy to get carried away with a search for all possible meanings. It is only necessary to identify patterns of meaning relevant to your project focus.

4.1 Option 1

Grid patterns

Initially you need to focus on the patterns of meaning revealed in your grid, specifically those which are relevant to your project focus. Depending on your focus you may be more interested in analysing relationships between elements or constructs or the associations between elements and constructs. (For clarity, elements and constructs are given as numbers while ratings are written in full.)

First, look at the elements (grid columns). Are any construed as particularly similar or different? In Nick's grid in Figure 3, elements 1 and 2 are construed as very similar, i.e. their ratings on the generated constructs are very closely matched, there is a difference between them of only five in ratings over all constructs. Elements 7 and 9 are also viewed as fairly similar, a total difference in ratings over all constructs of thirteen. If you wish to distinguish between very similar elements you may introduce another construct at this stage on which such elements differ. Do not use a triad this time, just identify a construct which differentiates for you the two elements that you have construed as very similar. The construct label thus elicited needs to be added to the difference pole list (right-hand pole) and its personal contrast identified and added to the similarity pole list (left-hand pole). Each element must then be rated on the newly elicited construct.

In Nick's grid, elements 3, 5 and 8 are also construed as similar and very different from element 6. Interestingly, element 3 is viewed extremely positively – all ratings are either ones or fives. On the other hand, element 6 also attracts extreme ratings on all constructs bar one, but is viewed negatively.

Turning to construct patterns (grid rows) Nick, not surprisingly, experiences all those viewed as 'committed' as also 'effective', with the exception of one colleague. The corollary being that those experienced as treating work as 'just a job' also 'fail to get things done'. This may be an association worthy of elaboration (see the section on conversational elaboration below). Another clear association is that for the most part those seen as 'rambling communicators' are also construed as 'inhibitors' rather than 'facilitators', as 'socially clumsy' and 'not to be trusted'. This is useful information as it implies that this worker may link these constructs. For instance, a new colleague, initially experienced by Nick as lacking in social skills, may also then be construed as one who rambles, inhibits and is not to be trusted. Such construing is likely to affect their future interactions. Remember when searching for associations between constructs to look also for opposites or mirror images. An example from Nick's grid is the association between the constructs 'facilitative–inhibitor' and 'rambler–clear communicator', the ratings are almost all on the opposite poles, either fives and ones or twos and fours. This implies that Nick construes those as 'facilitative' to be 'clear communicators' and those who 'inhibit' to 'ramble' (positive associations), the corollaries being a negative association between 'facilitative–rambler' and 'inhibitor–clear communicator'.

One way of checking for similarity/dissimilarity is to record all the ratings given to element one, for example, on a vertical strip of paper as illustrated in Figure 4. Then run the strip across the grid noting the numerical differences between the ratings for each construct between elements 1 and 2, 1 and 3, 1 and 4, 1 and 5, 1 and 6, 1 and 7, 1 and 8 and 1 and 9. Continue with each element until all pairs of elements have been compared.

	Elements								
	1	**2**	**3**	**4**	**5**	**6**	**7**	**8**	**9**
C	2	2_0		2	5_3				
O	4	4_0		4	2_2				
N	1	3_2		1	5_4				
S	4	3_1		4	1_3				
T	5	5_0		5	1_4				
R	1	1_0		1	5_4				
U	4	5_1		4	2_2				
C	4	5_1		4	1_3				
T	5	5_0		5	3_2				
S									
Difference	5				27				

Total difference elements $1 + 2 = 5$
$1 + 5 = 27$

Figure 4 *Using Nick's grid as an example*

You could follow the same procedure for constructs, but this time the ranking strip will be horizontal and will need to be run down the grid comparing each pair of constructs across elements.

Take care not to become caught up in fragmentary understandings
– i.e. looking only at parts of the picture and neglecting the overall
patterns. You are likely to need both macro and micro understandings. Be guided by your project focus.

For Nick's grid, looking at the associations between elements and constructs in this way, it can be seen that elements 3, 5 and 8 are currently
experienced, on these nine constructs, as highly polarized in the same
direction, with the exception of element 8 on one construct ('disinterested' rather than 'challenging') and element 5 who is given a three
on the 'committed–just a job' construct. Otherwise all three are seen as
'astute', 'effective', 'professional', 'creative', 'facilitative', 'clear communicators', 'challenging', 'socially skilled' and 'committed'.

Interestingly elements 1, 2 and 6 are similarly polarized on the opposite
construct poles, they are construed as 'lacking awareness', 'failing to
get things done', 'not to be trusted' (apart from element 2 who has a
rating of three), 'limited', 'inhibitors', 'ramblers', 'disinterested', 'socially
clumsy' and treating work as 'just a job'. Elements 4, 7 and 9 are experienced differently from both the other clusters of elements. To fully explore the personal implications of this understanding of work colleagues,
we would need to know a little more about Nick and her work context.

For further examples of analysis, you could also look at Tindall (1994),
pp.78–82, for a brief analysis of Alex's single grid. You may also find it
worth commenting on the overall picture exposed by the constructs
elicited. See Tindall (1994), p.78 for an illustration of the two very different work cultures experienced by Jo and Alex and revealed via their construct choices.

Conversational elaboration

Your completed grid partially represents (according to PCT) your current
experiencing of a specific area within your personal reality. What you
need to do now, bearing in mind the caution (section 1.3), is to make
use of your reflexive awareness by conducting a constructive critical conversation with yourself about the grid. Are you aware, on reflection, of
any omissions? What are the implications of the associations revealed by
the grid? In Thomas and Harri-Augstein's (1985) terms, use the '... grid as
a vehicle for a journey into inner space' (p.110). You may wish to use
the understanding you have gained to complete further grids, including
yourself in different roles perhaps, or including your ideal self. Maybe it
would be appropriate to discuss grid findings with a trusted friend or colleague who would be prepared to offer their views. If you elect to do
this, remember that you are dealing with two personal realities and two
different ways of experiencing what is going on. To increase self-awareness and understanding you need to remain open to their views rather
than impose your reality on them or accept their reality as more valid

than yours. The purpose of elaboration is to extend understanding and there are a number of ways to achieve this. When selecting what and how you might elaborate be mindful of your project focus.

Laddering

For this option, Hinkle's (1965) laddering technique is recommended as it enables you to explore a construct identified as pertinent both to you and to your project focus, with the purpose of gaining new insight.

During your reflexive exploration of the grid, or maybe at an earlier stage in the process of grid elicitation, you are likely to be aware of constructs that might usefully be elaborated. It is likely that the construct that you decide to ladder will almost select itself. It may be one that surprised or puzzled you, or one that provoked thought, or was emphatically stated, or was problematic in some way. Of course it must also be pertinent to the purpose of the study. You can ladder up your personal construct hierarchy to core constructs – as explained and illustrated in the extract from Tindall (1994) reproduced as Appendix 2 to this chapter – or ladder down (Thomas and Harri-Augstein, 1985) by requesting that the construing become more specific. This is done by asking questions such as, 'What does it mean to be ... facilitative/limited, traditionalist/professional or whatever?' Once examples have been offered about what it means to be facilitative, for instance, then the same question is asked about the opposite pole. 'What does it mean to be an inhibitor?', for instance. This construct example may give rise to descriptions such as: 'Facilitative colleagues open up possibilities, challenge, support and offer enabling strategies, often from a different perspective. Whereas, an inhibiting colleague may be described as critical, one who closes down possibilities, destroys rather than builds.' In these ways laddering offers the possibility of a fuller exploration of the implications of constructs and thus understanding of the personal meaning of specific constructs.

4.2 Option 2

Grid patterns

Your first step is to combine the two grids. The clearest way to do this is to take a blank grid framework and split each square with a diagonal line. Next include both sets of ratings in the same divided square using two different colour pens, one for you and a different colour for your participant.

In this way you can identify the extent to which you are able to view the chosen topic 'as if' you were your participant. In addition, the completion of the combined grid should also highlight areas of understanding and lack of understanding with regard to both elements and constructs. You might want to list both elements and constructs in order of current understanding. Essentially, it is a matter of looking for patterns of understanding (as this was one of the main purposes of the option) in the combined grid.

Elements

Constructs	1	2	3	4	5	6	7	
1	3 ⟍ 3	2 ⟍ 1	3 ⟍ 2	1 ⟍ 1	5 ⟍ 4	4 ⟍ 3	(4)	
2	1 ⟍ 2	1 ⟍ 1	3 ⟍ 1	2 ⟍ 2	2 ⟍ 1	5 ⟍ 2	(7)	Constructs differences
3	5 ⟍ 4	5 ⟍ 4	4 ⟍ 2	2 ⟍ 3	2 ⟍ 1	1 ⟍ 4	(9)	
4	2 ⟍ 2	3 ⟍ 3	1 ⟍ 1	5 ⟍ 4	5 ⟍ 5	4 ⟍ 4	(1)	
Element differences	(2)	(2)	(5)	(2)	(3)	(7)		

Figure 5 *Part of a combined grid*

Using the partially completed grid in Figure 5 as an illustration, there appears to be a good understanding of elements 1, 2, 4 and 5, within the limitations of the grid. Elements 6 and 3 appear to be less well understood. Similarly, there appears to be a good understanding of the way the person uses construct 4, and a reasonable understanding of the use of construct 1. However, it seems that the uses of constructs 3 and 2 are not well understood.

There may well be connections between the areas of understanding and misunderstanding. For instance, maybe you have little experience on which to base your understanding of your participant's contact with elements 6 and 3 (if they are people) or, if they are roles, of your participant's performance within those roles. It is up to you to identify connections and diversities relevant to your purpose, within the combined grid.

It may be interesting to compare areas of understanding and lack of understanding with the comments you made immediately before completing the grid. Were you right, or has the grid highlighted unexpected areas and degrees of understanding? Similarly, if you completed your own grid on the project topic before attempting the understanding grid, you may wish to comment on the degree of similarity between your own view and your participant's. Was a huge or slight shift required in order for you to understand your participant's understanding?

Conversational elaboration

It is useful, highly appropriate and very much in keeping with Kelly's theory that you offer feedback to your participant. This is best done in the form of a conversation which may, with permission, be audio-recorded. If recording is not possible for some reason, make notes of the key points of the conversation.

Your feedback discussion needs to be dealt with sensitively. Remember the focus is on the extent of understanding *you* managed to achieve. Remember, too, the ethical requirements presented in section 2.3. You are likely to learn more about this if you discuss it with your participant, rather than work on it alone. However if your participant declines your offer of feedback you clearly have no choice but to work alone.

PCT focuses on the individual's personal construction of reality which is inevitably influenced by the personal meaning attached to the social context. It is appropriate at this point to take a wider focus and consider the explanations a social constructionist might offer.

Consider also the interaction between personal and social construction and how they might mesh. You are likely to find reading Wetherell and Maybin (1996), and Tindall, 1994, pp.86–90 useful at this point.

Do remember that you are dealing with your participant's personal reality, which is probably different from, but no less or more valid than, yours. However, occasionally one of you, particularly if you are in the role of teacher, manager or similar, may have a more institutionally valid view. If this is the case, be aware of the power differential. Proceed with sensitivity, allow your participant to comment on meanings and personal links between constructs apparent to them from their own grid and the degree of understanding you have managed to achieve which is apparent from the combined grid. If your participant does not identify and verbalize obvious connections made explicit by completion of the grids, then it is not necessarily your role to voice them. Emergent implications may be sensitively checked out with your participant, but be aware of the possibility of harm. The grid may highlight sensitive issues that your participant chooses not to acknowledge at this time. Use the feedback session as an opportunity to explore the personal meanings underlying the verbal labels and to share commentary about your need to understand your participant's view and the possibility of learning from each other. You may find the laddering technique outlined in section 4.1 particularly useful in highlighting your individual personal meanings. It might be useful to ask your participant to comment on the degree of understanding they think you have in the chosen area from their experience of you. Does this match with the grid? Are there any surprises? What explanations can you suggest for the degree and areas of match and mismatch? Remember that our understanding of any one person differs across roles and contexts. In using the combined grid in this way as a basis for constructive conversation, understanding can be enhanced.

4.3 Option 3

Grid patterns

Although this option is exploring the extent to which you and your participant's views of the chosen topic harmonize – that is, the focus is on the degree and areas of agreement between your views rather than on understanding – the procedure outlined above for Option 2 is also appropriate for this option. Follow the instructions above (in section 4.2) for combining the grids, calculating differences and identifying areas of similarity and difference. However, as the focus is on agreement within your independently rated grids, it is a matter of identifying patterns of agreement within the combined grid.

Conversational elaboration

The conversational elaboration procedure is also similar to Option 2. However, as this option involves collaboration, the agreement patterns revealed by the combining of the negotiated grids ideally should be jointly identified. Remember the caution detailed in section 1.3, the ethical guidance given in section 2.3, and the fact that you are dealing with different personal constructions of the topic. Neither is any more 'correct' than the other, although in an institutional setting one view may be more institutionally valid.

PCT focuses on the individual's personal construction of reality which is inevitably influenced by the personal meaning attached to the social context. It is appropriate at this point to take a wider focus and consider the explanations a social constructionist might offer.

Consider also the interaction between personal and social construction and how they might mesh. You are likely to find reading Wetherell and Maybin (1996), and Tindall (1994, pp.86–90), useful at this point.

The next step is to jointly engage in constructive exploration of the patterns revealed. Do explore the personal meanings that each of you attaches to your negotiated construct labels. The laddering technique detailed in section 4.1 may be useful here. Similar use of the same terms may not necessarily imply agreement, while apparently different construct labels may have very similar underlying meanings. If you both agree, it may be useful to audio-record this conversation. If recording is a problem, keep field notes of your conversation. It is important that each of you remains open to the other's views, whether or not you are in agreement. It is through such open conversation, which is likely to highlight areas of agreement and disagreement and your different understandings of negotiated aspects of the grid topic, that the problem-solving potential inherent in this option may be realized. At the very least you will have been exposed to each other's understanding and the possibility of identifying an area of current disagreement, which you may jointly elect to work on. It would be useful during this constructive exploration of agreement to share your initial individual grids to reveal your unnegotiated views and the areas of expected agreement and disagreement. Note the similarities and differences between your views as represented in your initial grids. Consider omissions, which are often very informative, as well as inclusions. What view of the topic, in a general sense, does each of the grids suggest?

Compare your initial grids with the negotiated grid. What are the similarities and differences? Is the negotiated grid more similar than might be expected to one of your initial grids? If so why might that be? Were you both aware that one of you was shifting more than the other during the negotiation? Negotiation by definition distorts personal reality somewhat, at least temporarily, while also offering the potential for new understandings. During this joint exploration of the patterns revealed in the grids, a particular construct may be highlighted as significant. If you wish to explore the individual meaning of this construct further, it may be useful for each of you to use the laddering technique detailed in section 4.1.

5 The write-up

Your write-up of the project should be divided into the following sections.

Title

Your aim here is to provide the reader with a clear indication of what your project is about.

Abstract

This should provide a succinct summary of the purpose of your study, what you did, what you found, and your interpretations.

Introduction

The intention in this section is to provide the background to your study. You should initially set the general context, and go on to present the theoretical and personal rationale for your study. The aspects of Kelly's PCT relevant to your particular study need to be presented and you need to make clear to the reader the ways in which PCT is relevant and appropriate to your study. Although PCT is relevant to both the process and content of this project, you should have grounded the content in additional social psychological theories and research. Relevant aspects of these also need to be presented here. The rationale you provide for your study should readily lead to your specific *project focus* and be grounded in your chosen *area of interest*, which should be clearly stated at the end of the introduction.

Method

This section should provide sufficient detail to allow the reader to replicate your study. The following areas need to be addressed in an order appropriate to the study.

Design – make the scale of the study clear. Justify your use of PCT grids and elaboration techniques by presenting the reasons why you considered them to be particularly appropriate tools with which to explore your project focus.

Participants – details of participants relevant to your study should be presented. Do not forget yourself as participant. Pseudonyms are often used to preserve anonymity. This may not be possible for you of course and may be problematic also for your participant, particularly if they have a clear relationship with you. You may of course use actual names as long as you have your participant's permission.

Procedure – a step by step chronological account of exactly what you did including the inviting of participants if relevant, through to detail of grid generation, the organization of feedback and grid elaboration plus the type of analysis selected. Make use of any procedural notes kept. Aim to be clear yet concise.

Ethics – details of how you gained informed consent, facilitated negotiation of topic to construe, if necessary, and your debrief procedure should be included here. Also include any procedural issue which you incorporated to democratize the process of conducting your project (see Tindall, 1994, pp.152–6).

Analysis and discussion

Include the completed grids, plus any notes made either before the grids were generated or during the elaboration process, as appendices. Remember to refer the reader to the appropriate appendix.

This section presents the personal patterns of meanings, areas and degrees of understanding or agreement revealed as they relate to your project focus. You are not required to present all patterns and links, only those which relate to your purpose. Do ensure that you support your analysis with illustrations from the grid and your elaboration process.

Option 1

Look also at what additional meaning has been revealed by your choice of elements to include and those which might have been included but were not. Similarly, what about the general picture exposed by your choice of constructs? Which construct did you choose to ladder and why? How does your choice link with your focus? Was your understanding extended via elaboration? If so, how?

Option 2

Remember your analysis should be guided by your project focus.

To what extent were you able to understand your participant's view of your chosen topic? Identify and justify, with grid illustrations, apparent areas of understanding and lack of understanding. Is there a pattern of understanding evident? How does your analysis link with the notes you made prior to grid completion on expected areas or degree of understanding? It may also be worth commenting on the meaning revealed by your participant's choice of elements and constructs. If you elected to complete your own grid prior to the understanding grid, do your elements and constructs reveal a similar or very different view of the topic? What does this degree of match imply?

You may also want to include some analysis of new understandings reached during your feedback conversation. If so, support your claims with verbatim quotes or notes you made at the time if you did not record the conversation.

Option 3

Remember to structure your analysis around your project focus. How well does your view harmonize with your participant's? Justify the level and areas of both agreement and disagreement with illustrations from the combined grid. Is there a pattern apparent in the areas of agreement and disagreement? Bear in mind the difference between verbal labels and underlying personal meanings.

Does the grid analysis match with your pre-grid comments or are there unexpected findings? What views are revealed in your individual grids, completed prior to the negotiated grid? Compare the combined grid with each individual grid. Are any patterns evident? Does the combined grid reflect one individual's grid more than any other? If so, why might this be?

Include any new understandings gained during your conversational exploration of the patterns revealed. Support any claims to new understandings with illustrative verbatim quotes or notes you made during the feedback session. Include also any new agreement insights made explicit by laddering or other elaboration techniques.

All options

Your discussion should make links to both the theoretical and personal reasons for doing the study presented in the introduction. Link findings to previous work or identify them as novel to your study. You should critically consider the personal meanings revealed, present possible explanations and discuss their implications. Remember Kelly's notion of constructive alternativism. Make sure when discussing your findings that you acknowledge them to be *your* constructions, your interpretations, not fact.

Reflexive and method issues

Include a brief reflexive analysis which '... is about acknowledging the central position of the researcher in the construction of knowledge' (Tindall, 1994, p.151). Consider how you have influenced the research throughout the entire process, from choice of particular project option and specific purpose, to particular emphases and selection of patterns and links during analysis and discussion. Remember that constructions are fluid and should be judged only in terms of their usefulness. Comment on how you as researcher and the procedures you adopted shaped your project and final write-up. Reflexivity is a central concept within PCT so make links to the theoretical background

Next consider method issues. What do you consider to be the strengths and limitations of your study? To what extent were your personal goals for the study realized? What problems did you encounter? How did your choice of tool of analysis affect the process and thus the outcome? How might you modify the study if you were to repeat it? Has your study highlighted any ideas for further work?

You now need to step outside the framework within which you have been working and consider PCT in the context of social psychology. Specifically, you need to locate and evaluate PCT in the context of other social psychological perspectives. How might other perspectives react to the assumptions, methods and theoretical concepts of PCT? A good starting-point might be for you to think about the notion of personal construction in relation to social construction.

References

Provide a full reference list, using the conventional format, of all texts cited.

Appendices

Include clearly labelled copies of your grid(s), comments etc. as appendices.

References

Banister, P. Burman, E. Parker, I. Taylor, M. and Tindall, C. (1994) *Qualitative Methods in Psychology: A Research Guide*, Buckingham, Open University Press.

Dallos, R. (1996) 'Creating relationships', in Miell, D. and Dallos, R. (eds) *Social Interaction and Personal Relationships*, London, Sage/The Open University.

Hinkle, D. (1965) 'The change of personal constructs from the viewpoint of a theory of construct implications', unpublished PhD thesis, Ohio State University.

Kelly, G. (1955) *The Psychology of Personal Constructs*, Volumes 1 and 2, New York, Norton (reprinted by Routledge 1991).

Stevens, R. (1996) 'The reflexive self: an experiential perspective', in Stevens, R. (ed.) (1996).

Stevens, R. (ed.) (1996)*Understanding the Self*, London, Sage/The Open University.

Thomas, L.F. and Harri-Augstein, E.S. (1985) *Self-Organised Learning: Foundations of a Conversational Science for Psychology*, London, Routledge.

Thompson, B. (1975) 'Nursery teachers' perceptions of their pupils: an exploratory study', in Whitehead, J.M. (ed.) *Personality and Learning*, vol.1. London, Hodder and Stoughton.

Tindall, C. (1994) 'Personal construct approaches', Chapter 5 in Banister *et al.* (1994).

Wetherell, M. and Maybin, J. (1996) 'The distributed self: a social constructionist perpective', in Stevens, R. (ed) (1996).

Further reading

The following provide further reading on PCT and the use of this research method.

Burr, V. and Butt, T. (1992) *Invitation to Personal Construct Psychology*, London, Whurr.

Cross, M.C. and Watts, M.H. (1997) 'Personal construct contributions to the conceptualisation and treatment of post traumatic stress disorder', *Counselling Psychology Review*, vol.12, no.4, pp.158–69.

Dallos, R. (1991) *Family Belief Systems, Therapy and Change*, Open University Press, Buckingham.

Duck, S. (1994) *Meaningful Relationships*, London, Sage.

Fournier, V. and Payne, R. (1994) 'Change in self construction during the transition from university to employment: a personal construct psychology approach', *Journal of Occupational and Organisational Psychology*, vol.67, pp.297–314.

Fransella, F. and Dalton, P. (1990) *Personal Construct Counselling in Action*, London, Sage.

Fransella, F. and Thomas, L. (eds) (1988) *Experimenting with Personal Construct Psychology*, London, Routledge.

Houston, J.C. (1998) *Making Sense with Offenders Personal Constructs, Therapy and Change*, London, Wiley.

Klion, R.E. and Pfenninger, D.T. (1996) 'Role construction and Vietnam era combat veterans', special issue on traumatic stress, *Journal of Constructivist Psychology*, vol.9, no.2, pp.127–38.

Smith, J.A. (1990) 'Transforming identities: a repertory grid case study of the transition to motherhood', *British Journal of Medical Psychology*, vol.63, pp.239–53.

Smith, J.A. (1995) 'Repertory grids: an interactive case study perspective', in Smith, J.A., Harré, R. and Langenhove, L.V. *Rethinking Methods in Psychology*, London, Sage.

Vinney, L.L. (1996) 'A personal construct model of crisis intervention counselling for adult clients', special issue on traumatic stress, *Journal of Constructivist Psychology*, vol.9, no.12, pp.109–26.

Appendix 1: Kelly's personal construct theory (PCT)

George Kelly was an American psychologist and psychotherapist and one of the founders in the 1950s of the Association for Humanistic Psychology. It is probably true to say that his influence has been greater in the UK than in his own country, largely because of the enthusiasm of two British clinical psychologists, Don Bannister and Fay Fransella, for his ideas. Kelly's work has had a particular appeal to clinical psychologists in the UK where training has tended to be experimental and research-oriented. Qualified clinicians often encounter difficulty in applying this approach when confronted with the messy and complex problems of their clients. It is hard then to focus only on what is observable (as their training encouraged) and not get drawn into trying to make sense of their clients' experience. Kelly's approach provides them with a solution to the tension between the two worlds of their training and of their clients in the forms of a theory (personal construct theory) and, in particular, a method (the repertory grid) which promises to do justice to them both. Kelly's approach makes it possible to chart the nature of each person's world as she or he experiences it: but it makes it possible to elicit this from each person individually, rather than by imposing pre-set categories upon their experience.

Part of Kelly's particular appeal is that he spans the divide between cognitive and phenomenological psychology. On the one hand, he offers an 'outside', general way of understanding the way people make sense of the world. On the other, he provides a means of understanding and gaining access to the standpoint of a particular experience.

The main concept in Kelly's theory, as its name suggests, is *personal constructs*. These are the bipolar dimensions which constitute the discriminations we make in our experience of the world. So one way in which a particular person may classify a specific experience, for example, is as 'pleasant' as opposed to 'unpleasant'; or an ageing hippie may think of it as 'groovy' as opposed to 'square'. A construct has a focus and range of convenience. This means it may apply especially to some aspects of our world, be peripheral to others, and to yet others (which are outside its range of convenience) it may not apply at all. 'Tame–savage' might be used by a person to classify dogs, for example, but it is less likely to be applied when distinguishing between theories in psychology (though it might be by some people!). It is important to realize that Kelly is not talking about the concepts a person has but rather the key dimensions of discrimination which underlie his or her experience of the world. Most people will not be consciously aware of what constructs they are using to make sense of their experience. A construct is best thought of, Kelly suggests, as a 'reference axis devised ... for establishing a personal orientation toward the various events (encountered)'. A person can use this 'portable device for ordering symbols along scales, for placing events into categories, or for defining classes in the various familiar ways that suit his [*sic*] needs ... the construct is much more clearly a psychological guidance than it is either a limited collection of things or a common essence distilled out of them' (Kelly, 1979, p. 11).

The idea of constructs becomes clearer if we consider one of the main methods which Kelly devised to find out what constructs a person is using – the repertory grid technique. You might like to try a limited version of this.

ACTIVITY

Repertory grid technique

Think of five people you know who are (for the purpose of this exercise) fairly different kinds of people and write down their names. These are 'elements'. (By elements Kelly refers to any object, person or aspect of your personal world.) Now take three of these people (or elements) and think of a way in which two of them are alike and the other one is different. (For example, Ted and Jane might be seen as 'good fun' but Peter as the opposite, as a 'wet blanket'). Then continue with another combination of three elements (taken from your sample of five) and find a way in which two of these are alike and the third one is different. Keep on going until you have exhausted all possible combinations of three elements from your set of five. In the example I give above, the first bipolar construct is 'good fun–wet blanket'. You may well manage to extract ten or more bipolar constucts of your own, for there are ten possible combinations of three elements from a set of five, and you may want to generate more than one construct in the case of some triads.

Note that these constructs are *individual* to you. No-one suggested which particular constructs you should use. They were generated by the ways in which you distinguished between the people in your set, They provide a sample of the kinds of construct which you typically use when construing people. We would of course need to elicit quite a few more in order to get a proper idea of the way you see others.

What would also be interesting to add to an activity like this would be to work out the ways in which your constructs interrelate with each other. It might be the case, for example, that whenever you use the construct 'physically attractive–unattractive' you also tend to apply the construct 'arrogant–sensitive'. If so, this might indicate that you tend to see attractive people as arrogant. Before doing the grid, you may, not have been aware of this association in the ways you construe. Generating constructs and analysing a construct grid (i.e. of the repertory of constructs that you use) can often bring surprises. It can also open up understanding of your own or someone else's behaviour. Knowing how constructs are related may help us understand why a person persists in a particular kind of behaviour. For example, suppose Sarah is constantly criticized for being unreliable. If we were to investigate her construct system, we might find that the construct 'unreliable–reliable' was strongly related to the constructs 'spontaneous–predictable' and 'interesting–boring'. Although she may want to become more reliable, she may find it difficult because such a change implicitly carries with it the danger that she will become boringly predictable.

As you can see from these examples, Kelly did not think of constructs as operating in isolation but as being *organized* or interrelated. One way to explore the organization of the constructs a person uses is to follow the strategy above and see how they are interrelated in the ways in which they are used.

Some constructs are more *central* than others. There is a technique for finding out which are the more central ones called 'laddering' (developed by Hinkle, 1965), which is illustrated in the following activity.

Laddering   ACTIVITY

Select one of the constructs you elicited in the previous activity. Ask yourself on which side of the bipolar construct you would prefer to be (e.g. if it was 'organized–disorganized', perhaps you might prefer 'organized'). Then decide why you prefer this, eliciting a higher order construct in the process (e.g. perhaps you prefer 'organized' because it means being efficient. so 'being inefficient–being efficient' becomes your higher order construct). Repeat this process with the new construct and so on until you can go no further.

The higher up the hierarchy a construct is, the more central it is for that person's functioning. Kelly considered that if central constructs come under threat of invalidation this arouses a strong emotional reaction. So if one of the central characteristics of the person I see myself to be is 'tolerance', and someone accuses me of 'intolerance', I will feel as if my whole identity is under attack and may try desperately to justify myself.

Another way in which constructs vary is in their degree of *permeability*. This refers to the degree to which a construct is open to change and development through experience.

Think for a moment whether your construct 'educated–uneducated' has changed as a result of your studies.

Before a person embarks upon higher-level study, for example, he or she may often think that education is a matter of acquiring facts and knowledge. Later there may be realization that a more significant feature is a style of critical and analytic thinking.

Although, as we have seen, the pattern of constructs a person uses is essentially individual, there will, of course, be considerable overlap with the constructs which other people use. And it is on such *commonality*, as Kelly terms it, that communication depends. There is a considerable amount of evidence (see Duck, 1973) that we like people who construe things in much the same way as we do. This is probably because the fact that they do so helps us to validate our model of the world and, as our construction of the world to a large extent constitutes our identity, the latter also receives support. It may also, of course, be easier to communicate with them. (For the use of personal construct theory in understanding relationships, see Dallos, 1996.)

In this brief overview, I have indicated some of the key ideas in Kelly's theory of personal constructs. In fact, he published this in two volumes in which (perhaps reflecting his background in mathematics) he presented the theory in a formal fashion with a fundamental postulate and a set of corollaries developing from that. The fundamental postulate he expressed as 'a person's processes are psychologically channelized by the ways in which he [sic] anticipates events' (1955, p.46). (In other words, a person comes to process information about the world in terms of how he or she anticipates events will occur.) The corollaries each encapsulate the kinds of feature we have already considered, such as the dichotomous or bipolar nature of constructs, individuality, organization, commonality, and the extension and modulation of constructs through experience.

Kelly's approach not only offers a way of understanding and getting access to the way in which a person understands the world, but also emphasizes the active, constructive nature of experience. A premise underlying his theory is the idea of *constructive alternativism*. He assumes that people have considerable autonomy in the ways in which they can construe: there are usually alternative ways of construing open to us and, in this way, we have a part to play in ourselves determining the nature of our experience. As Kelly expresses it: 'Man [sic] creates his own ways of seeing the world in which he lives; the world does not create them for him' (1955, p.12). Events 'are subject to as great a variety of constructions as our wits will enable us to contrive. ... all our present perceptions are open to question and reconsideration ... even the most obvious occurrences of everyday life might appear utterly transformed if we were inventive enough to construe them differently' (1970, p.1). Kelly sees the person as developing constructs through active exploration, questioning and testing of the world. In this respect, the approach of the person is analogous to that of the scientist, for '... Both seek to anticipate events. Both have their theories, in terms of which they attempt to structure the current occurrences. Both hypothesize. Both observe. Both reluctantly revise their predictions in the light of what they observe ...' (1980, p.24).

[...]

The notion of 'constructs' holds the promise of providing a relatively precise way of conceptualizing and assessing the ways in which a person attributes meanings to the world. The danger is that constructs are easily reified (or made a thing of) and it is arguable as to how far eliciting constructs can reveal the complex interrelated fabric and fluid richness of subjective experience. But at least constructs are based on the distinctions an individual actually makes, rather than being (as is the case with personality inventories and attitude scales) measures imposed on a person as a result of whatever particular test happens to be used.

Kelly also makes the point that emotion arises from the ways in which we construe. So, as we noted earlier, anxiety may be aroused when central constructs are under threat. [...] Personal construct therapy focuses on modifying the way a client construes the world. Kelly found that a typical problem for many of his patients was that their constructs had become too fixed and rigid. The therapist's job, according to Kelly, is to encourage new ways of construing which may 'work better'.

Source: Stevens (1996), pp.162–6

References

Dallos, R. (1996) 'Creating relationships: patterns of actions and beliefs', in Miell, D. and Dallos, R. (eds) *Social Interaction and Personal Relationships*, London, Sage/The Open University.

Duck, S. (1973) *Personal Relationships and Personal Constructs: A Study of Friendship Formation*, London, Wiley.

Hinkle, D.N. (1965) 'The change of personal constructs from the viewpoint of a theory of implications', unpublished PhD thesis, Ohio State University.

Kelly, G. (1955) *The Psychology of Personal Constructs*, Vols. 1 and 2, New York, Norton.

Kelly, G. (1970) 'A brief introduction to personal construct theory', in Bannister, D. (ed.) *Perspectives in Personal Construct Theory*, London, Academic Press.

Kelly, G. (1979) 'Humanistic methodology in psychological research', in Maher, B. (ed.) *Clinical Psychology and Personality*, The Selected Papers of George Kelly, New York, Krieger.

Kelly, G. (1980) 'The psychology of optimal man', in Landfield, A.W. and Leitner, L.M. (eds) *Personal Construct Psychology: Psychotherapy and Personality*, London, Wiley.

Stevens R. (1996) 'The reflexive self: an experiential perspective', in Stevens, R. (ed.) *Understanding the Self*, London, Sage/The Open University.

Appendix 2: Laddering

Laddering (Hinkle 1965) is a particular style of interviewing which allows constructs to be revealed ... It may be used in addition to the grid or independently using constructs that crop up in conversations. It needs to be used wisely and cautiously (see Rowe 1988) and only when the participant is willing and keen to gain a deeper understanding. Often the grid gives rise to surface (subordinate) constructs that are not generally applicable. They have implications, but fewer than core constructs, which frame our reality as they are central to our being. Often subordinate constructs are sufficient. Laddering, however, not only allows elaborations of a more personal framework but also illuminates how constructs are personally (hierarchically) integrated, and has the advantage of being able to identify which of the revealed constructs is more important, thus offering a better understanding of how the person frames their reality.

We move up the hierarchy from subordinate constructs to those that form the core of our value system by asking where the person would prefer to be located on a particular construct and why. This is best achieved by using a conversational style, responding directly to their comments each time (rather than repeating the question why, which often feels interrogational). Occasionally laddering works neatly, when co-researchers move from initially stated superficial constructs through to more psychological core constructs fundamental to the person's understanding. Often this is not the case, and core constructs may be difficult to verbalize for a variety of reasons. Rather than climbing up the ladder of the hierarchy we can climb down to more subordinate constructs by pyramiding (Landfield 1971). This is done by asking the question 'What does it mean to be ...?' (organized, for example).

Alex and I used the laddering technique to try to gain a better understanding of what he means by 'political malleability'. We noted that he had put himself on the extreme position of less politically malleable. I began by asking what advantages there are to being less politically malleable.

A: Not a lot (said with a laugh) – I feel a bit more virtuous but it doesn't do a lot of good at the end of the day ... sometimes I feel things are right ... If I was politically malleable I'd have to go against my conscience. I'm not as politically malleable as some, but I'm not fixed – some of our managers duck and weave to stay in power ... that's their main aim in life.

CT: It's not yours?

A: I'm happy to be part of a team – to influence what's going on. If something is wrong I'm prepared to stand up against it, to put it right. I don't seek power for power's sake.

CT: Why don't you seek power?

A: Those who are power driven have a narrow, limited view ... some people need power.

CT: You'd prefer to put it right?

A: Yes ... although it doesn't necessarily win many friends – it's seen as a negative position. I'd prefer a more positive job. People have said to me 'I wouldn't have your job'.

CT: Is there anything positive about 'putting it right', about your position?

A: It helps achieve the company's aims.

CT: Which are?

A: To lower costs, to offer better value for money – which would secure more jobs and satisfy customers.

We now have a fuller view of what Alex means by politically malleable, although we have moved to a more pragmatic rather than psychological construct. It is tied up with power seeking and the consequent limitations of view. He experiences those in power as generating problems, ones that he has to 'stand up against' and 'put right' for the good of the organization and his conscience. His stated aim aligns with the company's aims, to lower costs and thus secure more jobs and to satisfy customers. In contrast, he construes the politically malleable as mainly aiming to stay in power. Although his stance does not 'necessarily win many friends' we can see that he and others construe this negativity as at least partly to do with his position. At least one of the sources of his frustration at work is now clearer.

Source: Tindall (1994), pp.82–3.

References

Banister, P. Burman, E. Parker, I. Taylor, M. and Tindall, C. (1994) *Qualitative Methods in Psychology: A Research Guide*, Buckingham, Open University Press.

Hinkle, D. (1965) 'The change of personal constructs from the viewpoint of a theory of construct implications', unpublished PhD thesis, Ohio State University.

Landfield, A.W. (1971) *Personal Construct Systems in Psychotherapy*, New York, Rand McNally.

Rowe, D. (1988) *The Successful Self*, London, Fontana.

Tindall, C. (1994) 'Personal construct approaches', Chapter 5 in Banister *et al.* (1994).

CHAPTER 7

SOCIAL REPRESENTATIONS OF GENDER IN THE MEDIA: QUANTITATIVE AND QUALITATIVE CONTENT ANALYSIS

by Nicola Morant

Contents

Introduction: overview and requirements

This project involves a primarily socio-cultural level of analysis. It uses the theory of social representations as a framework and the methodology of content analysis. This is a technique used by social psychologists and other social scientists to analyse a variety of material including individual interviews, discussion groups, observations of behaviour in natural settings, written texts and visual images presented on television. In this project you will be introduced to some of the various ways of conducting content analysis. You will use a combination of methods to analyse your material, combining both qualitative and quantitative approaches.

The material you will be using to conduct this project is printed media output. The media are increasingly becoming a focus of study for social psychologists interested in developing a more social and less individual-based form of social psychology. The topic you will be investigating is gender. Through analysis of magazine material, you will explore the meanings associated with femininity and masculinity that circulate in society.

Requirements

Part A of this material, 'Preliminary reading', is designed to equip you with all the theoretical and methodological knowledge that you will need to carry out this project.

All the instructions for carrying out the project are included in Part B, 'Conducting the project'. However, you should not start work on Part B until you have finished the preparatory reading. For this project you will be using gender-targeted magazines as your data source, so you will need to get hold of some recent copies of women's and/or men's general interest magazines. Part C contains some suggestions for variations of this project, including historical and cross-cultural comparisons, and an analysis of representations of health and illness in the daily press.

You will probably find that the most time-consuming parts of this project are the preparatory reading and the analysis of your data. However, compared with some other projects, the process of data collection is relatively quick.

PART A: PRELIMINARY READING

1 Theoretical orientation: the theory of social representations

The theory of social representations originates from French social psychology, and in particular the work of Serge Moscovici (1976, 1984). Moscovici was interested in the dissemination of psychoanalytic ideas into 1950s' French society, and was critical of the individualistic and cognitive approaches which dominated English language social psychology from the 1960s to the mid-1980s. He set out to develop a theory that would revive 'the social' in social psychology by focusing on shared and collective processes. For Moscovici, society is the focus of study rather than simply the backdrop to individual-based research. Social representations theory is essentially a theory of social knowledge, where 'knowledge' is defined broadly as not only factual information but shared belief systems and taken-for-granted social practices. Its focus is on the circulation of meanings and understandings in late modern societies characterized by diversity and an explosion of mass media and communication channels. The strength of the theory lies in its ability to conceptualize both the agency of individuals and the power of society, and to capture the ways in which they interact. Together with discursive psychology and social identity theory, the theory of social representations forms part of a significant shift towards more social approaches within contemporary English language social psychology.

The main features of the theory of social representations that are relevant to this project are summarized below:

- Social representations are common-sense theories of the world, or branches of knowledge about broad themes such as illness, women, the environment, AIDS or science. Social representations are more than the cognitive representations which exist in people's heads. They are often described as 'floating' in society. What is meant by this is that they exist at both individual and collective levels, pervading all aspects of our social life and of society. They can be detected in the talk and actions of individuals and also at a broader level in society; for example, in the media, in government policies, or in the organization of social institutions such as schools or health services.

- Social representations theory is a multi-level theory which attempts to integrate individual and interpersonal domains of analysis into socio-cultural levels of understanding. Studies usually draw on a range of methods which offer the different perspectives needed for multi-levelled analysis (for example, in-depth interviews with individuals, group discussions, analysis of media output and analysis of historical texts).

- It is through social representations that people, groups and societies make sense of the world in which they live. Social representations aid communication, allowing us to agree broadly *what* we are talking about (for example, science), even if we do not agree on specific issues (for example, government funding of scientific research). Social representations are lived out in social interaction. For example, those who hold a social representation of AIDS which involves a belief that it is predominant in one particular sub-group of society may avoid close contact with those they suspect are the main carriers of the HIV virus, such as young, gay men.

- Social representations can be thought of as the broad belief systems that underpin attitudes. However, compared to theories of attitudes, social representations theory attempts to provide a more *social* understanding of people's beliefs based on a social constructionist perspective. There are various forms of social constructionism (Gergen, 1985; Potter, 1996a; Sarbin and Kitsuse, 1994), but they are united by a basic assumption that rather than there being an objective reality 'out there', individuals and societies play an active part in constructing the world in which we live. Our understanding of any phenomenon in our social world – mental illness, adolescence, the royal family, even our sense of self – is constructed through language and communication, social practices, cultural beliefs and social institutions such as the media, the education system, and the law. It is precisely because meanings are socially constructed that social representations of phenomena, such as gender, change over time and vary from one society to another. The theory of social representations considers the beliefs of individuals to be importantly shaped by historical, social and cultural factors.

- One consequence of this approach is that social representations theory cannot provide universal or generalizable understandings. Because social representations develop within a specific social, historical and cultural context unique to a particular society at a particular point in time, the findings of social representations research cannot be generalized to other societies or historical times. (This comment also applies to many other approaches in modern social psychology.) However, this is not to say that such non-universal research is of no value; if social psychologists are interested in how we construct ourselves in Britain, then social representations theory and research provides a very rich, in-depth understanding of aspects of this. If we want to understand similar issues within the context of Japan, for example, we must recognize that different cultural, historical and social factors are at play.

- Social representations are generated and transformed in the activities of daily social life – for example, in the conversations people have over lunch; in the ways people interact with each other; in the reporting of news events on television and in the newspapers, etc. In modern society the media plays a crucial role in this circulation of ideas and in the development of new social representations. It transforms novel, unfamiliar or abstract concepts such that they make sense in terms of the existing stock of lay knowledge. Discussions of what we saw on television the night before or what we have read in the newspaper form a large part of our daily 'chat'. Many of us rely on the media to inform us about topics of which we have no direct personal experience – genetic engineering, or the developing world, for example. Analysing media output is thus one of many possible ways of detecting the social representations that circulate in our society. Social representations are both produced and reflected by the media. There is a complex and continual interplay between the ideas presented in the media and how they are taken on board, rejected, translated and negotiated by real people in ways that make sense for them (Livingstone, 1996). It is this active interaction between media output and its audience that makes the media a valid and important object of study for social psychology.

BOX I   The example of AIDS

An example of this dynamic interaction between the media, its audience and social institutions is the development of social representations of AIDS. When AIDS was first identified in Britain in the mid-1980s, medical understanding of the disease was limited and confused. The media played an important role in shaping lay knowledge and beliefs about what AIDS was and how it was transmitted. AIDS was often represented as 'the gay plague'. Gradually however, as medical knowledge became clearer, as AIDS was identified in the heterosexual community and as gay men reacted to stigmatization, media representations changed. Gay rights activists, health campaigners and the spread of the illness into other social groups all played a part in transforming social representations of AIDS as 'the gay plague' into representations which conceptualized AIDS as a disease that could affect anybody if they practised certain high-risk activities. (For an interesting and readable discussion of the social meaning of AIDS see Sontag, 1988.)

As social psychology has expanded in recent decades beyond individual and interpersonal domains of analysis, to incorporate more socio-cultural understandings, the media has become a topic of increasing interest for the discipline (Livingstone and Lunt, 1994; Rose, 1998). Media research provides many theories and approaches to studying the media, but as *social psychologists* we need a theoretical approach which allows us to study both media output *and* its relationships to individuals and groups. Using the theory of social representations is one way in which this can be done. It sees meanings as constructed in various ways, through the actions of individuals, through language and visual imagery, and through institutional practices.

The theory of social representations proposes that individuals, social groups and the media enact two processes in the development of social representations – 'anchoring' and 'objectification.' Anchoring involves categorization and naming processes which serve to make sense of something by linking it into another familiar sphere of knowledge. For example, by naming states of mental distress 'mental illness', our society has come to understand this phenomenon as an illness or dysfunctional state that should be treated in ways similar to physical illness (that is, by medically trained doctors and prescription of medication in a hospital environment). The second process, objectification, involves the transformation of an abstract concept into a tangible object or image. Art, television and advertising images are all places where objectifications of social representations can be found. Intangible concepts are often objectified in images of people. For example, war is objectified in the image of the injured soldier we see in television reports.

These two processes of anchoring and objectification should be incorporated into the analysis you do in this project. This will ensure that the theoretical bases of your work are reflected in the methods used. The project is not just a media analysis, *but a media analysis from the perspective of social representations theory.* So visual images will be considered as objectifications of social representations (for example, an image of a man in an aftershave advertisement can be considered as an objectification of a social representation of masculinity). Similarly, in conducting an interpretative analysis of the themes in your data, you should think of the associations they conjure up as anchors into other spheres which suggest certain ways of making sense of the phenomena (for example, anchoring health into the natural world).

It is suggested above that social representations can be thought of as underpinning specific attitudes held by individuals. The example of social representations of AIDS and attitudes towards condom use is given. Can you think of some specific attitudes which may be determined by social representations of the environment, of women, and of children? From a different perspective, what social representations might underpin the following attitudes: attitudes towards paternity leave; attitudes towards smoking; attitudes towards community care for the mentally ill?

Suggestions for further reading

Wider reading will give you a more in-depth understanding of the theory of social representations. Moscovici (1981), the first chapter of Farr and Moscovici (1984), the short preface to Herzlich (1973), and Augustinos and Walker (1995) are all recommended. Details of these can be found in the 'Further reading' section at the end of this chapter.

2 Methodology: content analysis

2.1 Researching social representations

So how do social psychologists actually go about studying social representations? The last two decades have seen the development of an increasing body of empirical work conducted from the perspective of social representations theory (Breakwell and Canter, 1993; Farr and Moscovici, 1984; Doise *et al.*, 1993). What is particularly striking about this body of work is its methodological diversity. There is no one particular methodology associated with social representations theory. In fact, it has been argued that one of the strengths of the theory is its methodological openness (Farr, 1993). Looking through the literature, one can find examples of studies using participant and non-participant observations, in-depth interviews, focus groups, analysis of media material, and even experimental studies conducted in laboratory settings. Some studies have used unusual and innovative methods to capture the non-verbal and collective aspects of social representations; for example, analysis of drawings (De Rosa, 1987) and of literature, film and architecture (Chombart de Lauwe, 1984).

Although there are no methodological imperatives associated with social representations theory, there are nevertheless some general methodological strategies which are suggested by the nature of the theory. Amongst the most important of these (and a feature which characterizes many of the best empirical studies of social representations) is methodological 'triangulation' (Banister *et al.*, 1994; Flick, 1992). The multilevel nature of social representations theory suggests that it is appropriate to search for social representations in several domains simultaneously, and to draw on a range of methods in the process. So, for example, in her study of how representations of madness were constructed in a rural French community, Jodelet (1991) relied on a combination of in-depth interviews, observations, survey data and historical archives. (See Box 2 for more details of this study.) Similar mixed methodologies were used by Moscovici (1976) in his study of psychoanalysis in 1950s' French society. Interviews and questionnaires were combined with analysis of media output read by various segments of society: the urban-liberal population, the Catholic community and members of the French communist party.

Several other methodological strategies are suggested by the theory. There is a need to take seriously content as well as process, and to recognise that it is as important to understand *what* is collectively known about any particular concept as it is to capture the processes through which this knowledge is produced. Social representations circulate through both communication and practice, so it is important to use methods which access not only the linguistic aspects of representations but also non-verbal features of collective belief systems, such as social

---

BOX 2:   Jodelet (1991): social representations of madness

Jodelet's in-depth investigation aimed to study how representations of madness were constructed in a unique rural French community where psychiatric patients had been living as lodgers with local families for over 80 years. In a sense, the scheme was an early version of 'community care' for the mentally ill. A range of methods were used during this four-year study: in-depth interviews were conducted with villagers and mental health professionals; the routines of daily life were observed in public spaces and in peoples' homes; and a survey of present-day and historical functioning of the scheme was conducted using questionnaires and analysis of historical documents in hospital archives. This multi-method strategy allowed Jodelet to access madness representations in this community in various ways, and to compensate for the weaknesses of particular methods by drawing on insights obtained from other methods. For example, she detected villagers' deep-rooted fears of the contagion of mental illness through observation of the minutiae of their daily activities, such as washing their mentally ill lodgers' clothes and cutlery separately from those of their own family. Through spending time in the community, she was also able to detect collective taboos against intimate or sexual relations with lodgers. Although Jodelet picked up veiled allusions to these practices in interviews, the basic processes of creating intergroup and interpersonal distance from mentally ill lodgers were never verbalized explicitly. It is unlikely that she would have produced such rich insights into these archaic, pre-verbal practices and representations if she had relied on verbal data alone.

The 'family colony' at Ainay-le-Chateau studied by Jodelet provided a unique opportunity to study how beliefs and reactions to mental distress are constructed in a situation of daily contact with people with mental health problems. Essentially, what Jodelet reports is a picture of massive social exclusion which is created through various subtle but powerful daily routines and unspoken assumptions. Despite the historical and cultural specificity of this study, it uncovers many of the basic processes involved when communities make sense of mental distress in their midst, and, as such, has broader implications for the success of integrationist policies more generally.

---

practices and visual images. Finally, social representations theory conceptualizes 'the social' as more than the summation of individuals. It is therefore important to use combinations of methods that can access representations as they appear, not only in the beliefs of individuals, but also in the collective practices of groups and social institutions.

It should be apparent from this brief review that researching social representations requires the use of in-depth, usually qualitative and often very time-consuming methods. Clearly your time is limited, and it will not be possible for you to conduct a full social representational analysis of gender. Instead, this project is designed as a 'taster' of the type of methods one might use to study social representations, and as an introduction to the media as an object of study for social psychologists. You should bear in mind while doing the project that sampling the media is only one of the many methods that should be used in a full study of gender representations. In a larger scale study, you would use a multimethod approach in order to capture how gender representations in the media interact with social and political factors and the ways people live their lives. You may decide, for example, to use group discussions on gender-related topics or analysis of recent legislation relating to gender. You will need to raise these methodological limitations in the 'Discussion' section of your report.

2.2 Content analysis: quantitative and qualitative approaches

Content analysis refers to *any* technique used to analyse textual or visual material. It involves the identification, counting and interpretation of aspects of content which the researcher assumes to be significant. For example, researchers using content analysis may record, count or interpret body movements in mother-baby interactions, stories about mental illness in daily newspapers, or images of women in television advertisements. As you will see, there are different *forms* of content analysis associated with various strategies for recording, counting and analysing material. Weber (1990) notes that there is simply no one 'right way' to do content analysis.

Various theoretical approaches within social psychology make use of forms of content analysis in different ways depending upon their aims and foci. As an illustration of this, Box 3 compares the analytic aims and methods of social representations theory with those of discursive psychology and discourse analysis.

The point to note from the comparisons made in Box 3 is that theory and method are always linked, and that although 'content analysis' is in some senses a generic method, it may be used differently by researchers located in different theoretical frameworks. The important thing to ensure in any piece of research is that the methodological strategies adopted are congruent with the theoretical aims and assumptions of the researcher. Accordingly, in this project we will be interested in both *visual* and *textual* aspects of media material, and we approach this material with an interest in how it both *constructs* and *reflects* societal beliefs, values and meaning systems (in this case surrounding notions of gender). Because we are working from within a social representational framework, we will be looking for examples of anchoring and objectification, and we will be interested both in what is present in the material and in what is absent, taken-for-granted or implied.

BOX 3:   A comparison of content-analytic strategies associated with social representations theory and discursive psychology

One of the most commonly used forms of content analysis in modern social psychology is discourse analysis, a method for analysing verbal and textual material which is associated with the growing area of discursive psychology (Edwards and Potter, 1992; Potter and Wetherell, 1987). Whilst both discursive psychology and the theory of social representations take broadly social constructionist perspectives, the two theories have rather different aims. Discursive psychology is primarily interested in how people and institutions *use* language to construct rhetorical and power positions, both within specific interpersonal interactions, and as part of a broader social landscape in which individuals, groups and institutions have varying access to different forms of power and social legitimacy. Discursive psychology sees language as a key social practice which is central to how social groups construct and position themselves. The aims of discourse analysis are to interpret how linguistic material is produced and used as a resource to construct, justify or challenge the practices, identities and claims of social groups. The theory of social representations, on the other hand, is more concerned with the construction of *symbolic meanings* in social life. This may occur through linguistic communication, but equally through various other non-verbal social practices which are imbued with symbolic and emotional significance. Social representations theorists are concerned as much with what is left unsaid, or taken-for-granted, as with what is said (or written). They are also interested in the role of visual images in social meaning construction; for example, through the 'objectification' of abstract or unfamiliar concepts in visual images in the media.

This difference between discursive psychology and social representations theory can be summed up (rather simplistically, perhaps) as differing interests in what linguistic communication *does* (discursive psychology), as opposed to what it *means* (the theory of social representations). As an illustration, Potter (1996b) offers a discursive re-analysis of some of the material collected by Jodelet (1991) in her social representational study of madness (see Box 2). Whilst Jodelet saw verbal communication as only one of many ways in which a community constructs and maintains its collective understandings of madness, Potter's focus is on how talk in interview interactions is used by villagers both to justify their ways of behaving with mentally ill lodgers and to manage the interview situation so as to avoid any implications of prejudice.

You may well be wondering at this point exactly *how* these forms of content analysis are conducted. Historically, social scientists have tended to adopt one of two rather different ways of conducting content analysis – quantitative or qualitative approaches. As these terms suggest, the former is concerned primarily with counting occurrences of aspects of content, whereas the latter is more interested in the interpretation of meaning. This section describes the basic approaches and techniques of quantitative and qualitative forms of content analysis, and argues that an integrationist approach which involves both numerical and interpretative aspects may be most fruitful.

Quantitative approaches

Content analysis is any technique for making inferences by objectively and systematically identifying specified characteristics of messages.

(Holsti, 1969, p.14)

'Classic' content analysis originates from the work of communications researchers in the 1950s and 1960s. Keen to demonstrate the scientific credibility of their work, researchers such as Krippendorf (1982), Holsti (1969) and Berelson (1952) developed detailed methodologies for analysing aspects of textual or verbal material in ways that could be shown to be systematic, rigorous and objective. The aims of this form of content analysis are to reduce the potential for researcher bias, distortion or impressionistic analyses by setting out explicitly formulated sets of methodological criteria which can be applied by any trained researcher. This approach usually assumes a perspective of 'realism' – that is, that there are fixed features of our social world, which can be objectively measured. The focus of quantitative content analysis is primarily on categorizing and counting occurrences of aspects of content. It is assumed that there is an association between the frequency with which a certain theme appears and its dominance. In other words, significance is synonymous with frequency.

Quantitative content analysis is useful for detecting patterns across large amounts of material and for testing out specific hypotheses. Results are often presented in terms of basic descriptive statistics (that is, averages, percentages or bar charts). If numbers are large enough, there is also the potential to test hypotheses using inferential statistics: for example, the number of references to the Prime Minister in a sample of newspaper articles, or the relative proportions of programmes on sports, religion, or the royal family on ITV compared with the BBC.

The essential feature of quantitative content analysis is the construction of a 'coding frame'. This is a set of categories which capture aspects of the material that the researcher is interested in, to which all the material to be analysed is allocated. The basic activities of quantitative content analysis involve three sequential stages:

1   *The construction of a 'coding frame'*

There are many possible ways of categorizing material. Origin of the material, numbers of people presented in visual images, topics of news items and gender of the person referred to in the article are just some of the categories a researcher may use. The choice of categories depends on the questions the researcher is interested in. Construction of the coding frame is usually done using a small sub-sample of data (say 10 per cent), and is the most difficult and time-consuming part of quantitative content analysis. It may involve several reworkings of categories to be used, until the researcher is satisfied that the coding frame can adequately account for all the variations in the data in which he or she is interested.

2 Allocation of all units of data to the categories in the coding frame

Once it has been established that the coding frame can be applied in a reliable and consistent way, the process of allocating all data units to these categories can be done. Units of data would be magazine articles, television programmes, or segments of speech. Decisions about what the unit of analysis is are discussed in section 2.3.

3 Analysis of relative frequencies of data units in each category

Results can be presented using basic descriptive statistics and graphical methods (for example, tables of percentages or means, histograms, pie charts, etc.) to compare frequencies across categories and across the material being analysed (for example, the percentage of articles on environmental issues in *The Times* compared with *The Guardian*).

In keeping with the 'social psychology as science' approach of quantitative content analysis, researchers demonstrate the rigour and plausibility of their analysis through measures of the reliability of their findings across different contexts and researchers, and by assessments of various types of validity. The credibility of quantitative content analysis lies primarily in the development and use of the coding frame. The coding frame must be *reliable* – two people coding the same material should allocate it to the same categories (inter-coder reliability). And if the same person were to code the material twice they should arrive at the same results each time (test-retest reliability). In order to achieve reliability, the rules for allocating units to categories must be clear and unambiguous. Usually the categories should be *mutually exclusive* – that is, a given unit can be allocated to one and only one category. The coding scheme must also be *exhaustive* – it should be possible to allocate all the data to the categories devised.

Qualitative approaches

The ever-expanding gamut of qualitative research methods in social psychology and the social sciences represents a radically different form of enquiry compared with methods of 'scientific' empirical investigations conducted in some areas of psychology and the natural sciences (Banister *et al.*, 1994). Within this, various forms of 'qualitative' content analysis have been used to investigate the meanings and themes conveyed and constructed in talk, texts, images and social practices. These include the work of feminist researchers (Burman, 1990; Hollway, 1989), structuralist and semiotic forms of analysing media material (Barthes, 1967; Hall, 1980), and the 'grounded theory' approach to textual analysis (Glaser and Strauss, 1967). There is not space here to go into the very substantial differences between the aims, assumptions and methods of these diverse analytic traditions. Instead, we shall focus on what unites the various forms of qualitative content analysis.

Qualitative content analysis is less concerned with counting and more concerned with the *meaning* of material. Rather than focusing on how often an image, behaviour or topic occurs, it investigates content in much more detail and attempts to decode the meanings and associations that may be hidden within this. Content is not seen as fixed and stable (as in classic quantitative content analysis) but as constructed by both its producers and its recipients. As such it may be a mediator or reflector of more latent cultural phenomena which are not easily categorized or readily quantified. Often there is a concern to use these hermeneutic forms of analysis to comment on issues of ideology and power.

Forms of qualitative content analysis are based on constructionist views of the social world and processes of researching this. The assumption is that meaning is not inherent in the material under analysis, but is socially constructed. So, for example, the meaning of media output is seen as constructed not only by those who produce it, but also by those who read, view or listen to it. This process relies on the implicit social knowledge, or 'referent systems' shared by producer and audience. For example, the impact of using a photograph of a famous film star to associate a product with glamour and success relies on the knowledge and values of the audience. Thirty-second television advertisements and image-based media output rely heavily on referent systems as 'shorthand' which can make an immediate link into complex networks of meanings and associations.

The implications of this are that analysing meanings and associations cannot be a neutral process. From this point of view, content analysis becomes less a matter of measurement and more of a constructive, interpretative process involving the investigator both as researcher and as social actor. Qualitative content analysts draw upon their own social knowledge and the symbolic meaning systems that they share with other members of their society or sub-culture. For this reason, qualitative content analysis is often accused of being less rigorous than quantitative content analysis. It does, however, offer a far richer way of analysing talk, texts, behaviours and images, which draws on the social symbols and meaning systems circulating in a particular society. There are clear parallels between the assumptions of qualitative content analysis and those of the theory of social representations described in section 1. In fact, social representations research frequently makes use of qualitative content analysis to analyse data obtained from the media, observations or interviews.

Compared with quantitative styles of content analysis, procedures of qualitative content analysis are less standardized. It is not possible to delineate a series of steps to be followed as it is with quantitative content analysis. As the examples in section 2.4 below will illustrate, analysis involves investigation of patterns and clusters of themes and ideas in the material. This in-depth interpretative work can be extremely time-consuming, and consequently analysis is usually conducted on relatively small samples of material. Compared with quantitative approaches, qualitative content analysis is less appropriate for making broad comparisons across material, but its strength lies in the detailed and in-depth analysis it can provide of single cases. When samples of material are small, counting frequencies of occurrence as an indicator of dominance or importance of themes or contents becomes less appropriate. Another reason why qualitative researchers shy away from counting is that they are interested not only in what is present in their material, but also what is absent from it. For example, media representations can work not only to privilege certain values and meanings, but also to exclude or suppress others. It is well known that ethnic minorities and older people are under-represented in many sections of the media. Many people would interpret this as illustrative of racism and ageism in society.

The findings of qualitative research are usually presented in a more narrative or 'wordy' style than quantitative content analysis. Often results concentrate on single units of material whose meanings are analysed in depth. Good qualitative research is presented in such a way that it is clear on which specific aspects of the material the researcher has based his/her findings. If textual material is used, this usually involves verbatim quotes of the relevant pieces of material. When visual material is used this should be clearly annotated.

The constructionist assumptions on which qualitative content analysis is based have important implications for the ways in which validity of findings can be ensured and evaluated. The numerical tests of reliability and validity used in quantitative research cannot be easily applied to qualitative data. In addition, many qualitative researchers would argue that there are fundamental epistemological incompatibilities (Flick, 1992; Silverman, 1993). Nevertheless, the methodological 'credibility' of qualitative research is particularly important. Despite their increasing popularity in social psychology over the past fifteen years, qualitative methods still suffer from the prejudices of psychologists of a more quantitative and 'scientific' orientation who see them as 'sloppy', lacking rigour, and used merely to bolster rather than challenge or advance the theoretical preconceptions of those who use them. Qualitative researchers have suggested many different non-numerical strategies for ensuring the credibility of their methods. One strategy over which there is general agreement is *reflexivity* (Banister *et al.*, 1994; Henwood and Pidgeon, 1992; Sapsford, 1998). Reflexivity refers to attempts by the researcher to be constantly aware throughout the research process of the assumptions, social knowledge, and preconceptions that are being drawn upon in conducting the analysis, and of the possible impact these may have on the construction of the research findings. For example, a researcher schooled in the ideas of feminism will probably interpret material in women's magazines very differently from a researcher with no knowledge of feminist theories. Related to this, *transparency* of methods is a second approach which helps ensure the quality of findings. If readers can see how and why the interpretative conclusions were reached from the material used, and if the researcher's values and preconceptions are made explicit and carefully outlined in the report, then they can at least form their own judgements as to the value of such an interpretation. This means that sufficient original material should be included in the report for readers to make their own independent assessments. (Incidentally, there is no reason why these two criteria of evaluation cannot also be applied to quantitative methods of content analysis.)

To summarize this section, Table 1 illustrates some of the principal features of quantitative and qualitative content analysis.

Table 1 A comparison of quantitative and qualitative forms of content analysis

	Quantitative content analysis	**Qualitative content analysis**
Philosophical assumptions	Realism, social psychology as science	Constructionism
Basic activity	Counting	Interpretation
Focus	Manifest aspects of material	Meaning, associations and underlying themes conveyed by material
Procedures	(i) Construction of a coding frame (ii) Allocation of units of material to categories (iii) Counting and quantitative analysis	Investigation of patterns of themes, ideas and associations implicit in the material
Most appropriate for	Detection of patterns across large amounts of material	In-depth analysis of single cases or small samples of material
Assessment	Measures of reliability as one guarantee of validity	Reflexivity, transparency

Integrationist approaches

Table 1 and the discussion which precedes it present quantitative and qualitative forms of content analysis as if they were fundamentally different and entirely separate methodological techniques. This dichotomization is reflective of a situation in the social sciences in which researchers using quantitative and qualitative methods have historically divided themselves into two distinct camps. It has been assumed that the two approaches to content analysis are fundamentally opposed due to their epistemological differences, and there has been little exchange of ideas between the two groups. However, there has been increasing recognition in recent years that this does not have to be the case, and that the two types of content analysis do not necessarily have different philosophical assumptions. After all, attempts to count aspects of material necessarily involve *some* interpretation, just as interpretative analysis must take *some* account of frequencies. It is important to remember that the construction of a coding frame emerges from a particular research question and that neither approach can claim to be entirely 'objective'. Research integrating quantitative and qualitative techniques is now frequently conducted, and this approach has proved extremely valuable. By combining methods, the strengths of the two approaches can be drawn upon – the broad sweep of quantitative analysis and its ability to describe and compare systematically across a sample of data, together with the in-depth, meaning-based interpretations of qualitative content analysis which captures the holistic meanings of media material rather than segmenting into its interrelated elements.

Similarly, there is the opportunity to overcome the weaknesses of each method. Use of qualitative analysis guards against the dangers of reductionism, segmentation and insensitivity to uniqueness associated with quantitative methods. Whilst counting techniques provide an indication of the relative frequency of themes, they are less able to capture the construction of meanings and associations. On the other hand, the techniques associated with quantitative content analysis ensure that conclusions are based on precise and systematic interrogations of all the data.

This combined approach to content analysis will be adopted for the analysis in this project. In other words, we will be interested in *both* frequency of occurrence and in meaning. One way to think of this is that quantitative content analysis looks at *what* is represented, whereas qualitative content analysis is stronger on investigating *how* it is represented – that is, the meanings and associations that are conveyed in the material. The development of an initial coding frame to which material can be allocated will provide a way of describing the general features of our sample of magazine material, whilst the use of qualitative analysis will allow us to capture the unique nuances of each item in the sample. We shall then be able to use the insights produced from these qualitative investigations to generate further ways of coding the data so as to analyse the frequencies and distributions of these themes within the whole data set and sub-groups of material within this.

2.3 Sampling material

In this section, we take a step back in the chronological sequence of procedures in conducting research. Before content analysis can be carried out, several important decisions have to be made about *what* material is going to analysed. The material you choose can ultimately shape the findings you obtain. Sampling decisions depend, obviously, on your area of investigation or research question. They are also influenced by your methodological stance. Quantitative researchers usually work with relatively large data sets and are concerned to obtain representative and unbiased samples of material. Qualitative researchers, however, usually work with smaller samples and may select material which is particularly loaded with social symbolism or in which a particular ideology is crystallized. In this project, we try to take account of both these considerations. We will target material which gives particularly good access into gender representations in the media, but we will also be concerned to ensure that we sample material in a consistent, transparent and unbiased way.

To illustrate these sampling decisions, suppose a researcher is interested in investigating how China is represented in the British media. There are several decisions to be made at an early stage: is he/she interested only in current representations or in how representations change over time? What aspects of China will be the focus of the study – representations of its culture, its politics, or the social climate of China? And what types of British media output will be used? Given the range and volume of media output – daily newspapers, television (which can be further divided into news, drama, soap operas, documentaries, radio, films, magazines, etc.) – the researcher may well decide to restrict the project to a certain medium, such as representations of China in the daily press. Having limited the research problem to a manageable size, the problem then becomes deciding how to obtain a sample of material which is an adequate reflection of the larger body of all media output from which it is drawn.

Sampling of material should be conducted in a logical and consistent way (for example, television news programmes should be recorded every weekday for four weeks, but not at weekends when the length and format of the news tends to be different). It is important to think carefully about this – often researchers introduce bias unwittingly into their findings at the stage of sampling. For example, in a study on the content of daily television news, if the researcher decided to sample the six o'clock news and the nine o'clock news over a two-week period, findings would be based on news output produced by the BBC only. If he/she was interested in national terrestrial television news presentation in general, it would be better to sample from the nine o'clock news, independent television's ten o'clock news and Channel 4 news which are all of similar format but produced by different agents.

Sampling can be thought of as a series of decisions which successively narrow down the material to be analysed. Having chosen what type of media output to analyse, one must decide how big a sample of this medium one needs (that is, how many daily newspapers, over how many days?). The next decision involves what material within this sample one will analyse – every article? a random sample of articles? every tenth article? the largest article on each page? all articles on a certain topic? As I have said, how large a sample is selected depends on the questions the researcher is interested in and the style of content analysis they intend to use. But it also depends on certain practical issues such as access to material, time, number of researchers, use of computer software, etc.

Units of analysis

Having collected the material for analysis, there is one further question before one can begin analysis. How is one going to segment this material into manageable chunks or units for analysis? For example, textual material can be divided into lines, sentences or paragraphs. Again, how researchers decide what their unit of analysis will be depends on their aims in conducting the research, the type of data and the type of content analysis they will conduct. Generally speaking, quantitative researchers tend to segment their material less than qualitative researchers. This is because the latter are concerned to capture *systems* of meaning (conveyed, for example, through the narrative structure of a drama programme or the juxtaposition of images and messages in a magazine), whereas quantitative researchers are concerned to create units which are broadly equivalent and can therefore be subjected to numerical analyses and comparisons.

Decisions about how to segment data depend on how the material divides into 'units of meaning'. Single news items, articles in a magazine, or television commercials could all be considered as units of meaning, in which a message or story is built up through the combination of visual images and the written or spoken word. Segmentation within these units allows more fine-grained analysis, but on the other hand it risks losing the semantic coherence of an item that was produced as an integrated whole, and intended to be received as such by its audience. In this project, you will need to think carefully about what you will take as your 'units of analysis' and justify this in your report. You will probably decide to use either *articles* or *pages* as your analytic units, but whatever you choose you should be aware of its methodological pros and cons and its potential impact on your findings.

2.4 A worked example: representations of motherhood

Having read through the descriptions of approaches to content analysis in section 2.2, you are probably wondering how *you* will conduct your analysis for this project. The worked examples that follow are designed to show you the sort of techniques and analyses you will be expected to use.

As an example of how one can investigate social representations in media output, I have chosen to look at representations of motherhood. Motherhood is traditionally represented in our society as something natural and positive. However, as Caplin (1992) points out, the influences of recent developments in reproductive technologies, consumerism and feminism have created a diverse range of representations of motherhood in modern society. I have chosen to look at representation of motherhood in magazines, and have taken single articles or advertisements as the unit of analysis. The two items that I analyse here are presented in Appendices 1 and 2. Appendix 1 is an article entitled 'The good care guide'. For reasons of space the whole article cannot be included but the two pages included here contain the bulk of the article. Appendix 2 is an advertisement for a baby carrier.

Quantitative analysis

I begin with *quantitative analysis*. Assuming that the two items I am using here are part of a larger sample, I would want to chart the variations in the nature and style of the material. Below are some of the codes I might use for the whole sample showing in brackets the categories to which these two items would be allocated.

Subject-matter

    Pregnancy/birth (Appendix 1)

    Technology

    Material goods (Appendix 2)

    Breastfeeding/nutrition

    Mothers' experiences

    Health problems

    and so on.

'Purpose' of the material

    Information (Appendix 1)

    Expressing opinions

    Selling (Appendix 2)

    Sharing experiences

    Reporting events

    Humour

    and so on.

Visual images: relationships

    With male partner

    With child(ren) (Appendix 2)

    In 'family group' (male partner + child(ren))

    With other adults

    In group of adults and children (not family group)

    Alone (Appendix 1)

Visual images: context

    Domestic environment

    Work environment

    Natural environment

    No specific environment (Appendices 1 and 2)

Woman's social role / position

    Nurturing role (Appendix 2)

    Domestic role

    In public sphere (e.g. work roles)

    No particular social role (Appendix 1)

I would also use other codes to record features of the material that may be relevant to how motherhood is socially represented in the media. These may include codes focused on the age and ethnic group membership of the principal woman in the article, more specific aspects such as her facial expression (serious, smiling, angry, sad, etc.), or the 'tone' of the writing (humorous, informational, political, sentimental, etc.). The aim in this initial quantitative analysis is to come up with clear, unambiguous codes which will enable all the sample material to be allocated to one category in each set. If I have been successful, the coding will be reliable and the same allocations should be made by a different researcher (a process you can check for yourself).

Qualitative / thematic analysis

For the qualitative analysis I look at each item in turn. My aim here is to take each item as a semantic whole and to consider how the juxtaposition of headlines, language style in the text, and features of the visual images (including colour which is obviously lost in this reproduction) combine to construct a 'package' of meanings and implicit messages. As a qualitative researcher, I recognize that this process cannot be neutral and that, in making these interpretations, I draw on my own socially positioned understandings of cultural codes. As such, my findings are one possible 'reading' of this material, rather than a single, definitive 'truth'. Here are the notes I made on the themes and associations that emerged from my reading of these items.

Appendix 1

The focus of this article is on informing and preparing readers for the experience of pregnancy and birth. The theme of care is dominant – a pregnant woman needs to be cared for by others, and the most appropriate people to do this are medical experts. There is a strong theme of pregnancy and birth as medical phenomena. At the same time it is recognized that the experience of medical care can be alienating. The terms 'impersonal' (used twice) and 'jargon' suggest this. Also 'it can sometimes feel as if you're being taken over by the professionals'. The overall message of the article is that pregnancy is an important personal experience, and the woman should be able to choose what type of care she wants. The mother is seen as a consumer of various types of medical health care. These themes are reflected in the section entitled 'Getting what you want' (for example, 'To understand the jargon and get the birth you want, it helps to arm yourself with some facts'; 'Most of all, though, think about what really matters to you and be persistent about getting it').

In the picture, motherhood is 'objectified' as a young, feminine woman. She seems to have the stereotypical 'rosy glow of motherhood' and looks calm and contemplative. She is presented alone.

Appendix 2

The picture is of a young, white, attractive mother carrying her baby in the 'Tomy cradle carrier'. The baby is sleeping peacefully and she is looking down at it with what appears to be a caring and contented attitude. This suggests a nurturant and caring mother. However, the fact that this woman needs this type of baby carrier suggests she is also an active person, who does not want to give up other aspects of her life just because she has a child. This is also suggested in the text: 'How can you stay close to your baby and still carry on with your life?' and the final sentence 'Trust Tomy to put more into carriers so you can get more out of life, together.' There is also an implication in both of these segments of text that being a good mother involves staying close to your baby. This product will allow the mother to combine caring for her baby with the rest of her life: for example, 'The Tomy cradle carrier (or how to rock'n'stroll)'; 'Come feeding time, just discreetly slip down the shoulder strap, instead of having to slip off home.'

The woman and baby are pictured alone, with no partner or other people present. This suggests a unique bond between mother and baby, and the text implies that at this stage the mother is the primary person involved in the daily care of the baby.

Integration

If these analyses were part of a larger study, I would then want to integrate findings across the whole sample, looking for themes which recur and patterns across the various types of material. It is unlikely that I would use all the details I have noted in the qualitative analysis. Instead, I might draw out the dominant themes and use these to construct categories for further quantitative analysis. For example, the categories of 'mother as carer', 'medicalized view of motherhood', 'mother as independent woman', 'mother as consumer' could be created. I would then be able to check the relative frequency of these themes across all items, and to compare their occurrence in different types of material (for example, across different types of magazines, or in advertisements compared with feature articles.) The themes and representations I had detected would form the basis of the report, and I would use some of the quotes and references to aspects of visual images to illustrate them.

3 Social representations of gender

3.1 Femininities/masculinities

As the substantive focus of this project is gender, it is necessary to have some understanding of work conducted within the broad field of gender studies. Obviously, there is not space here to review this huge body of writings and research, within which gender-related issues are approached from a variety of perspectives linked to disciplines across the social sciences. However, if we are interested in how women and men are socially represented in magazines, we need to be aware of the broad common themes which have emerged from research on gender and especially those studies which concentrate on the media as a way of understanding the themes, agendas and issues associated with being male or female in contemporary society.

We also need to remember the linkages between the specific focus of this research project (gender representations in magazines) and the experiences and aspirations of individuals, the development of changing social norms, and the many gendered social practices that structure contemporary society. The gendered images and ideas that we encounter every day in the media both reflect and construct aspects of our personal identities, our social lives, choices and our aspirations. More than many other concepts for which social representations exist, gender representations impact on personal lives through their invitation to identity construction. It would be very difficult for most of us to describe ourselves and develop a sense of selfhood without reference to our gender. As a study by Duveen and Lloyd (1990) illustrates, we are incorporated into a 'gendered' world from the earliest moments of childhood.

Any study of gender cannot ignore the issue of power. Which of the many possible social representations of women and men become dominant in a particular culture or sub-group of society is not arbitrary, but reflects current power struggles and ideologies. Too often we are blind to power inequalities in our own society. As we internalize the values and norms that social institutions such as the media present to us, they come to appear 'natural' or 'normal'. Uncovering and challenging these unequal power dynamics between the sexes has been the central project of much feminist research (Bordo, 1993; Ussher, 1997; Walby, 1990). Similarly, in studying 'common-sense' social representations, researchers try to remain aware of these naturalization processes and to question the origins of what has become unquestioned common sense. One way of implementing this in research is to consider what is absent or hidden as well as what is present in the content analysis of one's material. Media representations can work not only to privilege certain values and meanings, but also to exclude or deny others. For example, images of young, white, heterosexual, able-bodied women, which are the norm on the covers of women's magazines, work to define what forms of femininity are socially acceptable and desirable. But at the same time, they also 'render invisible' women of different race, age or physical ability.

However, while the power relations and ideologies supported by the media may make some representations more dominant or acceptable than others, we should not expect to find one single dominant social representation of women or men in media output. It makes more sense to talk about 'masculinities' and 'femininities' which reflect the diversity of contemporary society, rather than to posit a single gender construct (Wetherell, 1996). One of the most consistent themes that emerges from gender research is the multiple and frequently paradoxical meanings and messages which coalesce in gender representations. Not only is the modern man or woman faced with a range of ways of 'doing' masculinity or femininity, but they also have to grapple with the contradictions inherent in a complex array of media representations. Consider, for example, the coexistence in women's magazines of articles on health and slimming with adverts for chocolate and 'luxury' foods. Or the paradox of beauty products which aim to create a 'natural look' whilst simultaneously drawing women into continuing to put time, effort and money into their physical appearance. Whilst we should not assume that magazine readers cannot resist or re-frame these mixed messages, we should be aware in the empirical work for this project that we are likely to find a range of gender representations existing simultaneously.

Gender representations are often constructed in terms of dualities. In other words, representations of femininity are determined in part by representations of masculinity, and vice versa. In this sense, gender is 'relational'. This suggests that if we want to understand how gender is constructed in contemporary society, we should investigate representations of *both* masculinity and femininity. However, until recently this has not been the case – the feminist movement produced volumes of literature on the social position of women, but issues surrounding masculinity were rarely addressed. It is only since the late 1980s that gender research has included studies on masculinity, and men's studies have become an area of research in their own right (Connell, 1995; Edley and Wetherell, 1995; Kimmel, 1987; Segal, 1990). In comparison with women, however, there is still very little research on how men and masculinity are represented in the media. This project allows you to compare social representations of women and men. Even if you decide to focus on representations of femininity, you should bear in mind the implicit links between the representations you find, and those of men. This is an issue you could consider in the 'Discussion' section of your report.

Some researchers studying contemporary culture suggest that in today's society representations of both masculinity and femininity have diversified and become much more fluid and confused. They have argued that the dualities between male and female may be becoming less fixed. The old representations still exist but in parallel with newer representations which suggest a redefinition of the relationship between the sexes. However, it is debatable whether this represents fundamental changes and to what extent inequitable power relations between men and women still exist beneath these new representations. Walby (1990) argues that the entry of women into working life and the public sphere constitutes a shift from 'private patriarchy' to a new form of 'public patriarchy' in which women are segregated and remain less powerful than men in the public sphere while still retaining principal responsibility for domestic labour and child-rearing. Research by Livingstone and Green (1986) and Manstead and McCulloch (1981) has found that the portrayal of women and men in British television adverts conforms closely to traditional gender roles and stereotypes. Women are shown as product users, in dependent roles and associated with domestic products. Men are more commonly portrayed as autonomous authority figures, often in occupational settings and associated with a wider range of non-domestic products. On the other hand, Wernick (1991) suggests that new representations have developed out of recent social changes; women's entry into the world of work has been paralleled by men's increasing involvement in everyday purchasing activities which only a generation ago were considered as the exclusive province of women. As the norm of the nuclear family declines and more women go out to work, few men are entirely uninvolved in weekly supermarket trips and domestic chores. The recent rise in men's magazines reflects men's new position as consumers. The format of magazines such as *Arena, GQ,* and *Esquire* has much in common with women's magazines such as *Cosmopolitan, Elle,* and *Options,* suggesting to men that being a knowledgeable consumer of clothes, 'lifestyle accessories' and toiletries is no longer the exclusive preserve of femininity. These magazines encourage new representations of men as self-aware consumers, concerned with their looks and the image they present to the outside world. With the rise in electronic and communi-cation-related products, there may also be a weakening link between technology and masculinity. Personal computers, mobile phones and the like are increasingly marketed as user-friendly products used by both sexes.

BOX 4 Social representations of masculinity

Barthel (1992) investigated images of men found in American tele-vision and magazine advertisements. What this study illustrates, among other things, is that no single representation of masculinity is dominant. Rather, multiple images of masculinity exist simul-taneously, reflecting the diversity of contemporary society. A brief summary of the representations of masculinity found by Barthel is presented below:

- 'The Corporate Man': the successful businessman in a smart suit, presented in a sleek, modern office environment. Associations are with power, control and money.

- 'The Country Gentleman' whose clothes and environment suggest status derived not just from money but from an estab-lished family heritage. Such representations conjure up associ-ations with tradition, quality, sophistication and 'taste'.

- 'The Natural Man' is represented enjoying the natural environ-ment. Associations are with health and clean living. This man is both in touch with nature and with himself.

- 'The Sexual Man': Barthel found two quite different versions of the sexual man. In one, masculinity is associated with sexual prowess, power and control. In the other, the man is represented as a romantic lover, capable of successfully seducing beautiful women with his charm, good looks and sophistication. The former representation is commonly found in car advertisements while the latter is often used to sell alcohol or aftershaves. De-spite their differences, in both cases men are represented as sexually dominant and in control of their relationships with women.

- 'The New Man' recognizes the changing positions of the sexes and is not ashamed to express his feelings and invest emotionally in relationships. The New Man is relaxed and is frequently represented with children or babies.

- 'The Family Man' is represented as dependable and responsible – the breadwinner concerned for the safety, health and well-being of his wife and family.

These representations of men are probably recognizable to most people. They present idealized images suggesting that men can become more like these ideals if they buy the products on offer.

The repertoire of social representations of women that circulate in society has also expanded dramatically in the last few decades, reflecting the increased diversification of women's roles in society. Woman as car driver, student, mother, career woman, lover, shopper or home handy-woman are a few representations that spring to mind. Yet as Ferguson (1983) notes, the old representations still prevail, and women's magazines are one of the many social forces that skilfully rework old representations of woman to fit in with more modern values and ideologies (I am thinking, for example, of 'superwoman' representations in which the woman is represented as both mother and wife and as a career woman). The research described in Box 5 investigates how representations of women have changed over time.

BOX 5   Representations of femininity in women's weekly magazines: 1949–1980

Marjorie Ferguson, a sociologist, was interested in how representations of femininity have changed in Britain in the post-war period. She conducted a longitudinal study (Ferguson, 1983) of the three best-selling women's weekly magazines in the three decades following the Second World War – *Woman, Woman's Own* and *Woman's Weekly*. Using quantitative content analysis she found the following themes emerged. While there was a clear expansion in the range of female representations beyond the early emphasis on romance and marriage, two themes emerged as consistently dominant. First, love, marriage and the family were presented as peaks of female experience and satisfaction. Representations of women as wife and as mother have remained dominant throughout the three decades. Even with the emergence in the mid-1970s of newer representations such as the 'independent woman', women were still represented frequently as wives and mothers. In order to succeed in the competitive game of 'getting and keeping your man', women were urged to develop their domestic skills and dedicate themselves to their family.

The second dominant theme was an emphasis on the self – woman as a responsible, self-determining individual. It was towards the end of the period Ferguson analysed, from the mid-1970s onwards, that this second theme overtook 'love and marriage' as the most dominant representations (in quantitative terms). This theme emphasized women as self-helpers who take active steps to achieve perfection, whether this is the perfect hairstyle or the perfect soufflé. Self-help can also help women overcome misfortune. Magazines present multiple forms of excellence for readers to aspire to – there are articles on how to be a better mother, a better lover, a better wife, better looking, a better cook. Yet, as Ferguson notes, the messages of these most common representations are somewhat contradictory. On the one hand, women are represented as caring and nurturant of others (their husband and their children), while, on the other hand, they are represented as free to nurture and develop their *own* needs and wishes.

Another feature of social representations of women is the strong link between the perception and definition of women and their physical appearance. Whereas men are more frequently judged by their social status, intellect or material success, women have traditionally been defined in terms of their appearance and their relationship to men. A woman's character and status are judged by her appearance – the shape of her body and the clothes she wears. The staggering preponderance of advertisements in women's magazines for beauty products, fashion and clothes is a testament to the dominance of this representation of women as beauty objects (Betterton, 1987). Even when women are represented in other ways, for example the 'career woman', the focus on a woman's physical appearance remains. Bordo (1993, 1997) analyses the rise of eating disorders and concerns with body shape amongst women as an illustration of the way social power dynamics seek to control women and coerce them into repressive relationships with their bodies. Against a socio-historical context in which the female has been associated with unruly passions, urges and desires, slenderness has become an overdetermined ideal which symbolizes 'male' qualities of self-will, control and mastery.

The appearance of women is frequently tied up with sexuality. There is a 'surplus of sexuality' in many women's magazines (Ussher, 1997, p.80). Polarized media representations of women reflect the paradoxes and contradictions in how femininity is socially represented. Women are either presented as virginal, innocent and pure, or as the opposite – sexually experienced and seductive. This is an example of how current social representations of women are 'anchored' into historically established ways of representing women – in this case the virgin and the whore. However, while sexualized images of women were previously presented as primarily for the benefit of men, representations of female sexuality are now more complex. For example, is the woman in an advert for lacy underwear dressing this way for her husband or her lover, or for herself?

Finally, prevailing social representations have often attributed a lack of seriousness to women. In analysing visual representations of women and men in advertisements, Goffman (1976) notes how women are frequently portrayed in playful poses and costume-like clothing, creating associations with childishness. He suggests that male-female interactions are often portrayed in a similar way to those between parent and child, thus emphasizing the unequal power relations between the sexes and the subordination of women. Again, this is another example of social representations of women being 'anchored' into another social category – in this case childhood.

Before moving on, spend a few minutes thinking about the representations of women and men that form part of the social world in which you live. The research presented in Boxes 4 and 5 suggests some social representations of women and men which may be familiar to you, but others may also come to mind. If you have experience of a different culture, how do the gender representations in this culture differ from those discussed here?

Make a note of the representations you think of so that later on you can compare these with the representations you find in your data.

Suggestions for further reading

If you would like to read more widely about gender, the following material is recommended as relevant to this project: Bordo (1993), Coward (1984), Edley and Wetherell (1995). Details of all of these are given in the 'Further reading' section at the end of the chapter.

3.2 Women's and men's magazines

For this project you will be using magazines as your main data source. Magazines targeted at women form an important part of the wider cultural processes which define the position of women and the meaning of femininity in our society (Douglas, 1995). Ferguson (1983) sees the world of women's magazines as a powerful social institution that creates a 'cult of femininity' – a set of practices and beliefs into which women are socialized. The readership of these magazines is extremely large and includes all age groups, social classes and ethnic groups. Few of us, at some time in our lives, have not glanced through the pages of a woman's magazine, even if this was only in the doctor's waiting room. Many researchers interested in the social position of women and the social construction of femininity have taken women's magazines as the main focus of their analyses (for example, Ferguson, 1983; McCracken, 1993; Winship, 1987). But analysis of women's magazines can also offer insights into social representations of masculinity – it is not only women that appear in women's magazines – discussions of men and their relationships with women are a frequent topic, for example. A second important source for the analysis of social representations of masculinity is the expanding market of men's magazines which contributes to social definitions of masculinity and men's views of themselves. Having selected the type of material we will use, we also need to be aware that the specific nature of this material may have a bearing on the type of representations we are likely to find. To help you do this, what follows is a review of some features of gender-targeted magazines which media researchers have highlighted.

A good place to start is with the cover of the magazine. A magazine's cover is its prime selling point. Each magazine must vie for purchasers' attention on the newsagents' shelves against a range of other magazines targeting the same audience. Magazine covers can also reveal the representations of gender which are valued and judged attractive by the magazine's producers and the audience that buys them. Winship (1987) notes that the image on the front of most women's magazines is often a close-up of a young woman's face with blemish-free white skin and perfect hair and make up, usually smiling or seductive. She suggests that the success of these images lies in their ability to sell the female reader an image to aspire to. This is combined with cover stories offering a careful balance between practical items linked to daily life and those which tap into the reader's dreams and fantasies.

A second important feature of these magazines is the high proportion of visual imagery compared with text. Visual imagery using bold, bright colours tends to overshadow the written word. These visual images have a more immediate impact than text, as well as requiring very little effort on the part of the reader. From the point of view of our analysis, they also offer us many opportunities to analyse how social representations of men and women are 'objectified' in visual images. In analysing our material we should consider text and visual images as working together to convey a 'package' of meaning and associations. And we must use a style of content analysis which allows us to consider both visual images and text.

Popular magazines are intrinsically linked to advertising. Just a quick glance through any of the gender-targeted magazines shows that a large proportion of their content is advertisements. The social representations found in this study must, therefore, be considered within a context that is linked with advertising and consumer culture. They are often highly idealized images, which reflect more about the fantasies and desires that their producers wish to create in their audience than the reality of readers' everyday lives. Representations used in advertisements play on the aspirations of their audience, suggesting that by buying the product on offer they can become more like these desirable representations (Williamson, 1978). These implicit messages pervade both the advertisements and many of the editorial features in magazines, such that all sections of a magazine offer representations based on fantasy and consumerism.

This brings us to a final point about gender-targeted magazines. What is it that ensures their continued success and wide readership? Ussher (1997) suggests that women's magazines offer scripts for idealized femininity, while McCracken (1993) suggests their success lies in the generation of pleasure, achieved through linking the real and the imaginary in such a way that the boundaries between the two become blurred. Desire is linked to consumerism and commodity solutions are offered for our problems and anxieties. For example, the hidden message in an advert for face cream is that this product will guarantee blemish-free skin, which in turn will lead to success, happiness and attractiveness. In their colourful format, their glossy texture, their focus on glamour, beauty, fashion and on successful media personalities, magazines offer gratification in the form of fantasy and a sense of luxury. They also offer reassuring confirmation to readers of their values and their experiences and formulae for identity construction. So the woman who buys a copy of *Vogue* becomes a '*Vogue* reader' and can assimilate this label and its associations into her identity. Similarly, the continued success of weekly magazines such as *Woman's Own* lies in the reassurance they provide in helping women to construct and negotiate their identities in the domestic space.

PART B: CONDUCTING THE PROJECT

4 Data collection

Having worked through the preliminary theoretical and methodological reading in Part A, you are now ready to embark on the practical work for this project which involves the investigation of gender representations in contemporary gender-targeted magazines. To reiterate the arguments presented in section 3.2, the choice of gender-targeted magazines as the focus of investigation is justified by their important bridging role between the gender representations which permeate society and contemporary culture, and the identities, values, aspirations and experiences of their readership. It is up to you which type of magazines you choose to use for your project. You may, for example, want to use magazines targeted towards the younger market (for example, *Cosmopolitan, Elle, Marie-Claire* for women; *GQ, Arena* or *Men's Health* for men). Or you may be interested in traditional weeklies or monthlies (for example, *Woman's Own*). The only limitations are that the magazines should be gender-targeted (as opposed to special interest magazines).

As you work through the stages of data collection set out in the next four sections, you should refer back to the general points about selection of research material made in section 2.3.

4.1 Identifying a specific research question

The first decision you will have to make is what the specific focus of your investigation is going to be. Are you interested in social representations of women or social representations of men? Or (given the 'relational' nature of gender) perhaps you are interested in investigating social representations of both genders simultaneously. Are you interested in representations in a particular type of magazine (perhaps women's weeklies)? Or do you want to do a comparative study which involves investigations of representations in two or more types of magazine (perhaps monthly men's magazines compared with monthly women's magazines)?

Because of the complexities of sampling and the difficulties of dealing with large amounts of data in this form of analysis, it is probably better to limit yourself to a reasonably straightforward research question which either focuses on one particular segment of the magazine market, or involves no more than one variable in a comparative study. In other words, it is probably rather overambitious to attempt simultaneous comparisons of how women and men are represented as well as a comparison of different types of magazines. (Don't forget that each time you create a comparison between two types of data you will necessarily double the size of the data sample you need to analyse.)

Once you have decided on your research question and before you begin your practical work, spend a few minutes thinking about your 'hunches' or expectations regarding the sorts of social representation you are likely to find. This will probably be based on a combination of your reading of the material in this chapter (especially the themes discussed in section 3.1), knowledge of the specific media material you intend to investigate, your gender, and personal experiences and values. Make a note of these hunches so that you can refer to them later when conducting the analysis.

Although qualitative analysis of this type rarely aims to test hypotheses formally, you could think of this as informal hypothesis testing or as a way of 'getting started' with your analysis. However, it is important to ensure that such predictions do not structure your analysis entirely and that there is still space for other themes to emerge from your data. If you become too wedded to searching for certain themes that you expect to find, you may risk being blind to other themes in the data that you had not predicted. Examination of these preliminary notes will also allow you to take a reflexive stance which should enhance the rigour of your analysis by highlighting the assumptions from which you started your investigations. Referring back to your notes during analysis will help you identify any biases or preconceptions which you may have unwittingly introduced into your interpretations of the data.

4.2 Selecting material

Having decided on a specific focus for your research, you now need to decide what material you will use to answer your research question. Obviously, the type of magazines you analyse will have an impact on the representations you find. You will need to consider what sections of the population your magazines are targeted towards, and what the stated or implicit aims and values of the magazines are. In your final report you will need to provide an account of why you chose the material you used and what impact you think this may have on your findings. There are also a few practical issues to consider in selecting material. For example, if you are interested in representations of women and men, don't forget that men are represented much less frequently than women in women's magazines (and vice versa for men's magazines).

In order to draw reasonably generalizable conclusions from your analysis, you need to analyse material from more than one magazine. If you restrict your data collection to only one magazine, it is possible that findings could be specific to that particular magazine or even to that edition of the magazine. Therefore, you need to choose *at least two* examples of any particular type of magazine. Choosing magazines all published in the same month ensures that variations over time (or time of year) are held constant.

4.3 Units of analysis

The issue of how to divide up one's material into units which allow a sufficiently fine-grained analysis whilst maintaining the semantic coherence of articles or texts was discussed in section 2.3. For this project, you will need to collect somewhere *between 15 and 40 units of data* (depending on the nature of your research question). But first of all you will need to consider the format of the material you have chosen and decide on what you will take as your unit of analysis. The obvious 'unit of meaning' in most magazines is a single article, feature or advertisement. In some magazines, articles are generally fairly short and may cover only one or two pages. However, many of the monthly 'glossies' include articles or fashion features which span several pages. In this case, sampling 20 articles would provide a huge amount of data and your analysis may be less detailed than with a smaller sample. You may decide, therefore, that pages or double pages are more manageable units of analysis. However, you should balance these considerations against the potential difficulties of only analysing parts of articles in which representations and messages are constructed through the combination of various images and themes over several pages. As with many of the processes involved in this form of analysis, there is no perfect solution to this issue. What is important, though, is that you think carefully about the consequences (and potential biases or weaknesses) of whatever strategy you adopt and discuss these in your report.

4.4 Sampling

The construction of a sample of material for analysis is dependent on several factors – your specific research question, the format of the material you are using, and the style of analysis that will be conducted. It is impossible, therefore, to provide precise instructions on sampling. What follows are some suggestions on possible strategies. Whatever procedures you decide upon, you should aim to sample in a logical, consistent and transparent way. This may involve an amount of trial-and-error until you are satisfied that your sample captures the range of representations conveyed in your material in a representative way. You should aim to collate a sample of *between 15 and 40 units*. If you are doing a comparative study (for example, between representations of women in men's and women's magazines) you will need a minimum sample size of *10 in each group*, and you should ensure that the groups are of equal sizes.

The simplest ways of obtaining a sample from the total number of units in the magazines you are using is to number each of the units and then draw a random sample of the size you need. You can do this using random number tables. If you are dividing your material into two or more groups for a comparative study, you should do this for each group of magazines separately so that you obtain equal-sized groups. Another way of sampling is to select units at regular intervals from each magazine. Given that the content of many magazines is organized in a standard format (with 'news' and 'cultural events' sections preceding the main articles and items on travel or food usually placed towards the end of the magazine), this ensures that your sample includes units from all sections of your magazines. The front cover of any magazine is vital in attracting a readership and conveying a message about the general 'attitude' of a magazine, so you should include the front cover of all the magazines you use in your sample. Do not forget to keep a clear note of the magazine that each of the other selected units comes from.

Sampling in this way you are likely to obtain a diverse range of material. Some of the articles in your sample may not even appear, at first glance, to include social representations of women or men. An advertisement for a personal computer, a feature on homelessness or an interior design feature may not include visual images of women or men. Yet, if we consider the messages implicit in their content, and their very existence in the context of a gender-targeted magazine, these articles can still be informative about how women or men are socially represented in magazines. An advertisement for a personal computer in a women's magazine, for example, suggests that technology is no longer exclusively a male domain. Reading the text of the advertisement may offer you clues about the type of attributes the computer company uses to sell its products to a female market. What does this tell you about the values and lifestyles of the women implicitly represented in this advertisement? This type of analysis requires you to use the manifest content of your material – its visual images and text – to uncover the meanings, associations and messages implicit in this material.

Another way of sampling is to adopt a more 'purposive' procedure in which the pool of material from which the sample is drawn is limited. Many magazines rely very heavily on visual images in the construction of messages, meanings and themes. It would be possible to construct a sample which selects material containing 'objectified' gender representations in the form of visual images or photographs of women and men. You should use the same sampling procedure as described above of numbering you material and selecting a sample either randomly or at intervals. The only difference is that you will do this following an initial selection, excluding all material in which men or women are not visually represented in some form.

This procedure has the advantage of allowing you to focus specifically on gender representations, rather than confounding your analysis with the various other messages and social representations which are conveyed in magazines. It may also, one could argue, facilitate a more objective analysis, as there may be less reliance on inference and interpretation of a diverse range of material. However, such a selective procedure also has the potential weakness of over-reliance on a particular form of material and exclusion of gender representations constructed in other more subtle or indirect ways. There are also some practical issues to consider. For example, you will have to decide whether or not to include material in which women or men appear only incidentally (for example, a small photographic inset of the writer of an article, or an advertisement for a holiday location in which scenery rather than people is the main focus). When women and men are represented together, you will have to decide whether to include this material as representations of women or of men. (You could decide according to the gender of the central figure in the picture, or, if there are several pictures, the person in the main picture. Or you could create a third category which includes women and men represented simultaneously and may be informative about gender relations.)

These are two suggestions for how to sample magazine material. There are certainly many other ways of doing this which you may prefer to use. The process of sampling can often turn out to be more complicated than you had expected. However, careful sampling is a vital aspect of the credibility and rigour of any research. The reader of your report will want to see evidence that your sampling procedure was systematic and consistent. So it is important at this stage to keep clear notes of the technique you used, the decisions you made and the reasons for these, and the strength and potential weaknesses of the procedures you adopted.

5 Analysis

This is probably the hardest stage of your research. Having collected what may seem like a frighteningly large amount of data, what are you to do with it in order to arrive at some meaningful interpretations and conclusions?

To begin, I want to reiterate the point that there is no one 'right' way to conduct content analysis. Similarly, it is not possible to provide detailed instructions which can be followed to the letter. All I can offer are *guidelines* about what is expected of you, which you can apply to the unique sample of material you will be analysing. If you follow these guidelines, look back at the worked examples, and (importantly) consider the strategies for ensuring the credibility of results in section 2.2, you should be able to analyse your data without too many problems. Because of the interpretative and unstructured nature of content analysis (especially qualitative analysis), the experience of this type of work is often one of uncertainty and doubt. You may have the sense of not being sure if you are looking at the 'right' things, that you may be missing important themes, or that perhaps you are 'barking up the wrong tree' in making a particular interpretation. All I can do here is to reassure you that this sense of uncertainty is one experienced by all qualitative researchers, even those with years of experience. Good qualitative analysis requires a combination of rigorous methodological procedures and a certain degree of faith in one's ability to make valid interpretations. Think of the analogy of piano playing: the creation of beautiful music depends not only on the pianist's creative interpretation of the score, but also on their rigorous mastery of technique. The balance of 90 per cent perspiration and 10 per cent inspiration is probably about the same in sound qualitative analysis. Remember also that the aim of your report is to present your analysis and the rationale behind your conclusions, rather than an objective 'final word' on the topic.

Before you begin your analysis, look back at sections 2.2 and 2.4 to remind yourself of the issues involved in content analysis. Glance over the theoretical material in section 1 and research examples in section 3, making notes on any themes or ideas which you think may be applicable to your data. You should also have to hand the notes you made on your initial expectations after reading section 3.1.

Your analysis should aim to comment on *both* the visual and the textual aspects of your material, and to integrate quantitative and qualitative approaches. Remember, quantitative content analysis looks at *what* is represented, whereas qualitative content analysis is more interested in *how* it is represented – that is, the meanings and associations conveyed in the material. However, it is important to see these as interrelated processes. You should start with a quantitative approach as this can be a useful way of organizing and becoming familiar with your data. As you are conducting your quantitative analysis, keep a notepad handy and jot down any themes or associations which you detect. You will be able to explore these in more detail in the qualitative analysis. Similarly, when you are conducting the qualitative analysis you may think of ways of categorizing the data quantitatively which you may wish to add. Think of the analysis as an ongoing *process* in which new findings throw light on previous ones. You will need to adopt a flexible working style in which you can integrate and rework findings as you go along.

5.1 Quantitative analysis

The quantitative analysis should be used to describe the manifest features of your data. You will need to devise several coding frames into which all data can be categorized, and which covers all the features of your data that you are interested in. You should follow the stages described in section 2.2. Remember that the categories should be mutually exclusive and exhaustive (that is, it should be possible to categorize all articles into one and *only* one category for each of the features you are measuring).

This may require the addition of a 'not applicable' category. (For example, a code for the gender of the person presented would be inapplicable to visual images which did not include people.) Another strategy is to devise a category labelled 'other'. However, it is important to monitor what ends up in this 'other' category, to ensure that interesting patterns in the data are not being missed.

Some features of material which you may be interested in categorizing include:

- The context of material. Which magazines do the units come from? Are they located in particular sections of these magazines?

- The topic of the material. Units could be classified into health, clothes/fashion, work, relationship issues, lifestyle, political issues, etc.

- Social roles of the women or men portrayed.

- Social context/location of visual images.

You should add a few other codes which relate to your specific research question and the nature of the material you are using.

This analysis will produce results in numerical form which can be summarized in your report as tables of frequencies, histograms or pie charts. If you have used categorizing whose meaning is not initially obvious, remember to explain these clearly in your report. If necessary, you could include definitions of each category in an appendix.

You should wait until you have completed *all* the analysis before you write up these results, as qualitative investigations will suggest new ways of categorizing the data quantitatively. Once you begin to identify certain social representations it will be of interest to investigate their relative frequencies in different magazines. So keep the results of this analysis in note form for the time being and move on to a more fine-gained qualitative analysis of your material.

5.2 Qualitative analysis

You should use qualitative analysis to 'unpack' the meanings and associations in your material. You will probably find working with each unit in turn is the easiest strategy. Start by making rough notes on themes and associations in the material. These themes may appear explicitly in the data (at a manifest level); for example, in the wording of a headline, the text of an article, or in a visual image. Or they may operate at a more latent level; for example, through the use of certain colours and the associations they invoke, in the body postures or clothes, or in the type of language and metaphors used in text. Working with both obvious features of your material and with its more complex implicit messages and themes will allow you to investigate gender representations in a whole range of material. Take for example an article on cookery. We may take for granted that cookery articles appear regularly in women's magazines.

Cooking and its associations with a nurturing, home-based role are part of commonly held social representations of women as mothers, carers and home-makers. But how would you react to the same article in a men's magazine? The implicit message is that cooking is a socially acceptable activity for the modern man, an activity which interests at least a segment of the readership, and one which could (or should) be part of the male reader's life world. Don't forget also that what is absent from material can often be just as interesting as what is present (although it is obviously harder to draw definitive interpretations from absences).

You may find this style of working difficult to begin with, but it should get easier as you progress. You should try to maintain a 'reflexive' stance at all times. Ask yourself, 'Why did I make that interpretation?', 'Am I making use of particular social knowledge or making implicit judgements in doing this?', 'Is another interpretation possible?' This should help you adopt a questioning and critical stance on your own analytic process, and remind you of the epistemological basis of qualitative analysis. Meaning is not inherent in your material and simply waiting to be recorded. Rather, it is constructed through the way the reader or researcher interacts with the material. Think of your analysis as a 'reading' not a 'discovery'.

You may want to follow up your 'hunches' that you recorded earlier about the representations you expected to find in your data. You could conceptualize these as a series of questions which you address to your data, guiding the analyses you choose to do. However, at the same time you should try to remain open to your data, such that you are able to detect patterns and themes emerging from the data which you have not anticipated. Your analytic process should be as transparent as possible (see section 2.2), so you may want to include your notes in an appendix. Remember that you should be able to justify clearly any interpretations you make. So keep a note of which aspects of your material (sections of text, for example) you are basing your analysis on.

Depending on which magazines you are using, you may be analysing units of material of varying sizes, from a small section of a page to several pages. If you are using larger units, do not feel you have to analyse *everything*. Qualitative analysis is inevitably selective, and you should concentrate on picking out what seem to be the main themes. Some features of content that researchers have used to make inferences about meanings contained in media material include the following:

For visual images

Colour
Body posture
Facial expression
Background context
Clothes
Positioning of people in relation to each other
General 'feel' of the image.

For textual material

> Choice of headline message
>
> Relative emphasis of themes within the topic
>
> Perspective of the writing (that is, who is the subject of the story, from whose perspective the article is written, with whom the reader is intended to identify)
>
> Positive or negative associations
>
> Value judgements
>
> Metaphors
>
> 'Feel' of the writing (for example factual/impersonal, humorous, dramatic, chatty).

As you progress through this analysis try to move towards identifying constellations of themes, messages and images which convey particular social representations of women or men. You should look for examples of 'anchoring' and 'objectification' of social representations. (You may want to look back to section 1 to remind yourself about these concepts.) The social representations implicit in your material may be 'anchored' into other ideas or existing representations through the use of metaphors or linguistic linkages in text. Objectifications of social representations often occur in images of people.

5.3 Integration

Once you have worked through all your data qualitatively, you should collate all the notes you have made for each unit of material, and work on drawing out the most dominant themes occurring across the sample. You will probably have detected a diverse range of themes and generated a substantial volume of analytic notes. Now is the time to collate and reduce this material, drawing together the various themes into particular social representations of men or women, which are likely to consist of constellations of images and associations. A 'corporate man' representation, for example, may be constructed through images of men in city suits, an office or public domain location, and textual themes of competition, money or time. It is vital at this stage that you maintain a very clear link between data and findings. For each of the representations you identify, make clear notes on exactly which features of which material you are drawing on and why.

Having done this, you should use these collated findings to develop new ways of categorizing the data quantitatively. You should devise categories which correspond to the gender representations you have identified (clear definitions of each of these will be required) and use these to conduct quantitative analysis. This will allow you to explore the dominance or frequency of these representations in relation to each other. You should also use some of the quantitative categories you have already created (for example, origin of material, subject-matter) to compare social representations across your data set. Do certain social representations occur more or less frequently in material from different sources or produced for different markets? The results of these investigations could be presented using tables or graphs. In this way you will be integrating the two styles of content analysis, creating categories that are amenable to quantitative analysis from qualitative findings which capture the richness and complex meanings of your data. If you have time, you could check on the robustness and transparency of your analysis by asking a friend or fellow-student to code the data according to the new categories you have created.

Finally, a word of warning and some reassurance: at some point in this process of analysis you are likely to feel overwhelmed by the data or lost in the mass of findings and ideas. You may be so 'close' to your data that you 'can't see the wood for the trees'. If this happens – *stop*! Take a break and come back to it the next day. Often, with the sense of distance that this gives you, the main findings of your research will re-emerge. It is also a very good idea to take a break when you have finished your analysis before you write up your report. Re-read what you have done, checking for clarity of ideas and illustrations. Another good strategy, if you have the opportunity, is to ask a friend or fellow-student to read over your findings before you write them up. Discussing anything that doesn't seem clear to them can be a very good way of clarifying your own thinking and highlighting omissions.

6 Writing the report

The following comment by Banister *et al.* is good advice for writing up your project:

> A general guideline to bear in mind is that the shape of a report is ideally like that of an hourglass, starting off in the introduction with very general considerations, and going on gradually to focus in on the specific areas of interest. The methods and the results narrowly attend to the research itself, while the discussion gradually widens out again to encompass broader issues.
>
> *(ibid., 1994, p.164)*

Your write-up should be divided into the following sections:

Title

Abstract

The abstract should provide a brief overview of the whole project. It should summarize the aims, methods and principal findings of the research. Abstracts are often easier to write after completion of the main report.

Introduction

This should provide an introduction to the theoretical and methodological approach to your research, and to the substantive gender issue you are studying. It should give a brief overview in your own words of the theory of social representations, making clear why this is a good theoretical tool for social psychologists wishing to study the media, and how the theory of social representations conceptualizes media output. You should introduce the topic of gender. State why this is an appropriate topic for the theory of social representations and what particular issues you will be concerned with in this project. You should include findings from previous research that are relevant to your study.

Having introduced the project in general terms, the 'Introduction' should also serve to focus the reader's attention on the specific research you have conducted. You should state clearly how and why you arrived at your specific research questions and what material you have chosen to use.

Method

In the 'Method' section you should briefly describe and justify the strategy of integrating quantitative and qualitative approaches. Provide an account of any pilot work you conducted, and how this shaped your main study. Give full details of the sampling procedure you used and decisions made during this process. You should also describe in your own words the procedures used in the different types of content analyses. Make clear which aspects of the material you were interested in when coding the data quantitatively and qualitatively, and how these two processes were integrated.

Results

The focus of this section is on your data and the final findings of your analysis. You should present your results in a way that integrates the quantitative and the qualitative analyses, and focuses on the social representations you have identified. Quantitative content analysis results will be mainly numerical, but you should also describe the main findings in the text. Be careful to label all tables and graphs clearly. If you have constructed coding categories whose meaning is not immediately obvious, include details of these in a separate appendix. When presenting the social representations your analysis has revealed, be sure to support these using examples from the data, making clear the interpretations you have made. Remember that good content analysis should be 'transparent' – it should be clear to the reader what processes you used to get from your data to your interpretations, what assumptions you made, and on what specific aspects of the material findings are based. If this is textual material you should quote it verbatim, noting where the quote comes from. Interpretations based on visual material should refer to specific features that should be highlighted on the original material included in an appendix.

Discussion

This should aim to discuss the findings of your research, address methodological issues, suggest explanations for these findings, and set them back in the wider context from which the research originated. Some of the questions you may want to address include:

- How do your results compare with your initial expectations? How do they compare with the results of previous research? Can you speculate on the reasons for discrepancies or similarities? What impact do you think the type of material you used had on your findings?

- How useful were the quantitative and qualitative techniques of content analysis? What problems did you encounter? What do you see as the relative strengths and weaknesses of the two approaches? How would you rate the credibility or validity of your methods? And how would you test or demonstrate these? If you were asked to conduct the same research over again, what modifications would you make?

- How would you expect the social representations you have detected in this media material to be manifested in other social spheres? Give examples of the behaviour of individuals or groups, or of general social trends which you see as illustrative of the representations you have found. Is gender socially represented in other ways that you have not detected in your research? If so, why do you think these representations are not reflected in the media material you have used?

- How could you account for the social representations you have detected in terms of wider cultural and social patterns? For example, how do they fit into ideologies, politics and issues of power in society? You could speculate on this at several levels – at the level of the specific sub-group of society to whom your material is aimed; at the level of prevailing social values existing generally in society; and at the level of underlying cultural values.

Appendices

You should include all your original material in an appendix. Make sure it is all clearly labelled. Other appendices may include pilot work, details of your 'starting-point', preconceptions or social stance as a non-neutral qualitative researcher, categories used in qualitative analysis, and qualitative analysis notes on which final findings are based.

PART C: OTHER OPTIONS

This part provides three possible variants of the project described in detail above. All three of these include the same basic theoretical and methodological ingredients as the main project. Their theoretical base is the theory of social representations and they all rely on content analyses of media material. The first two options are most similar to the main project, suggesting ways of adding a historical or a cross-cultural dimension to an investigation of gender representations in gender-targeted magazine material. The third option provides brief notes on how to conduct a rather different variant. This centres on the topic of health and illness and uses newspaper rather than magazine material. It is not possible to provide full details of how to go about these options, and you should use the sections above on data collection, analysis and writing the report to guide what you do. But you should also think carefully (and show evidence of this in your report) about the specific methodological issues associated with the option you have chosen.

If you are particularly interested in another topic that could be investigated using content analysis of printed media material and the theory of social representations, you may wish to conduct a different variant of this project. However, you should consult with your tutor or the person marking your work before you begin.

7 Historical changes in gender representations

The theory of social representations stresses the dynamic and changing nature of our common-sense views of the world, that are constantly revised and renegotiated as society and its values change. However, whilst social representations are constantly changing, they also carry with them the values of the past which shape and define the development of new representations. Certainly it is without doubt that the last few decades have seen some dramatic changes in gender representations and in the position of women and men in society. But at many levels traditional gender positions and expectations remain, defining the scope of women's and men's lives in powerful ways. If you can get access to copies of magazines from previous decades (perhaps from library archives or second-hand bookshops), it would be possible to conduct a version of this project which investigates how social representations of women (or men) have changed over time.

If we compare current gender-targeted magazines with those from previous decades (which until the 1980s were almost exclusively targeted at the female audience), what differences do we find? Are there themes which remain the same? Have some old themes been reworked or given a modern gloss in the light of other social changes? An interesting comparison might be between contemporary women's magazines and those of the 1950s (*She, Vogue* and *Woman's Own*, for example, were all published in the 1950s). During this decade, Britain was primarily concerned with reconstructing itself after the war. The dominant representations of women perpetuated in the media were as wife and mother, helping lead the country into a future of stable family life and materialism (Ferguson, 1983; Winship, 1987). Another interesting comparison might be with the early 1970s when feminism was just beginning to find a voice (albeit often marginalized) in popular culture and women's magazines.

If you are interested in this historical variation of a study on gender representations in the media, you should use the procedures described in sections 4 and 5 on data collection and analysis as a template, and modify your strategy as appropriate. Because you are introducing a historical comparison, I would advise you to keep your research question relatively simple for this project. For example, you could set out to investigate how representations of women in a particular type of magazine vary between two time periods. The study by Ferguson (1983) described in Box 5 may provide a useful starting-point. As with the main option, you should aim to obtain equal-sized samples of between 10 and 20 units of analysis for each time period you are interested in. You should also include the cover of each magazine in your sample. Bear in mind the impact of technological and market changes in the changing formats of magazines over time, and try not to let these confound your analysis. Compared with their equivalents in previous decades, modern-day magazines tend to rely increasingly on colour and visual imagery. There is typically also a corresponding increase over time in page numbers and in the length of individual articles. You will have to consider how to tackle these historical changes when devising a sampling procedure and conducting your analysis. A finding that articles from 1950s' magazines contain a higher proportion of text than current day magazines is an interesting comment on changes in print media, but tells us very little about changing representations of women, which is your central research question.

8 A cross-cultural analysis of gender representations

Just as a historical dimension can be incorporated into this research project, so it is possible to devise a cross-cultural version. The theory of social representations emphasizes the construction of collective belief systems according to a unique interplay of the specific social, historical, political and cultural factors which permeate a particular society. Gender representations could therefore be expected to vary across cultures. But how exactly do they differ? And what aspects of the ways gender is socially represented are constant across cultures? It may be, for example, that gender is associated with similar values and expectations across European and North American countries that share a common set of historical, religious and cultural reference points.

In this variation of the project, you have the opportunity to work with gender-targeted magazines from two or more countries. This could be particularly interesting if you yourself have experience of more than one culture, or of life in countries other than Britain. You should use the procedures described in sections 4 and 5 on data collection and analysis as a template, and modify your strategy as appropriate. You will need to obtain at least two copies of magazines produced and distributed in each country. In these days of global media, some gender-targeted magazines produce several editions which are sold to different markets around the world. This would provide a natural comparison. A study comparing two countries is simplest, but if you are feeling ambitious you could include a third. Do not forget, though, that you will need a sample size of between 10 and 20 units of material for each country, and that cross-cultural comparisons can be complicated.

The most important issue associated with cross-cultural research that you will have to deal with concerns 'cultural equivalence'. How are you going to deal with language differences? (Obviously, you should not attempt a comparison of magazines unless you have a good grasp of the languages they are written in.) Even if a magazine has the same title in two countries, can you assume that it targets a similar readership or has the same social connotations? And as a non-neutral qualitative researcher, you should also be aware that the interpretations you make of material produced in your own culture are necessarily different from those you make of less familiar material from other cultures. On a more positive note, there are good theoretical reasons for conducting cross-cultural work such as this. The theory of social representations is concerned with collective belief systems which become 'naturalized' into a society's stock of common sense. Just as a period abroad can make you question the way things are done at home, comparisons across different cultures can usefully highlight the arbitrary and socially constructed nature of what any one society takes for granted or assumes is 'normal'.

9 Social representations of health and illness

This section provides brief guidance for a project exploring the meanings associated with health and illness in contemporary society by conducting a content analysis of newspaper articles. Because this is a different topic, some general background material is provided, followed by notes on the practicalities of collecting and analysing newspaper material.

9.1 Health, illness and the media

Social representations of health and illness encompass broad branches of knowledge, beliefs and behaviours which operate simultaneously at individual and collective levels. Our everyday conversations are replete with discussions of health and illness. Individuals organize their lifestyle and diet according to their beliefs about health and illness, making daily decisions about what foods to eat, how much to drink or smoke, whether to take exercise, and so on. As individuals and as a society we continually enact social rituals which reveal certain health/illness representations, such as visiting the doctor and our reactions to various health statuses such as pregnancy, flu or cancer. Implicit in this range of behaviours and talk surrounding health and illness are models and beliefs regarding the nature and causes of health and ill-health, and assumptions about who or what is responsible for these.

In modern western societies, lay representations of health and illness are dominated by medical knowledge and understandings. Most of us have a concept of bacteria, viruses, and how our biology is affected by lifestyle and medical treatments. However, research investigating popular conceptions of health and illness shows that while lay understandings are clearly influenced by the medical model, they are also made up of complex belief systems that fall outside of the realm of medical knowledge. For example, a study by Herzlich (1973) found social representations in which health was conceptualized as an internal resource, eroded by the demands of the outside world. Illness on the other hand was seen as originating outside the individual, generated, for example, by urban living. The natural environment was seen as one in which internal reserves of health can be maintained, whereas the urban environment was seen as toxic and an eroder of health.

Other researchers have found a range of conceptions of health and illness (Brody, 1987; Calnan, 1987, for example). Health is conceptualized as an absence of illness; the capacity to do things; an internal resource which is either a given or under the individual's control; or determined by emotional and psychological well-being. Illness is conceptualized variously as an unpleasant experience which undermines personhood; the subject of medical activity; degeneration of the body through maturation; enforced stillness; and disruption of social roles and relationships. Concepts of normality and normal functioning seem to be central to lay representations of health and illness. Furthermore, implicit value judgements are associated with this. Western cultural beliefs in individual responsibility encourage a view of illness as abnormality, with an implicit suggestion that individuals who become ill are somehow at fault or responsible for their illness.

In recent decades public interest in health and medical issues has expanded dramatically. This trend is reflected in changing lifestyles and diet, the huge market for health-related consumer goods, and in health-oriented media output. Media analysts note that of all the scientific areas, health and medicine is the one that now receives most media attention. Health is also marketed as a consumer product and is increasingly being used by advertisers to market other products. Health-related media output comes in a range of guises: scientific documentaries on medical advances, health magazines, food-related articles and television programmes, radio phone-ins, and so on. However, for this project option you will be focusing on one particular type of media output – daily newspapers. So you will need to consider the specific nature of the daily press and the impact of this on the type of representations you find. Issues such as diet, exercise and lifestyle are more likely to be discussed in magazines, whereas the imperative to capture up-to-date events determines the content of daily newspapers.

The nature of daily news reporting, focusing on the most recent events, means that there is an emphasis on dramatic events rather than long-term issues. The 'importance' of these events is determined by, among other things, their unexpectedness, their drama, their relation to other news stories, and their reference to elite persons. Negative events, disasters and scandals seem to be particularly newsworthy. News stories tend to follow familiar set formats. For example, Karpf (1988) identifies the following categories of health-related news: the breakthrough; the disaster; the ethical controversy; the scandal; the strike; the epidemic; and the official report or speech. However, the recent proliferation of regular health or medical sections in most national daily newspapers allows for a different style of writing. Because these articles can be prepared in advance, they allow issues rather than events to be covered in more detail, and more space can be allocated to background information.

Karpf (1988) also identifies four styles of media treatment of health and illness issues. Medical news tends to be dominated by the 'medical approach' which casts doctors as legitimate sources of authority and promotes the standard medical model of health and illness. The curative powers of medicine are celebrated, and better health is equated with better medicine. The second style of media treatment is the 'consumer/patient' viewpoint which addresses issues from the perspective of patients' experiences, often provides information designed to be helpful to patients, and is critical of the inequality of the doctor-patient relationship. A third style is the 'look-after-yourself' perspective which focuses on preventative health measures and calls for changes in individual behaviour and lifestyle. Finally, the 'social approach' stresses the environmental or social origins of illness and focuses on prevention rather than cure of health problems. Karpf also notes several features of current news reporting of health and illness related issues. Stress has become a big issue recently, with the emphasis on the personal management of stress rather than its social and environmental causes. The role of politics has also increased in recent media output. Much critical media discussion centres on the current changes and problems within the NHS, aided by similar critiques of the NHS by the powerful medical establishment. The medical approach to health and illness is often questioned, and there is increasing debate surrounding the role and effectiveness of alternative medicine and its treatments.

In a large-scale study of health coverage in the British press, Entwistle and Hancock-Beaulieu (1992) found a significant increase since the early 1980s in health related articles, especially in the area of preventative medicine. Sampling nearly 3,000 articles from eight broadsheet and tabloid newspapers over a two-month period, they found that the most common topics of health-related news were diseases, preventative medicine (including diet and exercise) and the NHS. Class inequalities in health was the least frequently addressed issue. A clear difference in the style of reporting of quality and popular newspapers was found. Broadsheet papers provided more scientific information about health, paid more attention to political contexts, and made more use of authoritative journals and reports than tabloid papers which focused on individual case histories and tended to promote a lay viewpoint. Articles in the popular press were generally more sensationalized and less objective in their reporting style. The authors also found evidence for all four of the media treatment styles identified by Karpf (1988). In general, the broadsheet papers made more use of the 'medical approach' than the tabloids, where the 'consumer/patient' and 'look-after-yourself' treatment styles were common. The 'social approach' treatment was the least frequently used style of reporting.

9.2 Practical guidance

It is up to you which type of newspapers you choose to use. You may want to focus on the 'quality' or broadsheet papers or on the 'popular' or tabloid press. Or you may want to conduct a comparison between the two. Whatever you decide on, you should use more than one title, so that findings relate to a type of newspaper rather than one specific paper. You will need to think carefully about what material to include. For example, do you want to include articles on mental health, or to limit yourself to physical health and illness? Where is the boundary between articles on politics and those on political issues relating to health? Does using the headline of an article as an indicator of its content bias your sample? You should aim to come up with a clear definition of what you are studying, which will allow you to make reliable decisions about the inclusion and exclusion of articles for your sample. You should sample material over a reasonable period, say five consecutive weekdays, to ensure that the sample is an adequate reflection of daily newspaper output. As with the other projects, you will have to decide on your 'units of analysis', although, given the standard format of newspapers, whole articles are probably the easiest units to work with. You should aim to obtain a sample of between *20 and 40 articles*, with no fewer than 10 in each comparison group.

When analysing your material, use the notes in section 5 for guidance, although in this case most of your material will be written rather than image-based. Newspaper headlines fulfil a similar function to photographs in magazines, grabbing the readers attention and offering a promise of more in the article. So you will need to give serious consideration to analysis of headlines. As a guide, you may want to address the following questions in your analysis:

- How are health and illness conceptualized?

- How are health and illness explained (e.g. lifestyle, diet, stress, viral/contagion, genetics, maturation, etc.)?

- Who or what are presented as responsible for health and illness (e.g. the government, health-care professionals, individuals)?

References

Augustinos, M. and Walker, I. (1995) *Social Cognition: An Integrated Introduction*, London, Sage.

Banister, P., Burman, E., Parker, I., Taylor, M., Tindall, C. (1994) *Qualitative Methods in Psychology: A Research Guide*, Buckingham, Open University Press.

Barthel, D. (1992) 'When men put on appearances: advertising and the social construction of masculinity', in Craig, S. (ed.) *Men, Masculinity and the Media*, Newbury Park, CA, Sage.

Barthes, R. (1967) *Elements of Semiology*, London, Cape.

Berelson, B. (1952) *Content Analysis in Communication Research*, Glencoe, IL, Free Press.

Betterton, R. (ed.) (1987) *Looking On: Images of Femininity in the Visual Arts and Media*, London, Pandora.

Bordo, S. (1993) 'Reading the slender body', in Bordo, S. *Unbearable Weight: Feminism, Western Culture and the Body*, Berkeley, CA, University of California Press.

Bordo, S. (1997) 'Anorexia nervosa: psychopathology as the crystallization of culture', in Gergen, M. and Davis, S. (eds) *Towards a New Psychology of Gender: A Reader*, New York, Routledge.

Breakwell, G. and Canter, D. (eds) (1993) *Empirical Approaches to Social Representations*, Oxford, Clarendon Press.

Brody, R. (1987) *Stories of Sickness*, New Haven, CT, Yale University Press.

Burman, E. (ed.) (1990) *Femininities and Psychological Practice*, London, Sage.

Calnan, M. (1987) *Health and Illness: The Lay Perspective*, London, Tavistock Publications.

Caplin, E.A. (1992) *Motherhood and Representation: The Mother in Popular Culture and Melodrama*, Routledge, London.

Chombart de Lauwe, M.J. (1984) 'Changes in the representation of the child in the course of cultural transmission', in Farr, R.M. and Moscovici, S. (eds) *Social Representations*, Cambridge, Cambridge University Press.

Connell, R. (1995) *Masculinities*, Cambridge, Polity Press.

Coward, R. (1984) *Female Desire: Women's Sexuality Today*, London, Paladin.

De Rosa, A. (1987) 'The social representations of mental illness in children and adults', in Doise, W. and Moscovici, S. (eds) *Current Issues in European Social Psychology, Volume 2*, Cambridge, Cambridge University Press.

Doise, W., Clemence, A. and Lorezi-Cioldi, F. (1993) *The Quantitative Analysis of Social Representations*, London, Harvester Wheatsheaf.

Douglas, S. (1995) *Where the Girls Are: Growing up Female with the Mass Media*, Harmondsworth, Penguin Books.

Duveen, G. and Lloyd, B. (eds) (1990) *Social Representations and the Development of Knowledge*, Cambridge, Cambridge University Press.

Edley, N. and Wetherell, M. (1995) *Men in Perspective: Practice, Power and Identity*, London, Harvester Wheatsheaf.

Edwards, D. and Potter, J. (1992) *Discursive Psychology*, London, Sage.

Entwistle, V. and Hancock-Beaulieu, M. (1992) 'Health and medical coverage in the UK national press', *Public Understanding of Science*, vol.1, pp.367–82.

Farr, R.M. (1993) 'Theory and method in the study of social representations', in Breakwell, G.M. and Canter, D. (eds) *Empirical Approaches to Social Representations*, Oxford, Clarendon Press.

Farr, R.M. and Moscovici, S. (eds) (1984) *Social Representations*, Cambridge, Cambridge University Press.

Ferguson, M. (1983) *Forever Feminine: Women's Magazines and the Cult of Femininity*, London, Gower.

Flick, U. (1992) 'Triangulation revisited: strategy of validation or alternative?', *Journal for the Theory of Social Behaviour*, vol.22, no.2, pp.175–97.

Gergen, K. (1985) 'The social constructionist movement in modern psychology', *American Psychologist*, vol.40, no.3, pp.266–75.

Glaser, B.G. and Strauss, A.L. (1967) *The Discovery of Grounded Theory*, Chicago, IL, Aldine.

Goffman, E. (1976) *Gender Advertisements*, New York, Harper and Row.

Hall, S. (1980) 'Encoding/decoding', in Hall, S., Hobson, D., Lowe, A. and Willis, P. *Culture, Media and Language*, London, Hutchinson.

Henwood, K. and Pidgeon, N. (1992) 'Qualitative research and psychological theorising', *British Journal of Psychology*, vol.83, pp.97–111.

Herzlich, C. (1973) *Health and Illness: A Social Psychological Analysis*, London, Academic Press.

Hollway, W. (1989) *Subjectivity and Method in Psychology: Gender, Meaning and Science*, London, Sage.

Holsti, O. (1969) *Content Analysis for the Social Sciences and Humanities*, Reading, MA, Addison-Wesley.

Jodelet, D. (1991) *Madness and Social Representations*, Hemel Hempstead, Harvester Wheatsheaf.

Karpf, A. (1988) *Doctoring the Media: The Reporting of Health and Medicine*, London, Routledge.

Kimmel (1987) *Changing Men: New Directions in Research on Men and Masculinity*, Beverly Hills, CA, Sage.

Krippendorf, K. (1982) *Content Analysis*, Beverly Hills, CA, Sage.

Livingstone, S. (ed.) (1996) *Making Sense of Television: The Psychology of Audience Interpretation*, Oxford, Butterworth-Heinemann.

Livingstone, S. and Green, G. (1986) 'Television advertisements and the portrayal of gender', *British Journal of Social Psychology*, vol.25, pp.149–54.

Livingstone, S. and Lunt, P. (1994) *Talk on Television*, London, Routledge.

Manstead, A. and McCulloch, C. (1981) 'Sex-role stereotyping in British television advertisements', *British Journal of Social Psychology*, vol.20, pp.171–80.

McCracken, E. (1993) *Decoding Women's Magazines: From 'Mademoiselle' to 'Ms'*, London, Macmillan.

Moscovici, S. (1976) *La Psychanalyse: Son Image et son Public* (2nd edn), Paris, Presses Universitaires de France.

Moscovici, S. (1981) 'On social representations', in Forgas, J. (ed.) *Social Cognition: Perspectives on Everyday Understanding*, London, Academic Press.

Moscovici, S. (1984) 'The phenomenon of social representations', in Farr, R.M. and Moscovici, S. (eds) *Social Representations*, Cambridge, Cambridge University Press.

Potter, J. and Wetherell, M. (1987) *Discourse and Social Psychology: Beyond Attitudes and Behaviour*, London, Sage.

Potter, J. (1996a) *Representing Reality: Discourse, Rhetoric and Social Construction*, London, Sage.

Potter, J. (1996b) 'Attitudes, social representations and discursive psychology', in Wetherell, M. (ed.) *Identities, Groups and Social Issues*, London, Sage/The Open University.

Rose, D. (1998) 'Television, madness and community care', *Journal of Community and Applied Social Psychology*, vol.8, pp.213–28.

Sapsford, R. (1998) 'Evidence', in Sapsford, R., Still, A., Wetherell, M, Miell, D. and Stevens, R. (eds) *Theory and Social Psychology*, London, Sage/ The Open University.

Sarbin, T. and Kitsuse, J. (eds) (1994) *Constructing the Social*, London, Sage.

Segal, L. (1990) *Slow Motion Changing Men, Changing Masculinities*, London, Virago.

Silverman, D. (1993) *Interpreting Qualitative Data: Analysing Talk, Text and Interaction*, London, Sage.

Sontag, S. (1988) *AIDS and its Metaphors*, Harmondsworth, Penguin Books.

Ussher, J. (1997) *Fantasies of Femininity: Reframing the Boundaries of Sex*. Harmondsworth, Penguin Books.

Walby, S. (1990) *Theorising Patriarchy*, Oxford, Blackwell.

Weber, R.P. (1990) *Basic Content Analysis* (2nd edn), Series: Quantitative Applications in the Social Sciences, Newbury Park, CA, Sage.

Wernick, A. (1991) '(Re-)imaging gender: the case of men', in Wernick, A. *Promotional Culture: Advertising, Ideology and Symbolic Expression*, London, Sage.

Wetherell, M. (1996) 'Life histories/social histories', in Wetherell, M. (ed.) *Identities, Groups and Social Issues*, London, Sage/The Open University.

Williamson, J. (1978) *Decoding Advertisements: Ideology and Meaning in Advertising*, London, Marion Boyars.

Winship, J. (1987) *Inside Women's Magazines*, London, Pandora Press.

Further reading

Augoustinos, M. and Walker, I. (1995) *Social Cognition: An Integrated Introduction*, London, Sage.

A clearly written textbook which reviews the theory of social representations and other major social psychological theories such as attribution theory and social identity theory. Provides some useful comparisons of the various perspectives in modern social psychology.

Banister, P., Burman, E., Parker, I., Taylor, M. and Tindall, C. (1994) *Qualitative Methods in Psychology: A Research Guide*, Buckingham, Open University Press.

Provides a good introduction to qualitative research methods. Includes a clear account of epistemological issues, examples of a range of qualitative methods, a discussion of validity, and advice on writing up qualitative research.

Bordo, S. (1993) *Unbearable Weight: Feminism, Western Culture and the Body*, Berkeley, CA, University of California Press.

An interesting book by a powerful American writer who links issues of power and control to women's experiences of and relationships with their own bodies. The essay on 'Reading the slender body', in which Bordo analyses forms of bodily control such as dieting and body building with consumer culture, morality and the management of desire, is particularly recommended.

Breakwell, G. and Canter, D. (eds) (1993) *Empirical Approaches to Social Representations*, Oxford, Clarendon Press.

A collection of essays and empirical studies using social representations theory conducted mainly by British social psychologists.

Coward, R. (1984) *Female Desire: Women's Sexuality Today*, London, Paladin.

A highly accessible book, arguing that through a variety of cultural phenomena including the media, women's desires are both constructed and exploited within a consumerist and male-dominated society.

Edley, N. and Wetherell, M. (1995) *Men in Perspective: Practice, Power and Identity*, London, Harvester Wheatsheaf.

A good general review of research on masculinity and various perspectives on male identity development.

Farr, R.M. and Moscovici, S. (eds) (1984) *Social Representations*, Cambridge, Cambridge University Press.

A classic text which provides a detailed exposition of the theory of social representations, its aims, origins and basic assumptions. Chapter 1, 'The phenomenon of social representations', by Serge Moscovici, is particularly recommended. Later chapters provide some examples of empirical studies conducted by an international range of authors.

Herzlich, C. (1973) *Health and Illness: A Social Psychological Analysis*, London, Academic Press.

A study of collective beliefs about health and illness using interviews with a sample of Parisian lay people. This is one of the first published studies using the theory of social representations and includes an short forward about the theory written by Moscovici.

Jodelet, D. (1991) *Madness and Social Representations*, Hemel Hempsteaad, Harvester Wheatsheaf.

A fascinating detailed study using a social representational approach to investigate collective understandings of madness in a rural French community. One of the best examples of empirical work using the theory of social representations.

Moscovici, S. (1981) 'On social representations', in Forgas, J. (ed.) *Social Cognition: Perspectives on Everyday Understanding*, London, Academic Press.

A basic introduction to the theory of social representations. Moscovici explains here his notion of a 'thinking' society, and the function of social representations in making sense of the unfamiliar. The chapter also discusses processes involved in the formation of social representations, and the relationship between social representations and causal attributions.

Wetherell, M. (1996) 'Life histories/social histories', in Wetherell, M. (ed.) *Identities, Groups and Social Issues*, London, Sage/The Open University.

A clear discussion of social constructionist perspectives on identity construction using the example of masculinity. The chapter investigates forms of masculinity in modern society, the social factors shaping men's experiences of themselves, and notions of patriarchy.

Appendix 1: 'The good care guide'

Choosing your antenatal care and deciding where to deliver your baby are important decisions. We give you the facts to help you decide

The good care guide

O nce your pregnancy is confirmed, your doctor or midwife will ask what sort of antenatal care you want and where you'd like to have your baby. It can be hard to make this sort of decision, especially early on when you're still adjusting to the idea of being pregnant, let alone having a baby! But whatever you decide, you can always change your mind later on, providing there aren't any complications.

Here's an outline of the different types of care available to pregnant women.

Consultant care
With this, you have all your antenatal care at the hospital and see either your consultant or one of his or her team. You'll be advised to have this sort of care if you have a medical condition, such as diabetes or heart disease, or if you had complications during a previous pregnancy.

The pros You and your baby's health will be closely monitored and any potential problems will be spotted quickly.

The cons You could have to travel further for antenatal visits; you may have to wait longer when you get there, and you're unlikely to be seen by the same doctor or midwife at each visit, so it can be a bit impersonal.

Shared care
This is where care is shared between your GP or community midwife and the hospital. You will go to hospital for some tests, such as your routine ultrasound scan or special blood tests, and you may also visit the hospital at certain times during your pregnancy for extra checks.

You may be assigned one particular midwife (this is sometimes called the 'know-your-midwife' scheme) who will see you for most visits. She may also go with you to hospital for delivery — or she and your GP can arrange a home birth for you.

The pros You already know your GP and you may be able to build up a relationship with one or two midwives. You'll probably find it easier to discuss intimate worries with someone you know. Your GP's surgery is likely to be close to where you live.

The cons Care may still be a bit impersonal, as there may be up to four midwives operating between your GP's clinic and the hospital.

GP unit
With this scheme, you'll see a doctor and a community midwife for all your antenatal care, and when you go into labour your midwife, or possibly your doctor, will deliver you in the GP unit, which may be attached to your local hospital.

The pros You'll be delivered by someone you know in a small unit close to home.

The cons If there are any complications with the birth, you might have to be transferred to a larger hospital, which can be upsetting if you have to travel far.

Midwifery-led care
In this scheme, you won't need to see a doctor at all as a team of midwives will care for you at the clinic or health centre. Some checks can be performed at home. When you go into labour, one of the team on duty will assess and care for you or, if you're having a hospital delivery, will go in with you.

The pros You get to know all the team, usually no more than six. You get continuity of care.

The cons This scheme is only suitable for low-risk women. If a complication arises during pregnancy, a referral will be made to your GP or consultant obstetrician but it won't mean the midwives will stop looking after you.

Domino scheme
This stands for 'domiciliary-in-out' and means that a local team of community midwives and your GP will care for you throughout your pregnancy, either at home (domiciliary care), at a clinic, or at your doctor's ▶

Getting what you want

When you're pregnant for the first time and perhaps feeling emotionally vulnerable, it can sometimes feel as if you're being taken over by the professionals. To understand the jargon and get the birth you want, it helps to arm yourself with some facts. Read as much as you can, write off for information and discuss options with your partner, family and friends. If you've got questions write them down and take them with you to your next antenatal appointment. Most of all, though, think about what really matters to you and be persistent about getting it.

The Tomy Cradle Carrier. (Or how to rock 'n' stroll).

How can you stay close to your baby and still carry on with your life?

All you need is the uniquely adaptable Tomy Cradle Carrier.

Simply adjust the padded straps to fit and you're off and strolling, knowing your baby's protected by a padded head and neck support.

Come feeding time, just discreetly slip down the shoulder strap, instead of having to slip off home. (The carrier even comes with a washable Terry bib.)

Either way, you can keep your baby snug inside with the detachable all-weather cover.

And when you are back home, you can lift out your sleeping baby undisturbed in the removable inner seat.

Trust Tomy to put more into carriers so you can get more out of life, together.

CHAPTER 8

DISCOVERING SUBJECTIVE MEANINGS: DEPTH INTERVIEWING

by Jane Henry

Contents

1 Introduction

This project asks you to use an interview – a discussion between two people in the context of a research setting – to find out about the meanings one individual attributes to some aspect of their personal world or sense of self, with a view to gaining insight into another person's experience and view of the world.

The aims of this project are to:

- Give you experience of qualitative interviewing and analysis and enable you to recognize some of the problems and advantages of depth interviews.

- Show how your own attitudes, values and beliefs, and the interviewee's perception of the situation can influence the outcome of the interview and thus highlight the role of interpersonal and personal constructions of reality.

- Help you gain some insight into your own and another's subjective meanings and sense of self.

- Complement theoretical exposition on perspectives on the self with a small-scale field investigation into this topic.

- Raise questions about epistemological limits to any analysis of subjective experience and ground your understanding of the purpose and difficulties of empirical work in experiential psychology.

2 Qualitative interviews

2.1 Interviews

Interviews are a widely used tool in social psychology, but they come in a variety of shapes and forms, ranging along a continuum from the highly structured to the open-ended.

In highly structured interviews the interviewer sticks to the order and wording of precisely phrased questions and predetermined precoded answers; in semi-structured interviews the interviewer asks more open-ended questions; in depth interviews the interviewer uses an interview guide to remind them of areas that might be worth asking; and in completely open-ended exploratory interviews the interviewer merely has a topic area but is not at all sure exactly what will be covered.

Since structured interviews employ standard questions where the researcher supplies predetermined codes for each type of answer, they generate standardized information which can be quantified and analysed relatively easily. For example, this kind of interview data has been used in social psychology to generalize about the attitudes of groups of people, either by contrasting responses from different subgroups (e.g. men and women), or seeing which variables correlate or co-vary with each other (e.g. experience and belief).

The drawback with this type of approach is that the information which is obtained tends to be superficial and limited. This is because the standard questions may be interpreted differently by different respondents; also the question and answer codes may not cover areas that are salient to the respondent. (Quantitative attitude techniques are discussed more fully in Potter, 1996.)

In contrast the qualitative, open-ended interviewing style which this project employs has no set questions, though the interviewer normally has a topic to focus on and often possible areas within this. Here the course of the interview is determined to a large extent by the interviewee's contributions. The task of an interviewer is to get the subject to talk freely around the research topic and thus convey his or her values and beliefs about this area.

More complex topics often lend themselves to more open-ended interviews. For example, the open-ended nature of the depth interview is more likely to offer a rounder, fuller and deeper picture of the interviewee's perspective on the issue under consideration and is therefore better suited to deal with complex and sensitive psychological issues, such as the nature of an individual's life experience. However, such interviews place many demands on the interviewer, are time-consuming, the information they produce can be hard to analyse and the analysis is likely to be coloured by the researcher's perceptions. Depth interviews also assume the informant has access to relevant information and is willing to reveal it to an interviewer. (For an example of a well-known piece of social psychology based round qualitative interviews see Levinson et al.'s 1986 book on adult male development.)

Qualitative interviews are also often used in an exploratory way at the start of a quantitative research project. Here the interviews are focused on a particular topic and are used to develop hypotheses and pertinent questions which are subsequently tested on a larger sample, often via a questionnaire.

In psychology, open-ended qualitative interviews are commonly used in clinical and psychotherapeutic as well as research settings. Personal history interviews, in which clients are encouraged to talk about their life, circumstances and feelings, are used as the basis for assessment by various caring professionals, such as social workers and counsellors. Humanist psychotherapists may use a totally unstructured approach to interviewing originating in the non-directive interview style advocated by Rogers (1945). Here, the therapist attempts to restrict questions to non-directive probes about areas raised by the client.

Many other traditions also employ qualitative interviews. For example, the qualitative approach to interviewing has been used for decades in anthropology and sociology, in the ethnographic tradition of research that derives from anthropology (e.g. Hammersley, 1997). Feminist

(Spender, 1981) and new paradigm (Reason and Rowan, 1981) research are among other traditions that also rely heavily on a qualitative approach to interviews, but here the participant is normally given a much greater role in determining the nature and direction of the research process.

See Banister *et al.* (1994), especially Chapter 4 'Interviewing', for further discussion of different kinds of qualitative interviewing and research not addressed by this project.

ACTIVITY

2.2 Analysis

In qualitative research, the processes of data collection and analysis are often interwoven. In the course of the interview(s) the researcher inevitably begins to develop ideas about the informant's thinking, and these are almost certain to be amended as the interview goes on. Ideally, the interview itself tests out the researcher's ideas by asking questions that could provide falsifying or confirming material. In this project, you will have to think fast to achieve this in the course of one or two interviews.

In analysing qualitative interview data, researchers make every attempt to be systematic – examining all the data, noting points which support and conflict with the researcher's conclusions, possibly reformulating the picture in the light of evidence that is not happily accommodated in the original version. In other words, the analysis involves a lot more than just picking out a few quotes to support a picture which, at first glance, seems coherent and plausible. Researchers strive to avoid over-generalization or misinterpretation. It is important to test the preliminary conclusions, as qualitative research is easily open to the criticism that the analysis has been selective and is therefore biased. Many researchers ask the interviewee whether they feel the analysis is an accurate reflection of their views or not.

However, no matter how conscientiously this process is carried out it is still one person's account, a partial account, and will almost certainly reflect the concerns of the interviewer at least in part. Therefore, good researchers include a reflexive account in which they make public any ways in which they might have affected the outcome, by describing the research process, considering the nature of the relationship between interviewer and interviewee, and acknowledging their own preconceptions and intentions.

In ethnographic research and a number of other qualitative approaches, the researcher's interpretation is checked against some other source of information. Since any research procedure has some strengths and some weaknesses, there is a lot to be said for using different methods or different researchers to investigate the same topic. In a small way, each option within this project uses different methods or different researchers to investigate the same topic.

Banister *et al.* (1994) provide further background on analysing and reporting on qualitative interviews, particularly in Chapter 1, 'Qualitative research', Chapter 9, 'Issues of evaluation', and Chapter 10, 'Report writing'.

2.3 Experiential research

Subjective experiences and the meanings people ascribe to them are the subject-matter of this project and the primary concern of the experiential tradition within psychology. Experiential psychologists often use depth interviews to ask people to describe their experiences, as it is difficult if not impossible to observe other's feelings, thoughts and intentions, their experience of the world or themselves and the meanings and significance they attach to events and their own actions.

Experiential research has grown out of phenomenology, humanistic psychology and existential concerns. The focus in all these traditions is on an analysis of experiences from the point of view of those who have the experiences – understanding human behaviour from the actor's frame of reference. This is sometimes referred to as first person rather than third person research. Like phenomenology, the experiential perspective stresses the importance of studying reality as people imagine it to be, and phenomena that occur naturally. It focuses on the meaning people ascribe to their experiences and their context and the relationship between subjective states and behaviour. Similar concerns are shown in humanistic and phenomenological psychology.

The experiential approach's antecedents of phenomenology, humanistic psychology and existentialism emerged in reaction to the dominance of behaviourism and the experimental method in the 1950s. Their concern is less with measurement than meaning, with what people experience rather than what can be observed. Hence it is no surprise that experiential research is often qualitative in nature. (See Banister *et al.*, 1994, Chapter 1 for an outline of the qualitative research undertaken by related traditions.) We see a similar split between the experientialist's concern with meaning and subjective experience shown in Stevens (1996a) and the experimental tradition demonstrated in Toates (1996) and Lalljee (1996). Unlike the cognitive-experimental and biological perspectives described there, experientialists rarely make any attempt to reduce information to numbers. Rather, experiential researchers strive to understand the phenomena and the situation as a whole, on the assumption that an understanding of the context is essential to understanding the person.

Another difference is the predominance of deductive versus inductive methods. The quantitative and experimental traditions in social psychology usually rely heavily on a deductive research strategy (i.e. hypotheses are specified before collection of evidence begins and the research is aimed at testing the validity of these hypotheses). In contrast, the qualitative tradition in experiential research, of which this project is an example, often begins with an inductive strategy – the researcher moves from empirical observations to generalizations about the topic being studied and, in a large study, from there to theory. In practice, this means the researcher enters the field open to discovering what the participant thinks are salient issues, rather than seeking his or her opinion on *a priori* issues which the researcher has deemed pertinent, and tries to keep as open a mind as possible about the outcome.

2.4 Methodological issues

Whilst some methodological issues affect many approaches to conducting interviews, a number are particularly pertinent for experientially-oriented interviews. These include the following points.

In undertaking an interview aimed at identifying the key features in another person's life, experiential social psychologists tend to assume that there is a meaningful perspective there, and that there is an underlying pattern in people's actions that can be known and seen by another. Yet some people, as Dahrendorf (1959) puts it, 'get by with a minimum of reflection' and may not have many views or much insight into themselves. Views on abstract psychological notions may be particularly hard to elucidate or may simply not be present. For example, Cottrell (1979) concluded that her middle-class sample neither had any coherent notion of the meaning of life nor felt the need for one, but were content to get on with immediate projects.

Experiential researchers also tend to approach interviews assuming that their interviewee's values are fairly stable, their accounts of their behaviour bear a close relationship to their actions and that there is a 'core' self that can speak fairly knowledgeably about the interviewee's intentions. Though perhaps of less concern to researchers working within certain other traditions such as discursive psychology, these assumptions can be problematic for those working within an experiential tradition.

For example, people's opinions are often inconsistent or ambiguous. For instance, in studying images of the class structure, Goldthorpe *et al.* (1969) discarded 7 per cent of their sample because their responses were so uncertain or contradictory that the researchers failed to discern any communicable image at all. There is also the question of the stability of views over time. Would the views of someone two weeks before and two weeks after they were made redundant be the same?

There is then the question of the validity of the qualitative information – to what extent are the verbal descriptions and explanations offered by the respondent plausible, coherent and accurate? The information the interviewee offers may be accepted at face value, yet is it a real reflection of the way the informant experiences the world or just a *post hoc* rationalization? The relationship between intentions and behaviour has been shown to be tenuous from LaPiere (1934) onwards (see Potter, 1996, for discussion of this issue). Powerful evidence for our need to explain away our actions is provided by split-brain research and post-hypnotic suggestion studies (see Toates, 1996, for examples). Split-brain patients are left with a largely mute right hemisphere which is unable to describe objects presented in the left visual field, and an articulate but less spatial left hemisphere which is unable to draw objects presented to the right visual field; neither hemisphere appears to know what the other is doing. Subjects invariably attempt to rationalize apparent inconsistencies caused by the experimenter presenting separate objects to each side of the visual field. Gazzaniga (1967) concluded that each hemisphere actually has a separate consciousness. Similarly, in post-hypnotic suggestion studies, subjects told to raise an arm on coming out of hypnosis, and then asked why they did this, invariably offer an explanation they believe – such as they felt like stretching. Further, if we accept Freud's notion of the unconscious as a driving force, many of our utterances may be little more than creative story-telling. Increasingly, evidence from cognitive psychology suggests that the really crucial factors are processed at an unconscious level and are unavailable to our conscious minds (see Claxton, 1994, for an accessible review).

There is another issue. From an experiential perspective, each one of us has not one but several different selves: a private self and a public self, for instance, or, if you prefer, competing subpersonalities. The private self is normally only revealed to our intimate friends, if at all. The public self will vary according to the context and power relations – virtually everyone reacts differently towards persons of different sex, age, 'race' and social status. A research-interview subpersonality might be quite different from a party subpersonality. Is one 'real', or do they all represent valid sides of the person? Even if there were a 'real' self there is the question of whether it is likely to be revealed to an interviewer?

Interviewing involves a social interaction between two people, and the outcome depends very much on the quality and setting of that interaction plus each party's expectations and attributions. The outcome is affected by the characters of the interviewer and interviewee, their perception of the situation, their understanding of the task, and their motivation and verbal skills. The interviewer needs to attempt to disentangle the effects of their intentions, perceptions and relationship to the participant on the situation.

It has been known for many years that how much the informant reveals or which sets of behaviour are shown is heavily dependent on his or her impression of the interviewer. Numerous studies have shown that the interviewer's appearance can affect the responses given on sensitive issues. For example, Robinson and Rhodes (1946) found that fewer anti-Semitic opinions were given to interviewers who looked Jewish (though people might have been particularly sensitive to this issue at that time). Katz (1942) found that the interviewer's apparent social class influenced the social and political opinions given by working-class respondents. The age, clothing and 'race' of the interviewer have also been found to affect what the interviewee says.

Various studies show that informants are likely to answer in ways that they believe the interviewer perceives as *socially desirable*. For example, views that are embarrassing or just divergent from one's self-image may not be reported at all, or may be changed to make them more acceptable. Even with a stranger, people seem constrained to make a good impression. For instance, income and voting have been shown to be consistently over-reported (i.e. there is a tendency for people to state that they earn more than they do and claim that they have voted when they have not done so). Similarly, mental and physical illness tend to be under-reported.

Equally important are interviewer expectations. Hyman *et al.* (1954) showed how *interviewer expectations* could affect what was reported. They identified three areas: role expectations, where the interviewer expected certain responses from members of particular groups, e.g. women, businessmen, etc.; attitude structure expectations, where the interviewer expected the interviewee to be consistent in his outlook; and probability expectations, where the interviewer expected beliefs to concur with his own ideas about sentiments in the population. In practice, for example, by offering leading questions or adopting a certain tone of voice or other non-verbal signals, interviewers can communicate their beliefs to respondents who often tailor expressions of their own beliefs accordingly. There are ways of questioning which aim to minimize interviewer bias; these are discussed in section 5.3.

The recording and analysis of data may also be biased; for example, by overemphasizing portions of the interview that reflect the interviewer's hobby-horses (i.e. points of issue he or she feels particularly strongly about). The additional information provided by each follow-up option is partly designed to counteract the danger of selective analysis. You should bear these points in mind when evaluating your data.

Whilst acknowledging these issues, most psychologists would accept that interviews can provide us with a useful means of learning how others perceive and make sense of their experience (assuming that the informant is motivated to disclose their opinions). Psychologists working within the experiential tradition assume that there is a subjective authentic truth that can be conveyed at least approximately by the interviewee to the interviewer. Social constructionists would have a very different view about the type of meaning that arises. When an interviewee struggles to put an experience into words they might question whether this reflects the informant's cognitive schema, instead suggesting it is an attempt to locate a common point in the discursive space shared by interviewer and interviewee. You might want to consider, for instance, the way discourse analysts view language (Wetherell and Maybin, 1996, section 4) and their emphasis on action orientation, the constitutive nature of language, and indexicality. How does this view of language compare with the experientialists' emphasis on people's accounts as a more neutral vehicle for conveying subjective truth (see also Still, 1998)?

3 Background

3.1 Overview

In this project, we want you to use a *qualitative depth interview* that aims to encourage the informant to answer in his or her own terms. We leave the choice of topic to you. You could, for example, pick one area of your interviewee's life – his or her work experiences perhaps, or the effects of a major incident such as redundancy, or you could opt for something more general such as his or her goals in life.

It is often difficult to know to what extent the researcher's understandings of the informant's views is a reflection of their own perspective, a transitory perspective unique to the dialogue between the two, or some more enduring aspects of the informant's ideas. Each of the project's follow-up options (see below) offers *a different way of developing* your initial ideas about the informant's thinking. These involve comparing the ideas you develop after an initial interview, with further information. In Option 1 this new information takes the form of a second interview and in Option 2 an essay; in Option 3 it comprises a feedback discussion with the informant and in Option 4 it is a second opinion provided by another researcher (a fellow-student). You will be asked to choose one of these to complete. Each offers a simple form of triangulation, a procedure which involves collecting evidence from different sources or perspectives which bear upon the same issue. (See Banister *et al.*, 1994, Chapter 9, pp.145–9 for amplification.)

A summary of these options follows.

3.2 Options

Option 1: two-stage account

Here, after a preliminary analysis of your first interview, you go back and carry out *a second interview* with the same informant. The purpose of the second interview is to allow you to focus in progressively on areas that seemed important, fill in any gaps, and perhaps test your ideas about the respondent's thinking by asking questions that could support and, more importantly, refute your initial impressions.

Your final report is based on data from both interviews. This has the advantage that if you are unhappy with the first interview you get a second chance to get more information.

Option 2: comparative account

Here you compare an interview with your informant about a particular topic with a *written piece of work in which he or she addresses the same or related areas*: for example, a 1,000-word autobiography. It does not matter if this written material is pre-existing or specifically written for the occasion. However, you need to establish details about the context in which it was produced: where, why, when and for whom the document was written, for example.

Option 3: negotiated account

This option involves interviewing an individual, analysing this data, and then going back to your informant to *discuss his or her opinion of the validity of your account*, both in terms of its accuracy as a summary of what went on during the interview and as a summary of his or her thoughts and feelings about the topic in question. This second stage will obviously throw up a lot more information, for instance about issues that were not covered first time round.

Your final report is based on information from the interview and the ensuing discussion. This has the added interest that the informant plays an active part in the data-analysis as well as the data-collection phase (unlike Option 1, where the conclusions drawn are entirely the responsibility of the researcher). Obviously this option requires a pretty robust informant who will not be too threatened by the second stage. It also requires a tactful interviewer.

Option 4: two-person account

This option involves a *comparison of your own and another student's account of the same person* after you have both interviewed them. First, you and your fellow-student need to agree the topic areas, then you each interview the informant, either separately or together, produce an account of your interview separately, and then meet to discuss your conclusions. Your final report will involve presenting your own ideas about the informant and comparing these with your colleague's. The results could be intriguing.

In all options, you should not expect to obtain perfect interviews or a fully formed picture of the way your informant sees the world: you should expect to explore a relatively small area of your informant's life rather than skim a wider area. However, you should be be aware of the shortcomings in the procedure and the ways in which you might have inadvertently influenced the outcome.

3.3 Requirements

To undertake this project you need to be comfortable with the idea of interviewing someone about his or her life. I mean this in an ethical sense, not that you should be bounding with confidence, as you may well be a little nervous at the start of your interview. The interview need not be concerned with any deeply personal matter; topics focusing on work life or dealing with how people spend their leisure time are perfectly acceptable.

However, we expect you to go beyond describing your informant's demographic situation – what they do, how many children they have, etc. – and ask for their opinions and feelings about their situation, with a view to gaining some insight into the way they 'make sense of' this aspect of their life. The use of an audio recorder to record the interview(s) is strongly advised.

It is important to bear in mind that this is a research interview, not a counselling session. You should stick to the researcher's role and refrain from giving advice. You are not asked to 'psychoanalyse' your interviewee, but rather to report back what they say and how they express their feelings in their own terms and what this evidence suggests about how the informant attributes meaning. It is extremely important that you stick to this brief and do not attempt to press the informant to reveal any more than he or she is willing to. This will require a certain amount of sensitivity on your part.

Talking about thoughts and feelings, one's present position and future plans can be quite a threatening and moving experience. To undertake this project, you need to be able to locate an informant who is prepared to undergo this kind of probing reflection. Your task will be made simpler if you pick someone who talks easily and is not too anxious about the process. Most people like to talk about themselves so this should not be too difficult. In selecting your informant, you need to be sensitive to power issues; for example, a junior member of staff may agree reluctantly because you are the boss rather than because they want to be interviewed by you.

3.4 Timing

The initial interview should last for at least an hour, possibly an hour and a half. Thus, for Option 1 your informant needs to have at least an hour to spare on two separate occasions, and in Option 2 rather longer, if they are writing an account especially for you as well as doing an interview. For Option 3, your informant probably needs to set aside over an hour for the first interview and up to an hour for the follow-up discussion. In addition, both you and your informant need to be open enough to discuss your preliminary thinking about the informant. For Option 4, you need to be able to locate another student to work with you in planning and conducting the interview and you must both be prepared to reveal your preliminary conclusions to each other. You also need to find an informant who is willing to talk about himself/herself to two people, for an hour or so on each occasion.

4 Preparation

4.1 Ethics

Naturally you need to satisfy yourself that the way you conduct the research and the information you give about it is ethical. The British Psychological Society (1997) ethical guidelines for conducting research with human participants make a number of points relevant to interviews. Researchers are encouraged to offer participants as full information about the project as possible, including the objectives of the investigation. They should also make plain the participant's right to withdraw from the research at any time and the right to require that their own data, including recordings, are destroyed. Participants have the right to expect that information they provide is treated confidentially and, if published, will not be identifiable as theirs. The BPS intend that participation in a psychological investigation should not increase the probability that the participant would come to any form of harm. Participants should be asked about any factors, such as a pre-existing medical condition, that might create a risk. At the debriefing the investigator should provide participants with all the necessary information to complete their understanding and discuss the participant's experience of the research in order to monitor any unforeseen negative effects or misconceptions. Participants should also be informed of procedures for contacting the investigators after the investigation should questions or concerns arise as a result of the interview.

4.2 Task

Your goal is to develop as full a picture as possible of the way your informant experiences and makes sense of the aspect of their life you chose to focus on. You obviously need some idea of your informant's situation, but remember we expect you to move beyond describing what your informant does and to find out what they think and feel about this aspect of their life, the meaning they place on events and the beliefs they hold.

In your final report, you will be expected to draw on the interview data and the additional information provided by your chosen follow-up option to support your conclusions about any patterns in the way the informant structures their thoughts and feelings about this area of their life. This will involve organizing your material in some way that conveys your story about your informant and illustrates the points you make with quotations from the informant.

You need a reflexive account that discusses the contextual factors that appear to have played a part in affecting the outcome (notably any part your role and perspective may have played in shaping the account), and offers some reflection on the reasons for your interviewee's views and on the strengths and weaknesses of the method and approach in comparison with other approaches, such as quantitative research, and other perspectives on language, identity and the self.

4.3 Topic

You may choose any topic, so long as it focuses on some aspect of the informant's sense of self. There are innumerable possibilities. Reading Stevens (1996a) may suggest topic areas to you. Other possibilities are outlined below.

One area of life

You could choose one *area* of your informant's life (e.g. friends, relationships, home life, work, leisure interests, peak or flow experiences – see Stevens, 1996a, section 2.2) and try to find out what they think and feel about this area of their life, how they make sense of these experiences, how important it is for your informant, why they have made particular decisions and what their goals are in this area. See Banister *et al.* (1994, pp.58–62) for a discussion of three examples – formative influences on occupational choice; political involvement with animal rights groups; and the importance of friendship. You might be able to make use of a visual aid. For example, you could ask the respondent to draw a lifeline, a line illustrating the high and low points (i.e. critical events, relationships and feelings) in their life (see Figure 1). Alternatively, a family tree could be useful, or a drawing showing the network of relationships in which the respondent is involved (known as a sociogram).

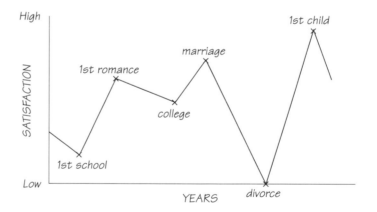

Figure 1 *A lifeline illustrates the perceived high and low points in an individual's life*

One period of life

Another approach would be to focus on one *period* of your informant's life; for example, their experience of childhood, parenthood, adolescence or old age. Here again it is the impact of these experiences on your informant and their feelings about this period that we are after, rather than an account of what they did.

Changes over time

You may opt to focus on *changes over time*. This may be the impact of a particular situation on the individual and their outlook (e.g. redundancy or becoming a parent; or something more wide-ranging, perhaps covering several periods of the life-cycle).You may document how your informant's existential concerns (or a specific existential concern) appear to have changed. You may discuss the extent to which you feel your informant has been able to create the kind of person they wished to become.

Key dimensions

Another alternative is to attempt to make sense of the informant's life in a more general way, focusing on the *key dimensions* in your informant's world (see Stevens, 1996b, for a discussion of key dimensions in three people's lives). For instance, if you decide on the dimension 'motivation', this might involve trying to identify your informant's concerns and goals, establishing how likely your informant feels it is that they will reach these goals and what they think will help and hinder them in reaching them. Alternatively, you might decide to try to find out about the informant's 'self-image' – how they see themselves – going on to discuss how far they feel this sense of self is socially constructed.

Whether you pick a narrow area or opt for something more general is really a matter of personal preference. Something narrow may be more straightforward, but a broad topic may be more interesting though somewhat superficial, given the time available. We suggest you avoid picking an overly sensitive topic. You may well tailor the topic to suit your informant's circumstances or select an informant who seems appropriate for the topic you wish to pursue.

You should inform your tutor or supervisor of your proposed topic before going ahead with the interview, so they can check that your plans are appropriate.

Whatever topic you pick, remember your task is to document how your informant makes sense of this area of their life; that is, to attempt to understand their point of view rather than judge what type of character you think they are. We are *not* asking for a clinical interview and you are *not* in the role of psychiatrist or psychotherapist. Rather, your role is that of a researcher trying to understand what it feels like to be like your informant.

4.4 Selecting an informant

Interviewers used to be advised not to interview someone they know, on the grounds that strangers have less reason 'to put on a false front' with someone outside their normal circle than with colleagues, relatives or close friends. Those with whom an interviewer has intimate relationships probably have a good deal invested in their relationships with the interviewer, which may well prevent them from being open or make them over-anxious to please. An interviewer will necessarily have all sorts of preconceived ideas about the way friends or relatives see the world, and these preconceptions are likely to colour the interviewer's interpretations of the data.

Whilst an amenable, open stranger would be ideal for Option 3, the negotiated account, these qualities can hardly be guaranteed; so an insightful, open and robust friend might be safer. Whether you choose a stranger, acquaintance or friend will also depend on the topic. You may feel the more intimate topics, such as relationships, have to be restricted to friends. In your report, you will be expected to make clear the basis of your relationship with the interviewee and discuss any ways in which this could have affected the outcome.

Before you approach any potential informant, you need to have in mind some account of who you are and what you want. You need to reassure them that the interview they give will be confidential, that you will use the material in an assignment, but that their name will be changed to a pseudonym. You will need to ask permission to record the interview. You could offer to return the audio-cassette recording of the interview to them. You should also tell them that the interview will take an hour or more. (Two interviews of an hour or so are required in the case of Options 1 and 3.)

5 Data collection

5.1 Preparing an interview guide

It is recommended that you read Chapter 4 on 'Interviewing' in Banister *et al.* (1994) or a similar text before planning and conducting your interview. As well as providing information on preparing for and conducting a semi-structured interview, it gives several examples of thematic analysis of interview data, and the authors also discuss a number of related approaches.

In a whole series of interviews with one individual there is time to allow the individual to talk freely, although much of the material may be irrelevant. In a single interview, time is precious and the interviewer is well advised to have in mind the areas they would like the informant's views on. In the heat of the interview it is very easy to forget what these are, so qualitative interviewers usually prepare an *interview guide*. This is a short list of areas you intend to include; under each item, list possible questions covering angles that may prove relevant. Use it as a checklist to remind you of topics you want to raise, rather than as a rigid structure for the interview. Of course, you may not cover all these topics and other interesting possibilities may turn up. Capitalize on the most promising ones as they arise and use the guide to remind yourself of any important gaps. The contents of your interview guide will vary according to the topic you decide to focus on. It should contain a list of headings covering the areas you think are relevant to the topic and that you want your informant's views on. Under each heading you need a list of questions that are designed to explore the informant's attitudes and feelings about this sub-topic. This can all be in note form, though people new to interviewing often find it helpful to include examples of exactly what questions they intend to ask their interviewee. An indication of the sort of information you might cover is given below, here in relation to an interview about an informant's work experiences. This has been divided into three areas: the past, present and future; this choice is quite arbitrary, and you could, for example, equally well have organized this under headings relating to your informant's feelings about the job itself, his or her colleagues, the job's effect upon your informant's life, self-image and family.

Past

- Kind of work done – for how long?

- How ended up working in this area? – factors affecting decision to stay, go, change jobs. How seen? e.g. conscious choice/pushed/happened.

- What aspects/which jobs liked/disliked – why?

Present

- What work as now – for how long? What's involved?

- What satisfactions/dissatisfactions experience at work now? – what you see as reasons for these likes/dislikes.

- Work with others or alone – how get on with colleagues, how do they see you? e.g. capable/incompetent, likeable/not, etc. Is this typical?

- Family/friends' reaction.

- Has work changed at all – how feel about that? How important is work – why?

Future

- Ever thought of doing anything else? – What is it that appeals about that? Why not pursued?

- Where do you see yourself in the next five years? – How likely is this?

- What do you think will help/hinder you reaching these goals? – Amount attributed to others and own efforts. Changes seen as desirable in self, others, situation.

This list is not intended to be exhaustive; no doubt you can think of other points that could be raised here. However, you only have an hour or an hour and a half so you cannot possibly cover everything that is potentially relevant. There is no harm in having a bit more material in the guide than you will be able to cover in the interview, but you need some system of highlighting the most important areas.

When you have drawn up this guide, use it in a *practice interview* with a friend or member of the family, ideally of the same sex and a similar age to your informant. This will allow you to get the feel of interviewing and give you some idea of how much information you can get in an hour and a half or so. You may also like to try to take notes, to see how practical you find this. You may well want to narrow the focus of your interview and revise the approach or content of the guide as a result of this pilot interview. You should also start to think about how you would analyse your notes. This may highlight the sort of questions and notes that would provide useful information for your report. It will be worth putting quite a bit of thought into your interview guide, both before and after the practice interview.

5.2 Recording the data

Qualitative interviews are often audio recorded so the researcher has a complete record of what was said. You might think that this would inhibit the informant, yet virtually everyone forgets the presence of the audio recorder after the first five minutes or so and talks freely thereafter. This is easiest if the audio recorder is small and placed out of the informant's line of sight.

In my view, a combination of recording and taking notes is the best bet. Taking notes of the key points during the interview can speed up the analysis and it allows you to note points you want to follow up later in the interview. You could also note the respondent's non-verbal behaviour, such as frowns and nods. At the same time, you do not have to worry about not getting everything written down as it is all on audio recorder. Later, when you come to analyse your data, you can do a preliminary analysis from your notes, replay the recording to find the exact wording of points that struck you as illustrating your ideas, and at the same time listen carefully so that you pick up on equally important points which you missed first time round. If you decide to use an audio recorder, you should ask your informant's permission first, explaining that you would like to record the interview simply to help you remember what was said. You could offer to give the interviewee the audio-cassette after you have used it to make your notes. However, do have a note-pad to hand as the informant will sometimes volunteer extra information after the audio recorder is switched off.

If you are unable to lay your hands on an audio recorder or do not feel happy about using one, you will have to adopt a slightly different strategy. During the interview, jot down key phrases verbatim from both your questions and your informant's answers. Immediately afterwards, use these notes to write up as full an account of the interview as possible.

You may think that taking notes of any kind will distract you from the task in hand, and you may favour relying totally on the audio recording. In fact, it can be quite uncomfortable to have someone looking at you all the time. If eye-contact is broken from time to time as you take notes, this can actually ease rapport. As mentioned earlier, notes can also ease the analysis by reminding you of what went on and the areas and statements which you felt were significant at the time. Researchers usually transcribe the whole interview, as this is the easiest and most reliable way of accessing and organizing quotations under different headings.

5.3 Conducting the interview

If at all possible, conduct the interview in a room in which you and your informant are unaccompanied. Not only will you probably both feel more comfortable, but there is less likelihood of interruptions or of some third party's comments influencing the way the informant presents himself/herself.

Questions

At the beginning of the interview, it is important to get a dialogue going and set the informant at ease. You should therefore start with something straightforward and concrete. A logical place to begin might be to ask the informant to tell you something about their background or past. If you were focusing on their work, you could start the dialogue along these lines: 'As you know, this interview is about your working life.' Alternatively, if it feels better to you, start by asking your informant about their current situation. The point is that you should start with some 'factual' questions that are easy to answer. Questions about future plans are harder to answer and, for some, are quite threatening; this type of question is best left until your informant has had time to review his or her past and present situation, probably towards the end of the interview. Leave more personal questions till later in the interview, when hopefully you have had time to become more comfortable with each other.

One way of helping people to think back to occasions they might not have thought about for some years is to provide some props to help them remember; for example: 'I'd like you to go back to an earlier time in your working life, which you may not have thought about for a while. Remember when you had just left college, you found a job and set off for your first day. Can you tell me about the experiences in those early days of working?'

Some people talk freely after just one or two questions while others need more encouragement. You may have to assist your informant by citing specific areas. For instance, if you are interested in feelings about school, you could ask, 'What do you remember about your primary school? And your infant school? Can you recall any of the children there? What about the teachers? What subjects did you do? Did you have any favourites?', etc. You may have to interrupt a more long-winded informant. Ceasing writing may be enough to give them the hint, but, if not, stop them in full flow, politely at first, for instance by saying: 'That's very interesting, but would you mind if I ask you about ...'; or by being more forceful if the problem continues, for example by saying: 'Let me stop you here for a moment. I want to make quite sure I understood something you said earlier. What did you mean by ...?'

As a general rule, you are more likely to keep the conversation flowing by keeping the questions as open as possible (e.g. 'What do you think of ... ?, How do you feel about ...?, How did you become a ... ?'), rather than phrasing questions in a way that suggests a 'yes' or 'no' answer (e.g. 'Was this important to you?'). Beware of presupposing an answer. Rather than asking 'How have you changed as a result of . . ?', when the answer might be 'I haven't', ask 'Would you say this experience has affected you personally in any way?', and if the answer is 'Yes' go on to ask 'In what way?' or 'Can you describe that to me?', as appropriate. Equally, avoid asking more than one question at a time (e.g. 'How well do you know and like your colleagues?'); it is less confusing to ask questions one at a time (e.g. 'How well do you know your colleagues?' and 'How well do you like them?').

Most of your questions are likely to be *non-directive*, but towards the end of the interview you might want to ask some more direct questions, and again these are best kept as open as possible. For instance, a general question like 'How do you see yourself?' leaves the informant free to answer in his or her own terms. If your informant focuses on just one aspect, it can be helpful to follow this up with a series of questions, which in this case might be: 'What would you say your strengths are? What about your weaknesses? What are some of the things you like about yourself? What about dislikes? Is there anything you would like to change about yourself?' Throughout the interview it is advisable not to give your own opinions, show surprise or voice strong agreement or disagreement. Though the interviewer's presence is likely to have an effect on the interviewee, nevertheless the interviewer's task is to minimize his or her own role. The questions asked should not lead the informant to answer in any particular way. For example, 'So it was really intense?' or 'You must have been upset?' put answers into the interviewee's mouth which, even though they may seem appropriate to you, may not be to the informant. It must be added that this is easier said than done. Watching TV interviewers at work will provide plenty of illustrations of how easy it is to fall into this trap.

Probing

To be in a position to draw some conclusions, albeit tentatively, about your informant's thinking, you obviously have to move beyond a purely factual account of events and ask for your interviewee's thoughts and feelings about events in their life. For example, 'I was made redundant' is a fact, whereas 'It's not right after all this time' is an opinion on the same subject, and 'I am very bitter about it' illustrates the informant's feelings. Novice interviewers need to guard against getting an interview full of 'facts' and devoid of 'feelings'. Getting a fuller account can be achieved by the use of follow-up questions.

In the early stages, restrict your probes to eliciting more detail about whatever is being described. This gives you a context in which to ask your informant for opinions and feelings about that event. Responses are also likely to be fuller if your informant has just 'relived' the experience by talking about it. For example, say your informant has just told you she is a lawyer. This is the time to ask 'Why did you decide to become a lawyer?' or 'What was it that attracted you to becoming a lawyer?' (The initial response to a 'What ...?' question is often fuller than that to a 'Why ...?' question.) Your informant may give you one reason, say money, when in fact there were several others: for example, status or the influence of her father; the follow-up 'Any other reasons?' may elicit these.

It is particularly easy to influence the informant's response when probing for an expanded answer. To avoid this danger, interviewers use non-directive probes. These may be designed to get an informant to elaborate on a statement (e.g. 'I'm beginning to get the picture, could you say some more on that'), or to clarify an ambiguous statement (e.g. 'How do you mean ...?'), or to fill in detail (e.g. 'In what way?'). Banaka (1971) suggests that around 50 per cent of a good qualitative interviewer's questions are probes designed to get a fuller response. Though the informant provides the content of the interview, you need to listen very carefully to the responses and direct the interview so it provides the type of information you want.

In most cases, you and your informant will probably enjoy this interview. Nevertheless, throughout this enterprise it is important to bear in mind that reviewing one's life can be quite a threatening and moving experience for some individuals, especially if they are not happy in themselves or with their present circumstances. If you have chosen a sensitive area, such as bereavement, you may find yourself quite moved by what you hear. Even if the respondent is talking freely, remember you are conducting a research interview not a psychotherapy session, so never push your respondent to reveal more than they are willing to, even if this leaves you with glaring gaps in your data. Equally, be very careful about pointing out contradictions unless you are sure your informant is capable of dealing with them. If you find yourself with an informant who is more interested in being counselled or analysed than being the subject in a research interview, present yourself as a student rather than psychologist, and stick to the researcher (rather than counsellor or therapist) *role*. This means asking open questions and non-directive probes and being non-interpretative (i.e. refrain from voicing any comment on what you think might be causing the informant's problems or giving suggestions as to how they should go about solving them). (Note: many, if not most, schools of counselling argue this is the best way to help people anyway.) It is harder than it sounds to stick to this role, hence it is really important to do a practice interview.

You might like to supplement the interview with some other forms of data. For example, this could be giving their hopes and fears for the future. Alternatively, a visual illustration like a lifeline, a sociogram or a family tree may be useful.

6 Preliminary analysis

The focus in an experiential analysis of a qualitative interview is on how informants make sense of themselves and the social world around them. This involves seeking out a pattern that reflects the informant's perspective (even if it appears illogical to an outsider). Your aim in this project is to understand your informant's thinking on your chosen topic and to document as much as you can about the informant's perspective from the information at your disposal; this means rooting out how they see things rather than commenting on why you think they are being defensive or whatever. Your final report should represent an attempt to reconstruct the informant's views, whilst acknowledging the shortcomings of the information on which this is based. You can think of the analysis in two stages, a preliminary and a final analysis.

The preliminary analysis is based on the information you gleaned from the first interview. No doubt you came to the interview with certain ideas in mind and developed others during the interview, and as you start trying to analyse the data other possibilities will probably present themselves.

Familiarize yourself with the data

Begin by familiarizing yourself with the data. The quickest way of doing this, if your notes are full enough, is to start organizing your findings under key points you noted in the interview. If you relied more heavily on an audio recording, replay it and note points that are relevant to your topic.

Identify key dimensions

These will be the major dimensions that your informant uses to make sense of the topic you have chosen: points that seem *important to your informant* and *issues they have raised a number of times*. It is hard to generalize about what kind of points these will be, as people have such a variety of different concerns. For instance, in talking about their jobs some people may stress the financial rewards a job offers or its security, while others might raise job satisfaction, a desire to be useful, or just the need to survive; others may raise a combination of these factors.

Select points relevant to your topic area

Concentrate on points that are relevant to your topic area and do not be afraid to ignore portions of the interview that are irrelevant. Many of these points will be *volunteered by the informant*. For example, in one interview I did, aimed at finding out about the informant's self-image, the informant referred to herself as guilt-ridden. Her feelings of self-blame centred largely on her family and concerned failing her husband, children and parents. It is also worth taking note of the *way informants describe their experiences*, as this too can reveal a lot about their thinking. For instance, various tales related by this same informant concerned her failings, which suggested feelings of inadequacy. These included clumsiness, lack of a sense of direction, not being very bright, lacking imagination, not understanding jokes and hating being teased.

Map out the pattern of findings and relate the themes that come up

Your task is to relate the themes that come up and map out the pattern of findings in as much detail as possible. Critical factors may well include whether the informant presents themselves in a good or bad light, how much control they feel they have over their own life and what part they feel circumstances have played in the way their life has unfolded.

Cite evidence for your interpretation

Cite all the evidence that you can muster in favour of a particular interpretation; that is, highlight and pull out quotations which support your ideas about the informant. In addition to the content of the interview, look at the metaphors your informant uses to describe their experiences: what images and self-concepts do these suggest?

Look for conflicting evidence

Resist the temptation to present a pat story. Look for evidence that conflicts with as well as evidence which supports your ideas about the informant, and note both kinds of evidence in your report. For example, I felt that the fact that the woman cited above dismissed apparent strengths supported my view that she felt inadequate and had low self-esteem. To take one instance, she knew she was considered a useful member of the firm and found work easy, but felt her job required little imagination, a quality she felt she lacked, even though she wrote stories in her spare time. On the other hand, these feelings of inadequacy were not all-engulfing; she acknowledged various strengths, for instance her capacity to get on with people.

Accept and report important contradictory evidence

Not all informants will have a clear set of perspectives. For example, in another interview I conducted, the informant seemed to have two contradictory pictures of the future. Despite his lack of direction and any firm prospects, one view was optimistic, which he justified on the grounds of innate ability (he presented a positive self-image) and the unexpected upturns in the lives of his friends and himself; the other view was pessimistic – a worry that things might not work out and that his optimism was just a rationalization.

Decide on follow-up areas

You need to complete the preliminary analysis before attempting the follow-up procedure entailed in your option. In the two-stage account, you use the preliminary analysis to work out which areas you want to ask more about and the kinds of question that might enable you to support and/or refute your ideas about the informant. In the negotiated and two-person accounts, you need to write up your preliminary analysis and discuss your ideas with the informant or with a fellow-student. In the comparative account, you do a preliminary analysis of the interview and the written account and then you compare the two. The more developed this first analysis is, the more productive the final analysis will be.

7 Follow-up options

You should carry out *one* of the following follow-up options.

7.1 Two-stage account

This option is based on two interviews with the same individual. The second interview allows you to test the ideas about the informant you developed in the first interview. This is probably the easiest option as, if you are unsatisfied with the first interview, you get a chance to collect more information.

First interview – cover ground thoroughly

Treat the first interview as though it were the only one you were going to do, covering as much ground as possible. This will allow you to spend more time refining and testing your ideas in the second interview.

Preliminary analysis

After your first meeting, undertake a preliminary analysis of the data, concentrating on those portions that throw some light on your topic. This exercise should help you decide which areas are worth pursuing in the second interview.

Second interview

Fill in gaps: Aim to fill in the gaps left first time round. This might be a whole area (e.g. your informant's family may not have been mentioned), or there may have been something that you meant to follow up and didn't, or perhaps were not clear about.

Ask more about key areas: To refine your ideas, you need to ask more about those areas which seemed important and relevant to your topic, perhaps probing more thoroughly than you did first time round.

Test your initial hypotheses: You need to make some attempt to test your ideas about the respondent by asking questions that could *support and, more importantly, refute* the impression you gained from the first interview. There will probably be opportunities to do this during the interview by the use of judicious questioning; for example, 'Did any other people influence your decision at all?' might allow you to test your idea that the informant sees X as the only influence.

Direct questions: Towards the end of the interview, you might want to ask increasingly direct questions: 'Would you say X was the most important influence on your decision to ... or not?', 'Would you say Y was what you think about Z or not?' It will probably be best to leave all direct questions until the second interview.

Final report

Base your final analysis on both interviews. Note whether the second interview provides evidence that concurs with that given in the first or not, and particularly if it has caused you to change your mind about the respondent.

7.2 Comparative account

Here your task is slightly different; you will be comparing two different kinds of data: some written evidence, such as an autobiography, provided by the interviewee, and an interview conducted and interpreted by yourself.

Written account

One way of approaching this task would be to ask your informant to write about the same topic as you propose to interview them about. Then carry out the first interview and preliminary analysis as described in section 7.1 above.

Alternatively, you might like to ask your informant to write about their life as a preliminary to your interview, to give a basis on which to paint a fuller picture during the interview.

Comparison

Either way, you need to compare their written account and interview data. Begin by doing a separate preliminary analysis of each. Then compare these and look for the similarities and differences between the two accounts.

Final report

In your discussion of the two pieces of evidence, you could consider whether different kinds of points have been made in the written and verbal accounts and, if so, why that might be. You could also consider any difference in focus between those issues you, as researcher, deemed most salient and those the informant singled out. Finally, you might like to give an account as to which approach was most useful; how they complimented or contradicted each other; whether your perspective or the informant's should be given primacy, why, and how you explain any differences.

7.3 Negotiated account

This option involves interviewing your informant about the topic you have chosen, drawing tentative conclusions on the basis of this interview, and going back to your informant to discuss his/her opinion of the validity of your findings. The second stage involves the interviewee as a more active participant in the research process than in the other three options.

Introduction

The way you introduce this option is important. If you explain the true purpose of both meetings it could make the informant self-conscious, which could, in turn, affect the type of information revealed. After the usual introduction about wanting to interview someone for a course and assurances about anonymity and confidentiality, you could play down the informant's role, and just ask if they would be willing to comment on the accuracy of the report you write about the first interview. Alternatively, you may feel happier explaining that you want to come back after the first interview and discuss in some detail how true a picture of the interview your informant thinks your summary is and how well it equates with their ideas about the topic.

First interview

The discussion is likely to be more fruitful if you cover as much ground as possible in the first interview, as this will allow you to present your interviewee with a more developed analysis. It may help to have a fairly detailed interview guide. Even more important is the need to listen hard to your informant's comments and follow up potentially relevant areas, probing for their thoughts and feelings about events and cutting short monologues that seem to be irrelevant to your purpose. A fairly open informant who talks freely will make this easier.

Preliminary analysis

After the interview, you need to undertake a preliminary analysis of the data. Then prepare a report summarizing what you feel the interview suggested about your informant's thinking. Feel free to make clear which conclusions you were fairly sure of, which ones you were much less sure of, and where you were confused or uncertain. When writing this tentative summary, you need to be aware that it will be presented to the informant and consider any material that might offend them, weighing up accuracy against ethical considerations. You may circumvent these problems by selecting a robust character as your interviewee.

Follow-up meeting

At the second meeting, give the interviewee a summary of points from the first interview that you feel are relevant to their views about the topic. This can be in note form. Ask them how valid they think the report is as a summary of the interview and of their views about the topic. This procedure is designed to offer some verification and involve the informant in the analysis. It will also throw up a lot more data, for instance on areas and issues that were not covered first time round. The informant may be more open than before, or your report may have set them thinking about themselves – their motives, values, satisfactions and dissatisfactions, etc., or it may just have given them a clearer idea of what you were after.

This exercise enables the informant to correct what they feel were erroneous impressions, and it allows you to refine your ideas about their thinking. However, it is important to bear in mind that your informant may not have been presented with a fully articulated view of themselves before, and this may lead them to change their views, and re-evaluate themselves, or present themselves in a different, perhaps more sophisticated, manner than they would have been able to, prior to this experience. In such cases, this follow-up procedure will become much more than just checking the accuracy of your initial impressions, and the weight of your comments in the final report should change accordingly. You need notes and/or an audio recording of this second meeting to assist you in compiling the final report.

Final report

In your final report, you will be expected to draw on data from both the first interview and the follow-up discussion and make clear how your opinion of the informant was altered as a result of the verification procedure. You might like to include the report prepared after the first interview and presented to the interviewee as an appendix to the final report.

7.4 Two-person account

This option involves a comparison of two students' account of the same person; both of you interview the informant either separately or together, conduct preliminary analyses independently, and then meet to discuss your conclusions.

Initial interviews

To undertake this option, you need to locate another student to work with. You need to discuss and agree a topic and interview guide, so that you are trying to find out the same things from the informant. You each interview the informant about all aspects of the topic, so if you decide on two separate interviews you need an informant who is prepared to give views on the same subject twice over. Differences between the informant's accounts on the two occasions are worth noting. The informant's account may well be more sophisticated second time round. They may also deliberately try to be consistent (or even inconsistent!).

Preliminary analysis

After you have conducted the interview(s), you each carry out and write up your preliminary analysis independently from your own notes. This report may be in note form if you like. Avoid discussing your thoughts about the informant or your reaction to the interview with your colleague prior to conducting your preliminary analysis.

Initial report comparison

Swap these reports and then meet to discuss their similarities and differences. Focus on why it was that you each stressed particular points and not others. Consider what might have caused these similarities and differences: for instance, the extent to which they reflect the particular sub-topics you covered in the interview; whether you asked questions first or second or were aware of each other's thinking. Equally, you should consider whether the similarities and differences between your reports reflect similarities and differences in your own preoccupations and perhaps situations and backgrounds. It will also be worth looking at any differences in the types of point you decided to note down in the interview. You need notes and/or an audio recording of this meeting for use in the final report.

Separate final reports

Each of you must write the final report separately, drawing on both the interview and follow-up discussion to form your final opinion of the informant's thinking. You should make clear who your paired student is. In your discussion of the findings, you should compare and contrast your own analysis with that of your colleague and attempt to account for any discrepancies and difference in emphasis. You should make it clear whether you have changed your perception of the informant as a result of this procedure.

8 Report

8.1 Final analysis

The main task here is to refine and revise your preliminary ideas about the informant by drawing on the data provided by your option's follow up procedures.

Evidence

In your final report, you need to explain how you came to your conclusions by citing the evidence for them, including quotations from your informant. If you have a transcript of your interview(s), you might like to number each line and then you can refer to line numbers when offering supporting evidence for your interpretation, as well as incorporating direct quotations in your account.

You may find that, while you are fairly certain of some conclusions, you feel much more tentative about other points. In your report, feel free to make clear which points you feel fairly happy with, where you are less certain, and where you should have asked for more information and did not do so.

In your discussion of the findings, you will be expected to make clear the extent to which, and the reasons why, your ideas about the informant were changed by your chosen follow-up procedure (e.g. the second interview or discussion with the informant or colleague, or the written account in Option 2).

8.2 Discussion

Banister *et al.* (1994), Chapter 10, on 'Report writing', may help you to write up your account.

Strengths and weaknesses of the interview process

It is insufficient merely to present an analysis of your informant's world view; in the discussion section of the final report you need to offer some evaluation of the procedure and the nature of the information it provided. This will involve a consideration of the research approach, including the use of a qualitative depth interview, analysis and the use of triangulation (evidence from different sources bearing on the same issue provided in each option). This should include your view of the significance of the content and usefulness of the procedure. Points to consider could include whether an informant is a good judge of their own condition, particularly the discussion of the tendency to interpret inner states according to context, or whether you believe that the role of agency is overemphasized or not. How stable did you think your informant's views would be? To what extent might the interview have been distorted by their expectation that a consistent and coherent story was expected? Would they have presented themselves differently to a different interviewer? Is the task a reasonable one, is it useful to try to identify enduring aspects of a person, or is this based on a flawed understanding of what it is to be a person and of the way language and people's accounts work (Stevens, 1996a, and Wetherell and Maybin, 1996, offer contrasting perspectives). Feel free to use the interview data as evidence for your views on the relative importance of the various influences on the person, their sense of identity and their attributions about others.

Reflexive account

You need to offer some sort of reflexive account concerning the research process, covering your relationship to the interviewee, his or her conception of you and the purpose of the interview, and the extent to which you were active in shaping the account given. You should question how far the outcome reflects your informant's beliefs and ideas and how far it was occasioned by your questioning: for example, you should check if any concerns you feel strongly about personally shine through. You should consider how far your interpretation of any ambiguous areas may have been influenced by judgements associated with stereotypical responses to the interviewee (e.g. see Duncan, 1976, in Lalljee, 1996, section 2.1).

You might also like to comment on the extent to which your interpretation of major influences on your interviewee coincides with your beliefs about the relative influence of these areas generally. As ever when answering educational assignments, point out parallels between points you are making and concepts introduced in your course material; for example, note the influence of personal and procedural reactivity (Banister *et al.*, 1994, pp.5–6). You may also find Marshall's reflective checklist useful (Banister *et al.*, 1994, p.152).

You should also point out the strengths and weaknesses of the procedure and make clear what you would have done differently in retrospect. Finally, you need to comment on any problems associated with the method you used and any implications for its reliability and validity suggested by discrepancies (or lack of them) between the data provided by the interview and the option you chose as your follow-up procedure.

8.3 Marking

In marking your report, the assessor will be looking at your analysis of the process – what went on in the interview – rather than just at your conclusions about the informant. You need to be aware of inadequacies – where you could have influenced the informant, what points you should have followed up and didn't and how this might have influenced the final outcome – along with any insights into qualitative research you derived from this experience.

8.4 Report format

Your report should include the following sections:

1   Introduction: a brief introduction to your topic.

2   Method: an account of the strategy you adopted.

3   Analysis: a summary of your findings.

4   Discussion: a discussion of factors that may have influenced the outcome and of the strengths and limitations of the approach.

5   Appendices: interview guide, raw interview notes and/or interview audio–cassette.

Sections 3 and 4 should form the bulk of your report. Please use *pseudonyms* when referring to your informant, their family and friends, to protect their confidentiality.

Your assessor is likely to look for a clear, concise, well-argued and insightful piece of work, which looks at both the content (outcome) and the process (context and procedures used).

References

Banaka, W. (1971) *Training in Depth Interviewing*, New York, Harper and Row.

Banister, P., Burman, E., Parker, I., Taylor, M. and Tindall, C. (1994) *Qualitative Methods in Psychology*, Buckingham, Open University Press.

British Psychological Society (1997) *Code of Conduct, Ethical Principles and Guidelines*, Leicester, British Psychological Society.

Claxton, G. (1994) *Noises from the Darkroom*, London, HarperCollins.

Cottrell, M. (1979) 'Invisible religion and the middle class', unpublished paper, Linacre College, Oxford.

Dahrendorf, R. (1959) *Class and Class Conflict in Industrial Society*, London, Routledge and Kegan Paul.

Duncan, B.L. (1976) 'Differential social perception and attribution of intergroup violence: testing the lower limits of stereotyping of blacks', *Journal of Personality and Social Psychology*, vol.34, pp.590–8.

Gazzaniga, M.S. (1967) 'The split brain in man', *Scientific American*, vol.217, no.2, pp.24–9.

Goldthorpe, J.H., Lockwood, D., Bechhofer, F. and Platt, J. (eds) (1969) *The Affluent Worker*, vol.I, Cambridge, Cambridge University Press.

Hammersley, M. (1997) *Reading Ethnographic Research* (2nd edn), Harlow, Essex, Longman.

Hyman, H., Cobb, W.J., Feldman, J.J., Hart, C.M. and Stember, C.H. (1954) *Interviewing with Social Research*, Chicago, University of Chicago Press.

Katz, D. (1942) 'Do interviewers bias poll results?', *Public Opinion Quarterly*, vol.6, pp.248–68.

Lalljee, M. (1996) 'The interpreting self: an experimentist perspective', in Stevens, R. (ed.) (1996).

LaPiere, R.T. (1934) 'Attitudes versus actions', *Social Forces*, vol.13, pp.230–7.

Levinson, D.J., Darrow, C.N., Klein, E.B., Levinson, M.H. and McKee, B. (1986) *The Seasons of a Man's Life*. New York, Ballantine Books.

Potter, J. (1996) 'Attitudes, social representations and discursive psychology', in Wetherell, M. (ed.) *Identities, Groups and Social Issues*, London, Sage/The Open University.

Reason, P. and Rowan, J. (1981) *Human Inquiry: A Sourcebook of New Paradigm Research*, Chichester, John Wiley.

Robinson, E. and Rhodes, S. (1946) 'Two experiments with an anti-semitism poll', *Journal of Abnormal and Social Psychology*, vol.41, pp.136–44.

Rogers, C. (1945) 'The non-directive method as a technique for social research', *American Journal of Sociology*, vol.50, pp.279–83.

Spender, D. (1981) *Men's Studies Modified: The Impact of Feminism on the Academic Disciplines*, Oxford, Pergamon.

Stevens, R. (1996a) 'The reflexive self: an experiential perspective', in Stevens, R. (ed.) (1996).

Stevens, R. (1996b) 'Introduction: making sense of the person in a social world' in Stevens, R. (ed.) (1996).

Stevens, R. (ed.) (1996) *Understanding the Self*, London, Sage/The Open University.

Still, A. (1998) 'Theories of meaning', in Sapsford, R., Still, A., Wetherell, M., Miell, D. and Stevens, R. (eds) *Theory and Social Psychology*, London, Sage/The Open University.

Toates, F. (1996) 'The embodied self: a biological perspective', in Stevens, R. (ed.) (1996).

Wetherell, M. and Maybin, J. (1996) 'The distributed self: a social constructionist perspective', in Stevens, R. (ed.) (1996).

Further reading

* Particularly recommended.

Atkinson, R. (1998) *The Life Story Interview: Qualitative Research Method*, Series No. 44, London, Sage.

One of a series of essays/booklets published by Sage on qualitative research methods. Notable for examining both the emotions and spirit of interviews, as well as the theories and practice. Many interesting references.

*Banister, P., Burman, E., Parker, I., Taylor, M. and Tindall, C. (1994) *Qualitative Methods in Psychology*, Buckingham, Open University Press.

A good, readable introduction to the various types of qualitative research used in psychology.

Glesne, C. and Peshkin, A. (1992) *Becoming Qualitative Researchers: An Introduction*, Harlow, Longman.

Introduction to qualitative research.

Guba, E.G. and Lincoln, Y.S. (1985) *Naturalistic Inquiry*, London, Sage.

A classic exploration of the philosophy, theory and practice of naturalistic inquiry, containing a detailed examination of ways of introducing reliability and validity in the qualitative context and of the analytical process.

Guba, E.G. and Lincoln, Y.S. (1989) *Fourth Generation Evaluation*, London, Sage.

Further explorations of evaluation of qualitative research methods.

Hammersley, M. and Atkinson, P. (1995) *Ethnography: Principles in Practice* (2nd edn), London, Routledge.

A detailed and readable review of the principles and practice of ethnography, including interviewing. Helpfully introduces the issue of how the 'truth' in interviews can be assessed.

Kvale, S. (1996) *InterViews*, London, Sage.

A practical and readable examination of the philosophy, theory and practice of research by interviews. Also contains a detailed examination of how to build validity into interviewing – a positive contrast to the Guba and Lincoln review.

Miles, M.B. and Humberman A.M. (1994) *Qualitative Data Analysis: An Expanded Sourcebook*, London, Sage.

A manual on qualitative data analysis. Detailed, sometimes technical.

* Sapsford, R., Still, A., Wetherell, M., Miell, D. and Stevens, R. (eds) (1998)*Theory and Social Psychology*, London, Sage.

Chapter 6 by Arthur Still, 'Theories of meaning'; Chapter 9 by Roger Sapsford, 'Evidence'; and Chapter 5 by Richard Stevens, 'Three epistemologies', provide useful background.

* Stevens, R. (ed.) (1996) *Understanding the Self*, London, Sage/The Open University.

Richard Stevens's Chapter 4 on the experiential perspective may be contrasted with Margaret Wetherell and Janet Maybin's Chapter 5, especially section 4 on discursive psychology.

Special Issue on Qualitative Methods (1995) *The Psychologist*, vol.8, no.3, March, pp.109–29.

A series of articles discussing key issues in qualitative research and offering examples of practice.

Spradley, J. (1979) *The Ethnographic Interview*, London, Harcourt Brace.

A readable review, and good 'how to' book.

Strauss, A.L., and Corbin, J. (1990) *Basics of Qualitative Research: Grounded Theory Procedures and Techniques*, Newbury Park, CA, Sage.

A classic on grounded theory. Criticized for making common sense technical and complicated, but giving a clear structure to analytical practice.

Studies based on qualitative research interviews

Bergquist, W.H., Miller Greenber, E. and Klaum, G.A. (1993) *In Our Fifties: Voices of Men and Women Reinventing Their Lives*. San Francisco, CA, Jossey Bass.

A positive view on the prospects for ageing.

Csikszentmihalyi, M. (1996) *Creativity: Flow and the Psychology of Discovery and Invention*, New York, HarperCollins.

A review of the life development patterns of 90 creative/exceptional people.

*Levinson, D.J., Darrow, C.N., Klein, E.B., Levinson, M.H. and McKee, B. (1986) *The Seasons of a Man's Life*. New York, Ballantine Books.

A classic and readable examination of male adult development. Includes the story of the research, as well as outcomes.

Levinson, D.J. and Levinson, J. (1996) *The Season's of a Woman's Life*, New York, Alfred Knopf.

The sequel to Levinson's earlier work.

Index

dogmatic individuals, and perseverance
effects 17
domains, and structured observation 114
Duck, S. 125
dyadic options
in diary research 4, 46, 48–9
agreement between diarists 77–8
co-diarist dropping out 56–7
qualitative 46, 48, 49, 50, 59, 71
quantitative 46, 50, 57–8, 59, 60–1,
76–8

educational research, survey work in 132
Electoral Register 140
emotionality, and personal construct theory
126–8, 227
emotions, and discourse analysis 65–6
ethical considerations 2
in depth interviewing 8, 297–8, 299, 313
in diary research 42, 48, 56
and the person perception project 22
repertory grids project 198–200, 215,
218
and structured observation 95–6, 107,
112
in surveys 132, 143
see also informed consent
ethnographic research, and qualitative
interviewing 290, 291
existentialism, and depth interviewing 292
experiential psychology
and depth interviewing 8
and personal construct theory (PCT) 193
experiential research, and qualitative
interviewing 292–5
experimental approach, and experiential
research 292–3
experimental psychology 3
and diary research 51, 53
and discourse analysis 64
and person perception 17
and personal construct theory (PCT)
193
experimental social psychology, and
framing effects 167
experiments
and the psychology of primacy and
perseverance 10
and surveys 130, 135
external validity, in personal relationship
research 43–4

face validity, of survey measurements 134
false information, and perseverance effects
14–17
family interaction, structured observation
on 95, 111–12
family trees, in depth interviewing 300, 308

femininities
social representations of 253–4
in women's magazines 256–60
feminism
and representations of motherhood 249
and social representations of gender
254, 273
feminist research
and qualitative interviewing 290–1
and qualitative research methods 243
and social representations of gender
253
Ferguson, Marjorie 256
Fowles, J.E. 117
framing effects *see* dilemma framing
France, social representations of madness
in 238, 239
Fransella, Fay 223
friendship groups, structured observation
of 95
friendship research 44

gender
in personal relationship research 44
social representations of 7–8, 233, 240,
252–60
cross-cultural 273–4
historical changes in 272–3
project work on 260–71
structured observation of differences 93,
97, 110
Goffman, E. 98, 102, 257

Harri-Augstein, E.S. 203, 212
headlines, in media representations of
motherhood 251
health, social representations of 274–8
health education pamphlets, framing effects
of different versions 165–6
Henley, N.M. 98
hermeneutic approaches
and diary research 40
and framing effects 167
and qualitative content analysis 244
histograms
and content analysis 266
and structured observation 109, 110
historical changes, in gender
representations, project work on 272–3
Holsti, O. 242
houses, selecting samples 140
humanistic psychology, and depth
interviewing 290, 292
Hyman, H. 295
hypothesis testing
in-depth interviewing 311
framing dilemmas 168, 170, 174, 179,
180, 181

Acknowledgements

Grateful acknowledgement is made to the following sources for permission to reproduce material in this book:

CHAPTER 7 APPENDICES: From 'The Good Care Guide', *Our Baby*, August 1995, pp.42–43, IPC Magazines; *The Tomy Cradle Carrier* advertisement 1995, by permission of The Hodges Consultancy and Tomy (UK) Ltd.

COVER ILLUSTRATION: Kasimir Malevich, *Sportsmen*, *c.*1928–32, oil on canvas, 142 × 164 cm., State Russian Museum, St Petersburg.